AF763171

Monetary Policy and Income Distribution

This book brings together a number of well-known post-Keynesian scholars who discuss the impact of monetary policy on both personal and functional distribution of income and even the gendered effect of monetary policy.

The impact of monetary policy (changes in interest rates) on income distribution is increasingly being recognized as a legitimate channel of monetary policy transmission. The study of this new channel – once the purview of post-Keynesian theory – is an important step in understanding the complicated and myriad effects of central bank policy. The chapters in this book raise a number of other questions about monetary policy that are still underdeveloped in the economic literature. This book is essential reading for students, scholars and policy makers interested in economic policy, monetary theory, income distribution and post-Keynesian economics.

The chapters in this book were originally published in the *Review of Political Economy.*

Sylvio Kappes is Professor of Macroeconomics at the Federal University of Alagoas, Brazil. His main areas of research are stock-flow consistent models, monetary economics and post-Keynesian economics. He is the co-editor of the *Review of Political Economy.*

Louis-Philippe Rochon is Full Professor of Economics at Laurentian University, Sudbury, Canada, where he has been teaching since 2004. He is the editor-in-chief of the *Review of Political Economy.* He is Founding Editor (now Emeritus) of the *Review of Keynesian Economics.* He has widely published in post-Keynesian economics, and monetary theory and policy. He has been Visiting Professor in over a dozen universities around the world.

Guillaume Vallet is Full Professor of Economics at the University of Grenoble Alpes, France. His main areas of research are monetary economics (particularly related to the Swiss case), the political economy of gender and the history of economy thought during the Progressive Era.

Monetary Policy and Income Distribution

Edited by
Sylvio Kappes, Louis-Philippe Rochon and Guillaume Vallet

Routledge
Taylor & Francis Group
LONDON AND NEW YORK

First published 2025
by Routledge
4 Park Square, Milton Park, Abingdon, Oxon, OX14 4RN

and by Routledge
605 Third Avenue, New York, NY 10158

Routledge is an imprint of the Taylor & Francis Group, an informa business

Introduction, Chapters 1, 3–5 and 7 © 2025 Taylor & Francis
Chapter 2 © 2023 Samuele Bibi. Originally published as Open Access.
Chapter 6 © 2024 Matheus Trotta Vianna. Originally published as Open Access.

With the exception of Chapters 2 and 6, no part of this book may be reprinted or reproduced or utilised in any form or by any electronic, mechanical, or other means, now known or hereafter invented, including photocopying and recording, or in any information storage or retrieval system, without permission in writing from the publishers. For details on the rights for Chapters 2 and 6, please see the chapters' Open Access footnotes.

Trademark notice: Product or corporate names may be trademarks or registered trademarks, and are used only for identification and explanation without intent to infringe.

British Library Cataloguing-in-Publication Data
A catalogue record for this book is available from the British Library

ISBN13: 978-1-032-97641-9 (hbk)
ISBN13: 978-1-032-97643-3 (pbk)
ISBN13: 978-1-003-59466-6 (ebk)

DOI: 10.4324/9781003594666

Typeset in Minion Pro
by codeMantra

Publisher's Note
The publisher accepts responsibility for any inconsistencies that may have arisen during the conversion of this book from journal articles to book chapters, namely the inclusion of journal terminology.

Disclaimer
Every effort has been made to contact copyright holders for their permission to reprint material in this book. The publishers would be grateful to hear from any copyright holder who is not here acknowledged and will undertake to rectify any errors or omissions in future editions of this book.

Contents

Citation Information

The following chapters in this book were originally published in *Review of Political Economy*, volume 36, issue 3 (2024). When citing this material, please use the original page numbering for each article, as follows:

Introduction
Monetary Policy and Income Distribution: A Symposium
Sylvio Kappes, Louis-Philippe Rochon and Guillaume Vallet
Review of Political Economy, volume 36, issue 3 (2024), pp. 887–891

Chapter 1
Monetary Policy and Income Distribution: The Post-Keynesian and Sraffian Perspectives
Antonino Lofaro, Guillermo Matamoros and Louis-Philippe Rochon
Review of Political Economy, volume 36, issue 3 (2024), pp. 892–918

Chapter 2
The Distributive Monetary Analysis of a (un)Sustainable Economy
Samuele Bibi
Review of Political Economy, volume 36, issue 3 (2024), pp. 919–952

Chapter 3
Foreign Price Shocks and Inflation Targeting: Effects on Income and Inflation Inequality
Lilian Rolim and Nathalie Marins
Review of Political Economy, volume 36, issue 3 (2024), pp. 953–973

Chapter 4
Dealing with Rising Inequality: Is the Fed Up for the Task, or Will Everyone Get Fed Up?
Steven Pressman
Review of Political Economy, volume 36, issue 3 (2024), pp. 974–993

Chapter 5
Monetary Policy and the Gender and Racial Employment Dynamics in Brazil
Patricia Couto and Clara Brenck
Review of Political Economy, volume 36, issue 3 (2024), pp. 994–1018

Chapter 6

Monetary Policy and Income Distribution in a Multisectoral AB-SFC Model
Matheus Trotta Vianna
Review of Political Economy, volume 36, issue 3 (2024), pp. 1019–1041

Chapter 7

Are Firm Markups Boosting Inflation? A Post-Keynesian Institutionalist Approach to Markup Inflation in Select Industrialized Countries
Guillermo Matamoros
Review of Political Economy, volume 36, issue 3 (2024), pp. 1042–1063

For any permission-related enquiries please visit:
http://www.tandfonline.com/page/help/permissions

Notes on Contributors

Samuele Bibi, Northumbria University, Newcastle upon Tyne, UK.

Clara Brenck, Federal University of Minas Gerais, Belo Horizonte, Brazil.

Patricia Couto, The New School, USA.

Sylvio Kappes, Federal University of Alagoas, Brazil.

Antonino Lofaro, University of Siena, Siena, Italy.

Nathalie Marins, Boston University, Boston, Massachusetts, United States.

Guillermo Matamoros, University of Massachusetts Amherst, United States.

Steven Pressman, Department of Economics, New School for Social Research, Monmouth University, USA.

Louis-Philippe Rochon, Laurentian University, Sudbury, Canada.

Lilian Rolim, Universidade Estadual de Campinas (UNICAMP), Brazil.

Guillaume Vallet, University of Grenoble Alpes, France.

Matheus Trotta Vianna, University of Manchester, UK.

Introduction: Monetary Policy and Income Distribution

Sylvio Kappes, Louis-Philippe Rochon and Guillaume Vallet

With the recent resurgence of inflation — which had been dormant for the better part of the last 3 decades — monetary policy has once again taken centre stage as the only possible policy solution to inflation or the only game in town. Fiscal policy was never considered, and there has been no mention of the possibility of using fiscal policy to fight inflation except in some heterodox circles. As such, the entire responsibility to fight inflation was laid at the feet of independent central banks.

And predictably, central banks resorted to a familiar theme or rather the only one they knew: raising interest rates in an attempt to bring inflation back to target — usually close to two per cent — while avoiding triggering a hard landing. Yet, this inflation-first policy carries important consequences for income distribution, and a number of post-Keynesians have been at the forefront of this discussion.

Post-Keynesians are generally against the use of monetary policy fine tuning, as Rochon (2022) explains, largely questioning the effectiveness of incremental increases in interest rates in impacting those interest-sensitive components of aggregate demand, and unemployment, let alone the discussion over the Phillips curve at the heart of the mainstream explanation of the transmission mechanism.

Despite the empirical evidence supporting the weakness of the mainstream story, central banks still pursued counter cyclical policies, and used interest rates as a blunt instrument, and raised them repeatedly until economies finally collapsed. Indeed, while incremental increases in interest rates may not have the predictable mainstream consequences, certainly the cumulative impact of, say, ten or eleven consecutive increases may indeed collapse the economy, raise unemployment and lower wage demands and inflation. And since we live in a world of Keynesian uncertainty, it becomes a guessing game as to how many increases are required, and more often than none, a game of too-many-too-late.

And regarding the latest spat of monetary policy austerity, the evidence on its impact on economic activity is mixed. While some countries have certainly experienced economic slowdowns, the United States seems to be going against the conventional wisdom — at least so far — although it must be stated that they also simultaneously enacted a very expansive fiscal plan, known as the Biden plan.

Given the above discussion, monetary policy in the last two years has shown one very real conclusion: the New Consensus model, which had been declared dead by many economists, including some post-Keynesians, has resurfaced in a very healthy way; it was simply lying dormant waiting for the appropriate moment to reassert itself. Indeed, the core assumptions of mainstream central banking theory were never abandoned. For instance, mainstream economists still insist on seeing inflation largely as a demand-pull phenomenon to which monetary policy is uniquely situated to fight it. This goes hand in hand with Fiebiger and Lavoie's (2020) conclusion that central banking thinking is still not that far from Friedman.

This said, there has nevertheless been some interesting development regarding the impact of monetary policy, or rather a rethinking of a possible new channel of transmission: the income distributive channel, or what Borio (2021) has called the 'Distributive Footprint' of monetary policy.

Indeed, the relationship between monetary policy and income distribution has recently emerged as a topic of renewed interest within the mainstream, certainly as a result of three events: (*i*) the lasting effects of the financial crisis of 2007, (*ii*) the current COVID crisis; and (*iii*) the public's increased interest in all-things distributional. Haldane (2018, p. 311) has claimed that until the crisis, 'There has been no particular clamour for published assessments of the distributional impact of monetary policy', leading some to argue that 'monetary policy is rarely mentioned as a likely candidate' in discussions over inequality (Coibion et al. 2017, p. 1); Mersch (2014) has called it an 'unusual topic', and Dietsch, Fontan and Claveau (2016) have argued 'the two trends are rarely connected'.

But this assessment is not exactly correct. Certainly, from a mainstream perspective, this may be correct, but post-Keynesians have been discussing this topic at least as far back as the mid-1980s. Indeed, since at least this time, post-Keynesians have made explicit links between interest rates and income — and wealth — distribution. Post-Keynesians like Niggle (1989), Moore (1989), Arestis and Howells (1991, 1994), Smithin (1994), Lavoie (1996), and Lavoie and Seccareccia (1988, 1999, 2016) have always considered the income distributive impact of monetary policy.

In fact, according to Niggle (1989, pp. 818–819):

> The processes connecting monetary policy to changes in the distribution of personal income through the transmission mechanism of the level of interest rates are complex, with at least three causal sequences operating: (1) changes in interest rates can affect the functional distribution of income, and thus the personal distribution; (2) changes in interest rates change the market values of financial assets, effecting capital gains or losses; (3) interest rates influence investment, aggregate demand, employment and income.

If this is correct, it should give us pause and rethink the purpose of monetary policy. Indeed, as Lavoie (1996, p. 537) is explicit:

> It then becomes clear that monetary policy should not so much be designed to control the level of activity, but rather the find the level of interest rates that will be proper for the economy from a distribution point of view. The aim of such a policy should be to minimize conflict over the income shares, in the hope of simultaneously keeping inflation low and activity high.

The topic of the impact of monetary policy and income distribution gained renewed attention and interest with the publication of Rochon and Setterfield's (2007, 2008, 2012) discussion of the interest rate rules and their emphasis on the 'parking-it' approach (see Lavoie and Seccareccia 2025). Recently, Lofaro, Matamoros, and Rochon (2023) have carefully traced this interest in both post-Keynesian and Sraffians traditions.

But the mainstream's approach to the topic, however, while a positive sign, should not be taken too far. Their interest, we would argue, is the outcome of some historical events. They result from the undeniable distributive consequences of unconventional policies, as little is said about the distributional implications of 'conventional interest rate policies'.

Moreover, while heterodox works are interested in the *functional* income distribution, reflecting their emphasis on the distributive conflict between different groups' income sources, mainstream economists are instead focused on the *personal* income distribution, given the common belief that each person belongs, in a sense, to many different income groups. For instance, a worker could also a rentier or a capitalist, since her/his savings are allocated in financial securities and companies' shares. This conceptual background drives the empirical strategies adopted by the mainstream, which seeks to assess the impact of interest rate changes on distributional metrics such as Gini coefficients or ratios between deciles, such as the 90/10 ratio.

The mainstream's empirical findings point to many directions, but the majority of the papers point to the conclusion that either *expansionary* monetary policy *decreases* inequality, or that *contractionary* policy *increases* income inequality (for a deeper discussion, see Kappes 2023). A very important finding, at least from a post-Keynesian perspective, appears in the work of Furceri, Loungani, and Zdzienicka (2018), who found that contractionary monetary shocks have statistically significant effects on income distribution, while expansionary shocks effects are not statistically different from zero. This points to long-run distributional consequences, since the impact of changes in interest rate do not net out over the business cycle. Despite this finding, mainstream economists claim that 'over the long run, inequality is not a monetary phenomenon' (Carstens 2021, p. 1) or that 'Over the longer horizon, the distributional impact is likely to die out given the temporary nature of the effects of monetary policy shocks' (Colciago, Samarina, and de Haan 2019, p. 220).

Yet, there are other important differences between the mainstream and post-Keynesian approaches. In fact, while the income distributive nature of monetary policy is not denied by the mainstream (Ampudia et al. 2018; O'Farrell, Rawdanowicz, and Inaba 2016; among others), the conclusion appears to be that it is a 'side effect', the 'unintended consequences' of disciplined — inflation-first — policy (Fontan, Claveau, and Dietsch 2016), and small (Inui, Sudou, and Yamada 2017, p. 3) and transitory (Bernanke 2015). In this sense, income distribution can be safely ignored in setting monetary policy and the pursuit of inflation targeting: 'Few [macroeconomists] would suggest that monetary policy should have targets for labor force participation, inequality, or the long-term real interest rate' (Mankiw and Reis 2018, p. 89). This can also be exemplified by a recent speech by Augustin Carstens (2021, pp. 1, 3), in which he affirms that '[...] the best contribution monetary policy can make to an equitable society is to try to keep the economy on an even keel by fulfilling its mandate' and that '[...] delivering on central banks' mandate of ensuring macroeconomic stability provides the best foundation for an equitable society'.

The implications of this debate for post-Keynesians cannot be underestimated. As the topic grows in interest among the mainstream, they will be able to set the terms of the discussion, as well as provide the empirical and policy conclusions. As such, it is imperative that post-Keynesians engage with the mainstream as quickly as possible to influence the debate on a topic that has been of interest to the larger heterodox community well before the advent of the financial crisis.

The Symposium

The papers in this symposium are the result of a workshop we held on 15–16 September 2022, at the Fields Institute in Toronto, funded partially by the Fields Institute and the Young Scholars Initiative, but mostly by the Social Sciences and Humanities Research Council. With this grant, we were able to bring together a total of 22 scholars over two days to discuss the relationship between monetary policy and income distribution, which is quickly becoming a dominant theme in post-Keynesian economics. Indeed, it has been an active area of research for the Monetary Policy Institute, which hosted the event. In addition to this symposium, we had previously published two books on the relationship between monetary policy and income distribution: Kappes, Rochon and Vallet (2023) was a more general discussion on the topic that began in Kappes, Rochon and Vallet (2022), while Rochon, Kappes and Vallet (2024) focused on the income distributive implications for gender.

This symposium publishes a number of the articles from this workshop, in addition to a few more. We would like to thank all those who participated and subsequently submitted their articles. We would also like to thank the referees who did a meticulous job at reviewing the manuscripts.

Disclosure Statement

No potential conflict of interest was reported by the author(s).

ORCID

Guillaume Vallet http://orcid.org/0000-0002-8359-649X

References

Ampudia, M., D. Georgarakos, J. Slacalek, O. Trist, P. Vermeulen, and G. Violante. 2018. 'Monetary Policy and Household Inequality.' Working Paper Series, n. 2179, European Central Bank.

Arestis, P., and P. Howells. 1991. 'Financial Innovations and the Distributional Effects of Interest Rate Changes in the UK.' *Eastern Economic Journal* 17 (3): 263–271.

Arestis, P., and P. Howells. 1994. 'Monetary Policy and Income Distribution in the UK.' *Review of Radical Political Economics* 26 (3): 56–65.

Bernanke, B. 2015. 'Why are Interest Rates so Low?' Brookings, March 30. https://www.brookings.edu/articles/why-are-interest-rates-so-low/.

Borio, C. 2021. 'The Distributional Footprint of Monetary Policy.' Speech at the Bank for International Settlement, June 29.

Carstens, A. 2021. 'Central Banks and Inequality.' Remarks at the Markus' Academy, Princeton University's Bendheim Center for Finance, May, 6.

Coibion, O., Y. Gorodnichenko, L. Kueng, and J. and Silvia. 2017. 'Innocent Bystanders? Monetary policy and inequality.' *Journal of Monetary Economics* 88: 70–89.

Colciago, A., A. Samarina, and J. de Haan. 2019. 'Central Bank Policies and Income and Wealth Inequality: A Survey.' *Journal of Economic Surveys* 33 (4): 1199–1231.

Fiebiger, B., and M. Lavoie. 2020. 'Helicopter Ben, Monetarism, the New Keynesian Credit View and Loanable Funds.' *Journal of Economic Issues* 54 (1): 77–96.

Fontan, C., F. Claveau, and P. Dietsch. 2016. '"Central Banking and Inequalities: Taking off the blinders", Politics.' *Philosophy & Economics* 15 (4): 319–357.

Furceri, D., P. Loungani, and A. Zdzienicka. 2018. 'The Effects of Monetary Policy Shocks on Inequality.' *Journal of International Money and Finance* 85: 168–186.

Haldane, A. G. 2018. 'How Monetary Policy Affects Your Gross Domestic Product.' *Australian Economic Review* 51 (3): 309–335.

Inui, M., N. Sudou, and T. Yamada. 2017. 'The Effects of Monetary Policy Shocks on Inequality in Japan.' BIS Working Paper n. 642.

Kappes, S. A. 2023. 'Monetary Policy and Personal Income Distribution: A Survey of the Empirical Literature.' *Review of Political Economy* 35 (1): 211–230.

Lavoie, M. 1996. 'Monetary Policy in an Economy with Endogenous Credit Money.' In *Money in Motion*, edited by E. Nell and G. Deleplace. London: Macmillan.

Lavoie, M., and M. Seccareccia. 1988. 'Money, Interest and Rentiers: The Twilight of Rentier Capitalism in Keynes's General Theory.' In *In Keynes and Public Policy After Fifty Years, vol. 2*, edited by O. Hamouda and J. Smithin. Aldershot: Edward Elgar.

Lavoie, M., and M. Seccareccia. 1999. 'Interest Rate: Fair.' In *Encyclopedia of Political Economy*, edited by P. O'Hara. London: Routledge.

Lavoie, M., and M. Seccareccia. 2025. 'Where do the Pasinetti Rule and the Pasinetti Index Come From?' *Review of Political Economy*, Forthcoming.

Lofaro, A., G. Matamoros, and L.-P. Rochon. 2023. 'Monetary Policy and Income Distribution: The Post-Keynesian and Sraffian Perspectives.' *Review of Political Economy* 36 (3): 892–918.

Mankiw, N. G., and R. Reis. 2018. 'Friedman's Presidential Address in the Evolution of Macroeconomic Thought.' *Journal of Economic Perspectives* 32 (1): 81–96.

Mersch, Y. 2014. 'Monetary Policy and Economic Inequality.' Corporate Credit Conference, European Central Bank, Zurich, October, 17. https://www.ecb.europa.eu/ press/ key/ date/ 2014/ html/sp141017 _1.en.htm.

Moore, B. 1989. 'The effects of monetary policy on income distribution.' In *Macroeconomic Problems and Policies of Income Distribution*, edited by P. Davidson and J. Kregel. Aldershot, VT: Edward Elgar Publishing.

Niggle, C. 1989, September. 'Monetary Policy and Changes in Income Distribution.' *Journal of Economic Issues* 23 (3): 809–822.

O'Farrell, R., Ł Rawdanowicz, and K. Inaba. 2016. 'Monetary Policy and Inequality.' OECD Publishing, Paris. OECD Economics Department Working Papers, No. 1281.

Rochon, L.-P. 2022. 'The General Ineffectiveness of Monetary Policy or the Weaponization of Inflation.' In *The Future of Central Banking*, edited by S. Kappes, L.-P. Rochon, and G. Vallet. Cheltenham: Edward Elgar.

Rochon, L.-P., and M. Setterfield. 2007. 'Interest Rates, Income Distribution and Monetary Policy Dominance: Post Keynesians and the 'Fair' Rate of Interest.' *Journal of Post Keynesian Economics* 30 (1): 13–41.

Rochon, L.-P., and M. Setterfield. 2008. 'The Political Economy of Interest Rate Setting, Inflation, and Income Distribution.' *International Journal of Political Economy* 37 (2): 2–25.

Rochon, L.-P., and M. Setterfield. 2012. 'A Kaleckian Model of Growth and Distribution with Conflict-Inflation and Post-Keynesian Nominal Interest Rate Rules.' *Journal of Post Keynesian Economics* 34 (3): 497–520.

Seccareccia, L. a. 2016. 'Income Distribution, Rentiers, and Their Role in a Capitalist Economy: A Keynes–Pasinetti Perspective.' *International Journal of Political Economy* 45: 200–223.

Smithin, J. 1994. *Controversies in Monetary Economics: Ideas, Issues, and Policy*. Aldershot: Edward Elgar.

Monetary Policy and Income Distribution: The Post-Keynesian and Sraffian Perspectives

Antonino Lofaro, Guillermo Matamoros and Louis-Philippe Rochon

ABSTRACT
This paper examines the post-Keynesian and Sraffian perspectives on the relationship between monetary policy and income distribution, highlighting their endogenous demand-led money approach and rejection of the neutrality of interest rates, and monetary policy as tool of redistribution among social classes. Both approaches acknowledge that the central bank can influence interest rates and hence, the functional distribution of income. These shared ideas recognize the political nature of interest rates and the distributive impacts of monetary policy. Although all are crucial common points, some differences persist; PK theory often emphasizes the impact of monetary policy on rentiers vs. non-rentier classes, while Sraffians focus more on wage earners vs. non-wage earners. Further, while PK theorists advocate for alternative monetary policy rules, Sraffians favor discretionary policy tailored to each economy's unique institutional framework. The paper concludes by suggesting that these shared critical conceptions, despite minor differences, should stimulate collaborative efforts to further develop heterodox theories of monetary policy and income distribution.

Introduction

After the great financial crisis (GFC), the distributional impact of monetary policy became a central topic in mainstream academia and policy circles. Most mainstream work, however, focus on *personal* income distribution, pointing out that the distributional effects of monetary policy would not be structural, but only temporary (Kappes, 2023). These results appear perfectly in line with the long-run neutrality of money historically assumed by mainstream New Keynesian economists.

On the other hand, there is a prolonged tradition within heterodox economics claiming that interest rates are primarily distributional in nature, focusing on social groups, and determined by convention, whose repercussions are long-lasting in essence. Notably, the post-Keynesian (PK) and Sraffian perspectives have advanced the relationship between monetary policy and *functional* income distribution since at least the 1980s.

In this paper, we aim to describe what has been the history of ideas of these two heterodox schools on this issue, trying to point out the points of convergence as well as the differences between them.

This paper is divided into the following two sections: first, we consider the views developed and proposed by post-Keynesians, and second, we turn our attention to the ones developed by Sraffians. In the next section, we address the post-Keynesian tradition by first commenting on how Keynes, Robinson and Pasinetti raised crucial issues on the topic, although in an early stage. Moving on, we discuss how these original contributions would be further developed all in the 1980s by who we call the 'post-Keynesian mavericks' — mainly the views of Eichner, Lavoie and Seccareccia, Moore and Niggle.[1] We argue that the crisis and stagnation of the 1980s — including the unprecedented economic policy austerity — played a key role in the advancement of an alternative monetary policy approach within post-Keynesian economics. Finally, we proceed to sketch out the post-Keynesian ideas that emerged in the 1990s and early 2000s, against the backdrop of the widespread dominance of the Taylor rule. Post-Keynesians reacted by formulating alternative monetary policy rules based on income distribution considerations.

In the second section, we focus our attention on the Sraffian theory (or classical-Keynesian or surplus approach), which originated in the works of Piero Sraffa and Pierangelo Garegnani, who revived the theory of value and distribution of Marx, Smith and Ricardo. We will do this by following a chronological order, as done in the previous section. The discussion will begin with an analysis of the thinking of the classical economists and Marx, who gave great importance to the conflict between social classes in determining the functional distribution of income. However, we will emphasize how, perhaps except for Marx, monetary policy did not play a decisive role in this process.

From here, we continue with the reinterpretation that took place after World War II by Sraffa, who showed how even within this approach, it may be possible to define a link between monetary policy and income distribution through a monetary determination of the profit rate. Afterward, we show how in the 1980s the ideas of Sraffa were developed by researchers in the classical-Keynesian tradition, such as Pivetti and Panico, in which specific relationships would be defined whereby, in line with the post-Keynesian strand and in antithesis to the neoclassical strand, monetary policy would not be neutral with respect to income distribution, even in the long run.

Finally, the last section concludes by drawing both commonalities and differences between the post-Keynesian and Sraffian approaches, pointing out how the elements of compatibility between these two theories would justify the need for further future research on these issues.

Monetary Policy and Income Distribution: The Post-Keynesian Tradition

This section reviews the post-Keynesian tradition of monetary policy and income distribution beginning with Keynes, Robinson, and Pasinetti, who on several occasions, covered monetary policy from a heterodox perspective, and discussed the rate of interest

[1]We call these post-Keynesians 'maverick' because their approach stood in contrast to much of what was discussed at that time in the post-Keynesian literature, which we contend was rather conventional, and amounted to what Rochon and Setterfield (2008) call the 'activist approach': the conventional use of fine-tuning interest rate policy to achieve a desired goal. Seeing monetary policy as distributional was certainly not widely accepted among post-Keynesians.

as a distributional variable. These views would only be further revied or developed decades later in the work of the so-called post-Keynesian mavericks in the 1980s. Finally, we describe some of the earlier advancements in the tradition that have to do with actual policy proposals based on a critical appraisal of Taylor-type rules that have dominated monetary policy discussions in recent decades.

Antecedents: John Maynard Keynes, Joan Robinson, and Luigi Pasinetti

In the first chapter of *A Tract on Monetary Reform* (1923), Keynes analyzed how changes in the inflation-discounted rate of interest — the real rate of interest — affected income distribution between rentiers (those who make a living chiefly out of interest-bearing assets) and non-rentier groups, in a world dominated by fixed interest rate contracts (see Seccareccia and Matamoros 2023, for more details). The chapter showed Keynes's preoccupation with the consequences of rising social discontent regarding the stability of Western Europe during the agitated interwar period.

This interest-income redistribution mechanism would put forward the essential fact that the interest rate is not only a price (or a cost) but also a source (or a loss) of income for someone. Furthermore, Keynes pointed out that a continuous increase in interest payments could bring about a vicious cycle of low investment due to its perverse effects on the behavior of entrepreneurs. For instance, high interest rates convey large financial returns that would discourage current and potential entrepreneurs to venture their capital in investment projects and instead incentivize them to engage in speculative activities or rentier behavior.

However, Keynes did not identify workers as the primary threat to peace. Rather, he was concerned with the dangers posed by a monetary policy put in place to favor the rentier class, thereby magnifying income inequalities. A 'rentier first' monetary policy would provide no incentive whatsoever to invest, and social life could be ultimately transformed into a casino. This idea of the perverse effects of a rentier-first policy would be carried forward to the *General Theory* (1936, 334), to the point where he advocated the 'euthanasia of the rentier' by keeping interest rates low, which in turn would minimize hoarding activities and promote full employment.

To be fair, however, the *General Theory* only touches tangentially on the distributional impacts of interest rate policies. In contrast, some of the founding post-Keynesians, notably Joan Robinson in the 1950s and later Luigi Pasinetti in the early 1980s, took up Keynes's insights to provide a clearer perspective on how monetary policy influences income distribution. In this vein, Robinson's exposition is almost a natural extension of the ideas that Keynes only sketched out previously; meanwhile Pasinetti has the virtue of modeling the rate of interest as a distributional variable within a pure labor economy — an economy composed only of workers.

In chapters 24 and 25 of her *magnum opus*, *The Accumulation of Capital*, Robinson (1956) analyzed the interest rate as a distributional variable with special emphasis on its effect on what she called the rentier share of profit, i.e., the income of the rentier class derived primarily from interest payments on loans, which are a deduction from business profits.[2] She did not hesitate to reveal the intrinsic conflict between entrepreneurs and

[2]Rochon (1999) was one of the first to draw attention to Robinson's (1956) understanding of money and monetary policy. Moreover, Robinson's view of interest payments as a deduction of profits has a clear connection with the Sraffian

rentiers over the distribution of profits, where the variable in dispute is the rate of interest. Furthermore, compared to Keynes, she was more incisive in how the distribution of income and wealth both within and among social classes impacted the rate of investment.

Firstly, she noticed that, apart from entrepreneurs differing in their psychological inclination to invest, the so-called animal spirits that were so important in Keynes, entrepreneurs differ as well in what Robinson termed 'borrowing power'. The borrowing power is the capacity of an entrepreneur to get a loan at a certain moment, and it depends on the entrepreneur's respective net income and wealth. It follows that the rate of investment would be conditioned by 'the distribution of borrowing power amongst entrepreneurs' (Robinson 1956, 244), such that, given a certain distribution, a reduction in the rentier share would increase the rate of investment because the borrowing power of the entrepreneur class has been strengthened and the mass of credit expanded.

In addition, Robinson explicitly stated the connections between changes in the money rate of interest, income distribution, and the rate of investment. In her endogenous money framework, she claimed that a monetary policy trying to stimulate investment through low interest rates would be effective if it increases capacity utilization rates. For example, she mentions the importance of the accelerator effect of private expenditure in cases of redistribution that provoke the reduction of the rentier share vis-a-vis the net-profits share. Like Keynes, Robinson was aware of the potential benefits for investment and capital accumulation of a reduction in the rentier share, something that could be accomplished by a policy of low interest rates (Robinson 1956, 253).

On the other hand, in his 1981 book *Structural Change and Economic Growth*, Pasinetti (1981) dedicated a chapter to the role of the rate of interest as a distributional variable (see also Pasinetti 1980). In it, in the simplest formulation, when he assumed labor is the only factor of production, the rate of productivity growth must equal the rate of real wage growth. Thus, the rate of interest emerges as soon as inter-personal credit relations are present, which implies people willing to postpone consumption (creditors) and advance consumption (debtors). It follows that the rate of interest that preserves distribution between creditors and debtors is the rate of interest that maintains the purchasing power of the sum lent in labor time, which occurs when the real rate of interest is equal to the growth rate of real wages (or labor productivity). This rate of interest would guarantee a constant income share of creditors — also known as rentier share — , which he called it the 'natural' rate of interest. Although there is no automatic tendency for the rate of interest to follow real wage growth, he concluded that any other rate would necessarily affect the distribution of income in favor of creditors (rentiers), if it is higher than real wage growth, and vice versa.

At that time, Pasinetti did not quite explore the monetary policy implications of his theory, but in subsequent work (Pasinetti 2002), he eventually came up with the normative implications of maintaining the rentier share constant through keeping the real rate of interest equal to real wage growth, so that he named this rate as the 'just' rate of

approach of the relationship between the rate of interest and the profit rate, in which, broadly speaking, interest payments are incorporated in the normal profit rate as a cost component to the firm. This will be developed further in the next section but, to be fair, as Lavoie (2022, 183) has pointed out, this view was shared among many post-Keynesians, such as Harrod, Kaldor, Graziani, Sylos Labini, among others. Similarly, Arestis and Howells (1994, 63) add Kalecki and J. K. Galbraith to the list, signaling that Kalecki first put forward 'that the redistributional effects of interest rates depend directly on the responsiveness of the markup to interest rates'.

interest. He suggested that monetary policy ought to be conducted with reference to the 'just' rate of interest to see how it is affecting distribution and who are the winners and losers of this policy.

The Mavericks: Post-Keynesians in the 1980s

Despite all these early contributions, the link between monetary policy and distribution remained a bit blurred. It was rather a side topic in the theories of the early post-Keynesians, such that it never took the center stage of analysis in their major books or research papers. In that sense, it was not until the late 1980s, when a few established post-Keynesians picked it up and provided a comprehensive form of understanding the effects of interest rate policy on the distribution of income and wealth.

Eichner (1987), Lavoie and Seccareccia (1988), Seccareccia (1988), Moore (1989), and Niggle (1989), all wrote original papers that constitute the foundations of the post-Keynesian perspective on monetary policy and income distribution.[3] It is not accidental that these authors, mostly associated with the horizontalist approach, all wrote in the 1980s. Those were hard times for the working class due to the severe crisis, coupled with the merciless dismantling of the welfare state. These were hard times as well for post-Keynesian economics because they were progressively isolated in mainstream academia and policy debates for not sharing the crucial assumptions of orthodox economics (e.g., the representative optimizing individual, the neutrality of money, and so on). But precisely because of this, post-Keynesians were able to develop an alternative explanation of the causes and consequences of the 1980s economic crisis which was tied to distribution and power relations between social classes.

To begin, post-Keynesians argued that the inflationary surge in the 1970s and early 1980s was supply-sided, having to do more with the oil shocks and specific supply-chain bottlenecks. Also, the 80s crisis was induced — at least partly — by a policy response to fighting inflation but did not tackle any of the major inflation pressures — what Tobin (1974) called 'inflation hysteria'. Indeed, according to him, 'hysteria about inflation may lead to policies that keep economic progress well below its potential'.

Instead, macroeconomic policies were oriented towards the redistribution of income away from workers through a combination of huge interest rate hikes associated with Fed Chair Volcker and a restructuring in fiscal policy focused on curtailing social spending and giving tax benefits for the wealthy. In particular, monetary policy switched decisively to an inflation first-and-only strategy at all costs, meaning that interest rates would overshoot upwards whenever the inflation rate picks up to keep real rates always positive and high, thereby prioritizing the share of rentier income over the income shares of workers and capitalists (Seccareccia and Matamoros 2023b).[4]

---

[3]As to the influence of Keynes, Robinson and Pasinetti in these foundational works, Eichner (1987) does not cite them directly, but he includes them as recommended readings; Lavoie and Seccareccia (1988) mention Keynes, Robinson and Pasinetti in several occasions; Moore (1989, 27) analyses Keynes's view of interest rates and distribution in the *General Theory*; and Niggle (1989) does not refer to them but he mentions a 1988 mimeo-version of Moore (1989).

[4]The fact that most recent evidence points that monetary policy affects income distribution primarily through changes in interest payments and employment levels, suggests that the main driver of rentiers as a social class is the rate of interest (see Kappes 2023, for a literature review). Yet, despite asset price appreciation and capital gains are also a source of distributional changes, they might be more important for intra-class redistribution within the rentier class, as

Mainstream economists argued that the Volcker policy was a painful but necessary medicine to cure high inflation, given that for them money is neutral and monetary policy could not have any long-term effects on income distribution (see Kappes 2023; and Seccareccia and Matamoros 2023, for recent reviews of the mainstream perspective). Conversely, post-Keynesians always rejected any notion of money neutrality and the existence of a unique 'neutral' rate of interest; as such it was obvious that the Volcker policy would have tremendous consequences on personal and functional income distribution and ultimately on economic growth. Several post-Keynesian economists like Smithin (1996) noted that the Volcker policy was just mirroring what he called 'the revenge of the rentiers' — although the expression predates Smithin's book by several years (see Morris 1982) — which was nothing but a rentier-first monetary policy aiming at defending the interests of the rentier (or financial) groups, which corroborated that central bankers were, so to speak, the executive committee of the rentier class.

The list of the 'maverick post-Keynesians' begins with Eichner (1987), who pointed out that the money rate of interest is just another distributional variable, such as the wage rate and the firm's markup. He claimed that if the supply of credit is perfectly elastic at an exogenous interest rate fixed by the central bank, it has nothing to do with time preferences or productivity, such that the rate of interest is an administered price that ought to be an outcome of policy decisions concerning a socially acceptable share of rentier income. His only explicit recommendation for monetary policy was to keep nominal interest rates equal or slightly above the rate of inflation.[5]

Almost simultaneously, at a Toronto conference in 1986 at York University in honor of the 50th anniversary of the *General Theory*, Lavoie and Seccareccia (1988) exposed the paramount increase in the concentration of income since the late-1970s because of a rentier first monetary policy, inspired not only by the ideas of Keynes, but also those of Joan Robinson and Luigi Pasinetti, which the authors cite explicitly.[6]

At that conference, Lavoie and Seccareccia argued succinctly that 'changes in the rate of interest have both a direct and indirect impact on the distribution of income between rentiers and the 'active earning class' of workers and entrepreneurs.' (Lavoie and Seccareccia 1988, 151) They underscored how, *ceteris paribus*, a rise in the rate of interest increases the rentier share, which in turn impacts unemployment not only by reducing the level of investment — as suggested by Robinson — but also by reducing the aggregate propensity to consume and impacting aggregate demand. Accordingly, the authors proposed what would later be known as the Pasinetti Index (PI): a measure of income redistribution trends between the rentier and non-rentier groups resulting from monetary policy.

The initial proposal of the PI was the difference between the real rate of interest and average labor productivity growth: $\rho - z$.[7] It had the objective of measuring the extent

mainstream literature has shown that capital gains affect primarily the wealthy households (McKay and Wolf 2023). Although perhaps more research is needed from post-Keynesian economics on this matter.

[5] This view amounts to what Rochon and Setterfield (2008) have called the Smithin Rule, that is a real rate of interest close to zero.

[6] As a side note, Pasinetti spent a few months in Ottawa as a visiting professor at the University of Ottawa and Carleton University the same year of the publication of his 1981 book. There is no doubt that both the book and Pasinetti's visit — and the discussion that ensued — would inspire part of the work of Lavoie and Seccareccia in subsequent years.

[7] There is an unresolved discussion on which rate of interest would be adequate (for instance, see Lofaro and Rochon 2023). To some extent, it depends on what precisely is expected to be captured with the index. Nonetheless, Seccareccia and Lavoie (2016) argue that a long-term interest rate (e.g., the rate on 10-year government bonds) would be

of income redistribution between rentiers and non-rentiers in the medium or long-term, to some extent emulating the traditional measure of income redistribution between workers and capitalists that is the wage-productivity growth gap (see Seccareccia 1988). If the PI is positive, meaning $\rho > z$, one would expect a net transfer of income from the non-rentier groups towards the rentier class, and vice versa. It is worth mentioning that Lavoie and Seccareccia (1988) also presented the index using output growth as a proxy for productivity growth, $\rho - g$, a measure that could be roughly compared to the now famous Piketty's (2014, 25) law of capitalism, but relying on very different theoretical grounds (see Seccareccia and Lavoie 2016; see also Rochon and Setterfield 2008, for a discussion). However, this simply shows that when the debate on distribution and macroeconomic policy was minimal in mainstream circles, post-Keynesians were already digging into the theoretical mechanisms and evidence of this subject.

Furthermore, Lavoie and Seccareccia (1988) argue that although the central bank is only able to fix the short-run money rate of interest and what determines the extent of the rentier transfer is the real rate of interest, monetary policy can be conducted with relative flexibility to make sure that money interest rates follow inflation with certain precision. In addition, monetary policy can also exert influence over long-term interest rates given that they generally mirror short-term interest rates — although the yield curve does have other determinants such as liquidity preference, risk premiums and markups (points also raised by Eichner 1987).

Along these lines, Moore (1989) stated that since the core of post-Keynesian price theory is based on imperfect competition and markup pricing, monetary policy might directly impact the wage share. In his words, 'the functional redistribution effect of changes in interest rates centers directly on the responsiveness of the mark-up to interest rates' (Moore 1989, 25). Obviously, this responsiveness would depend on several factors, for instance whether the change in interest rates is temporary, the degree of capacity utilization, and so on. But, in general, long-lasting increases or decreases in interest rates might be passed on to prices by firms to maintain their profit targets. If markups over normal unit cost are maintained, the trends in interest rates would be inversely correlated with the share of wages in total income.[8]

On similar grounds, Niggle (1989) argued that monetary policy affects the functional distribution of income through changes in the level of interest rates but also depending on the debt-income ratio for the economy. According to the author, 'The processes connecting monetary policy to changes in the distribution of personal income through the transmission mechanism of the level of interest rates are complex, with at least three causal sequences operating: 1) changes in interest rates can affect the functional distribution of income, and thus the personal distribution; 2) changes in interest rates change the

more appropriate to depict Keynes's original idea of rentiers as a class who makes a living chiefly out of interest-bearing assets.

[8]This last position by Moore appears interesting, indeed the hypothesis of an effect of monetary policy on markups, as we shall see in the same manner as the Sraffian theory, would point to an effect of monetary policy on the distribution of income due to the change in prices and real wages. Therefore, even if from an activist position, one could find in Moore a relationship between monetary policy and income distribution in line with the parking-it approach. It might be interesting to try to understand in future work whether this can also be a link within the post-Keynesian monetary policy debate between the activist and parking-it approaches. For an interpretation of Moore's monetary theory evolution, see Rochon (2020).

market values of financial assets, effecting capital gains or losses; 3) interest rates influence investment, aggregate demand, employment and income' (Niggle 1989, 818–9).

Furthermore, he and Moore (1989) put forth the many difficulties of trying to measure these effects due to, for instance, the fact that changes in interest rates might negatively influence financial asset values, whence affecting capital gains/losses and income distribution in the opposite direction as the income distribution channel would normally do. However, he stresses out that, at least with respect to financial assets (as opposed to, say, real estate assets), Keynes's view was that interest income payments would dominate capital gains as the primary redistribution force over time, since short-run capital gains would be offset eventually by lower future interest income streams in the overall functional income distribution:

> Keynes's interest rate redistribution argument overlooked the inverse effects of interest rate variation on wealth and so on income in the form of capital gains. As interest rates fall, the value of capital assets, as determined by the discounted value of their future income stream, necessarily increases, so that capital gains will occur in the process. While Keynes's explicit argument was that in the case of reproducible assets the future income streams would fall proportionately with interest rates, this would not be the case for land (Moore 1989, 29)

Interestingly, from the 1980s group of five post-Keynesian mavericks, perhaps only Marc Lavoie and Mario Seccareccia would adopt and develop the relationship between monetary policy and distribution as a dominant topic in their research agenda. For instance, they proposed the name 'fair' rate of interest to the 'rate of interest that will leave unchanged the distribution of income between interest and non-interest income groups, regardless of lending and borrowing activities' (Lavoie and Seccareccia 1999, 543), that is, the rate of interest that keeps the PI equal to zero. Furthermore, they have also worked on building bridges between post-Keynesian and other heterodox traditions on this topic (see Lavoie 1992a; 1992b; 1996)[9] and on advancing monetary policy proposals (Lavoie and Seccareccia 2020). Ultimately, their work became the common thread between the 1980s foundations and the subsequent developments in the PK approach to monetary policy and income distribution.[10]

A Long and Live Tradition: Some Subsequent Contributions

The decades that followed the turmoil of the 1980s were characterized by an increasing number of post-Keynesian economists writing extensively on monetary policy and distribution. On the one hand, a branch of research continued the focus on the income distribution channels of interest rate policy both in terms of their formalization and their empirical evidence (see, for instance, Arestis and Howells 1991; 1994; Argitis 2001; Argitis and Michopoulou 2010). On the other hand, a new branch of research emerged in the 1990s as a critical reaction to the inflation targeting regimes and Taylor rules that became so popular among central banks in those years. The post-Keynesian monetary policy toolkit was summarized in a series of interest rate rules

[9] Particularly, Lavoie (1992a; 1992b), inspired by the work of his colleague Henry (1982), argues that post-Keynesian and neo-Ricardian (or Sraffian) economics could be merged into a single paradigm called postclassical economics. On the concept of money, he claims that post-Keynesians and Sraffians agree on the fundamental notion that credit-money is endogenous and demand-led à la Kaldor, while the rate of interest is exogenous and determined by convention.

[10] Today, in many ways, Rochon has taken on this task by organizing workshops and editing books on these topics.

(See Rochon and Setterfield 2007, 2008 and 2012), which, combined with fiscal policy coordination, targeted inflation, employment, and distributional outcomes (for recent reviews, see Rochon and Seccareccia 2023; and Seccareccia and Matamoros 2022, 2023).

One of the first attempts to suggest a new monetary policy framework was Lavoie (1996), who while rejecting the fine-tuning approach to monetary policy, tried to summarize how monetary policy ought to be conducted in an endogenous demand-led money framework. He suggested:

> [...] monetary policy should not so much be designed to control the level of activity, but rather to find the level of interest rates that will be proper for the economy from a distribution point of view. The aim of such a policy should be to minimize conflict over income shares, in the hope of simultaneously keeping inflation low and activity high. (Lavoie 1996, 536)

Furthermore, several post-Keynesian economists pinpointed that the income distribution channels would likely have within class redistribution as well. For instance, Galbraith (1998) claims that monetary policy also has intra-class redistribution effects. As such, there would be income redistribution towards high income workers whenever there is an 'inflation first' monetary policy that keeps unemployment relatively high for long periods. He argues that some sectors or industries are more vulnerable to changes in interest rates and private spending, such as those industries within the services sector with lower wages and weaker bargaining power, so that they are also the sectors that suffer a great deal under high unemployment rates. These sectors tend to get below-average wage increments that rarely keep up with price inflation. Not all workers have the same bargaining power, and so they can be ranked in what Galbraith (1998, Ch. 4) called the 'wage structure', that depends on the wage rate, their bargaining and borrowing power, and their financial vulnerability.

In a similar vein, Argitis and Pitelis (2001), in a framework that combines the PK and Sraffian approaches (due to their similarities, which will be portrayed in the following sections), point out that monetary policy not only affects distribution between workers and capitalists, but also among financial and non-financial capitalists. An increase in the rate of interest means greater interest costs-prices for non-financial capitalists — following the cost channel — but the extent to which this would reduce real wages depends on the power of workers to negotiate higher nominal pay. According to their evidence, they conclude that 'monetary policy emerges, therefore, as a channel through which intracapitalist distributional conflicts directly affects the distribution of non-wage income between industrial and financial capital' (Argitis and Pitelis 2001, 632)

At the turn of the Twentieth century, innovative contributions tried to put together an alternative post-Keynesian monetary policy framework that considers inflation, distribution, and employment — in conjunction with fiscal policy. These post-Keynesian proposals were characterized for being very critical of the 'inflation-first' monetary policies and Taylor rules adopted by most central banks (at least until the GFC), but also this post-Keynesian alternative framework debated whether another interest rate rule (or 'automatic pilot') ought to be pursued e.g., a rule that targets certain distributional norm over a determined period. If so, what interest rate rule should be followed? As opposed to the mainstream Taylor rule that relies on the existence of a unique 'natural' interest rate that would supposedly stabilize price inflation, post-Keynesian interest rate rules were designed on the base of a strong skepticism over interest rate 'fine-tuning' or what Rochon (2022) calls the 'general ineffectiveness' of monetary policy.

On this new literature of post-Keynesian interest rate rules, that distinguishes from previous research for advancing concrete policy prescriptions, Rochon and Setterfield (2007, 2008, 2012) argue that there are basically three rules on the table. First, the Pasinetti rule proposes setting the real interest rate equal to the rate of growth in labor productivity i.e., the interest rate consistent with a zero PI ($\rho - z = 0$) and a constant rentier income share. Second, the Smithin rule recommends setting the real interest rate virtually at zero ($\rho = 0$), implying a declining rentier income share if there is positive productivity growth. And third, the Kansas City rule advocates fixing the money interest rate at zero ($i = 0$). Of course, when inflation and productivity growth are very low, such as in an environment of secular stagnation, the differences between the three rules are trivial in practice. But when inflation picks up, for instance in the current pandemic inflationary surge, the divergences between interest rate rules do matter in terms of their potential impact on income distribution, employment, and growth. In such circumstances, the nature of the inflation process (e.g., the type of price pressures) and the productive structure of the economy (e.g., how binding is the external constraint) both may suggest that interest rate rules, if adopted, should be targeted in long-term horizons and accompanied by central bank dual or multigoal mandates that guarantee certain coordination with fiscal policy to attain full employment, attenuate income inequality, and preserve financial stability (see Seccareccia and Matamoros 2022).

On another note, Seccareccia and Lavoie (2010) put forward that 'inflation first' monetary policy — that morphed into inflation targeting monetary policy in the 1990s — has been a tool used against workers by threatening them to raise interest rates and increase unemployment if they do not moderate their wage claims. In their pursuance of price stability, central banks have been repressed workers' demands for higher pay. The authors claim this procedure is not very different from the incomes policies put in place in the 1960s and 1970s to check inflation by setting voluntary guidelines on the wage claims. The difference is that monetary policy does not need to justify its actions other than on inflation concerns, and its effectiveness to control wage claims is based on fear rather than on deliberation and consensus. In that sense, monetary policy can be seen as a 'perverse incomes policy that raises the income of one group, the rentiers, while slowing the income growth especially of wages earners' (Seccareccia and Lavoie 2010, 40).

More recently, Lavoie and Seccareccia (2019) discussed extensively the PI. Hence, they propose a revised interpretation, the labor-commanded PI, that is defined instead as the difference between the money rate of interest and the growth in the money wage rate, $i - w$, which would be more in line with Pasinetti's original conception of preserving the value of exchanges in labor time. This labor-commanded PI is important because it accounts for long-term changes in the wage share produced by the divergence between real wages and productivity over time. However, to be fair, both PIs behave similarly over time particularly if they are looked in the medium or long run. In this regard, the PI has become a trademark present since the birth of the post-Keynesian perspective on monetary policy and distribution in the 1980s. Yet, PK economics was not alone in its endeavor, as we will put forth in the following section with the review of the Sraffian perspective.

Monetary Policy and Income Distribution: The Sraffian or Classical-Keynesian Perspective

Having discussed the relationship between monetary policy, interest rates and income distribution in the post-Keynesian approach, in this section we will focus on how Sraffian scholars — also known as the Classical-Keynesian approach — have dealt with this topic. Originating in the work of Sraffa (1960) and Pierangelo Garegnani (1978, 1979, 1984), it represents a revival of the theory of value and distribution of the classical economists (Smith and Ricardo) and Marx.[11] This theory, founded on the notion of social surplus, gave great importance to the conflict between social classes in determining the distribution of income. It was revived and developed in contrast to the neoclassical or marginalist theory, which was based on the mechanism of substitutability between factors of production.[12] However, with the exception perhaps of Marx, monetary policy would not have had an influence on functional income distribution in neither Smith nor Ricardo. Hence, having originated on such a basis, some post-Keynesian authors have concluded that the Sraffian theory had little discussion of the role of money (for instance, see Davidson 1999). In contrast, however, others such as Lavoie[13] (2013, 36) observe that:

> It is often claimed that Sraffians do not take into account financial and monetary factors. But what has been the contribution of the other Post-Keynesians in this regard, when analysing pricing and relative prices? The Sraffians were the first to claim that relative prices and real wages are affected by the trend level of the rate of interest, through its proportional impact on the normal profit rate, that is, the target rate of return embedded in the pricing mark-up.

Indeed, from the very beginning, in his seminal work, *Production of Commodities by Commodities* (1960), Sraffa introduced the relationship between monetary policy and income distribution. Consider the following: 'The rate of profits, as a ratio, has a significance which is independent of any prices, and can well be 'given' before the prices are fixed. It is accordingly susceptible of being determined from outside the system of production, in particular by the level of the money rate of interest' (Sraffa 1960, 33).

Later, Sraffa's suggestion was developed by Classical-Keynesian scholars, such as Panico (1988a) an Pivetti (1991) in what has been called the *Monetary Theory of Distribution*, which, in line with post-Keynesian theory, would theorize a decisive influence of monetary policy on income distribution. However, as done in the previous section, before analyzing this theory, we will discuss the relationship that exists between interest rates and income distribution in classical authors and Marx, to better emphasize the similarities and differences with the Sraffian perspective.

Monetary Policy and Income Distribution Before Sraffa's Work: The View of Smith, Ricardo, and Marx

For neoclassical economists, income distribution would be determined by real or 'natural' variables, each factor of production being remunerated according to its marginal

[11] Following Garegnani (1984) and other authors, the analytical differences between the classical economists and Marx are sufficient to consider them separately.

[12] See Garegnani (1970) on the various critical points of the marginalist theory of value and distribution.

[13] Also, Lavoie (1995, 147) expresses a similar position in the debate on the role of money in heterodox models of growth and distribution. For the current status of the theoretical discussion between post-Keynesians and classical-Keynesians, see also some considerations of Stirati and Zezza (2022).

productivity. Therefore, monetary policy would have no influence on it and, rather, would have to adjust to the natural rate of interest (the profit rate for this theory), which would be fixed by 'productivity and thrift' (Wicksell 1898; Robertson 1940). In contrast, for Smith, Ricardo and Marx, income distribution would not be based on natural laws but on the conflict between social classes. For example, the wage rate would not be equal to the marginal productivity of labor but to a 'subsistence level' determined by historical, social, and institutional circumstances.[14] Hence, in their analysis, the real wage rate was the independent variable, and given the technical conditions of production, the normal profit rate would be determined as a residual. However, in the next few pages, we will try to understand whether these differences with neoclassical theory also concern the role of monetary policy. Specifically, will interest rate changes in the work of Smith, Ricardo and Marx be able to influence the distribution of income among different classes?

A potential link between interest rate and income distribution can be found in the definition of the profit rate[15] (r), which, as pointed out by Adam Smith in *The Wealth of Nations* (1776, 70–71), is composed of the money interest rate[16] (i), taken in *real terms*, and the normal profits of enterprise (*npe*). At the level of social classes, the real interest rate would represent the remuneration for the class of financial capitalists. Normal profits of enterprise would correspond to the portion of the profit rate that would go to the non-financial capitalists who take the *risk and trouble* of employing capital productively.[17]

Therefore, assuming equality of normal profits of enterprise in the different spheres of production, we have:

$$r = i + npe$$

Hence, simplifying, monetary policy could have a dual influence on income distribution. Firstly, there would is the impact on the components of the normal profit rate (i and *npe*) and the distribution of profits between productive and financial capitalists. Secondly, there is the effect on the distribution of income between workers and capitalists, influencing the levels of the real wage and the profit rate.

However, Smith's and Ricardo's views would differ from Marx's with respect to the role of the interest rate and its effect on the functional income distribution.

For Smith and Ricardo, profits ($\bar{r}$), determined by the real wage rate and technical conditions of production, must be able to remunerate the *risk and trouble* of the productive use of capital ($\overline{npe}$). Neither of these variables would be affected by the interest rate. Rather, once we deduct from profits a remuneration for normal profits of enterprise,

[14]On the classical wage theory, see Stirati (1994), and Levrero (2011, 2012). In this theory, it is the disadvantage that workers usually have in wage bargaining that causes the wage to tend to its subsistence level, the historically determined minimum wage compatible with 'common humanity' and relative social stability. It was admitted, however, that that 'disadvantage' could change in the presence of rapid capital accumulation, or through the action of labor unions.

[15]For a more detailed discussion of how these economists interpreted the relationships between profit wages, interest rates, and normal profits of enterprise, see Pivetti (1991, 61–69) and Zolea (2022).

[16]Among the various monetary interest rates, the most relevant will be the real interest rate on long-term securities, which is the main rate for financing the purchase of capital goods and is the one that matters when analyzing the relationship between interest rates and the rate of profit, as clearly pointed out by Lavoie (1995, 145).

[17]Such normal profits of enterprise would vary from sector to sector, so industries might have different profit rates.

we obtain as a residual the rate of money interest[18] (Δi):

$$\bar{r} = \Delta i + \overline{npe}$$

It follows that monetary policy is neutral,[19] having no possibility of influencing the profitability of capital and, more generally, the distribution of income among different social classes. In contrast, capital profitability has effects on interest rate movements (see Ricardo 1821, 300). In this regard, Pivetti (1991, 8) points out that at least for the long run: 'An important implication of this way of conceiving the relation between the two rates [profit rate and interest rate] is the denial of any substantial power on the part of monetary authorities'.

On the other hand, Marx does not seem to accept the real nature of the rate of interest, especially in *Capital*, anticipating some elements that will be taken up by both post-Keynesians and Classical-Keynesians. For the German economist, the rate of interest is a monetary variable determined by convention[20] (Marx 1894, p. 362), and as such, it cannot continually adjust to changes in the rate of profit[21] (see Pivetti 1991, p.9). Therefore, the idea of an interest rate independent of the profit rate would imply that in Marx the residual variable would be the remuneration of productive capitalists, the normal profits of enterprise. Given the rate of profit ($\bar{r}$) and the rate of interest ($\bar{i}$), the normal profits of enterprise (Δnpe) must adjust to maintain this equality:

$$\bar{r} = \bar{i} + \Delta npe$$

This conventional nature of the interest rate would also mean for Marx an effect on the distribution of income. Indeed, according to Marx, financial and productive capitalists, while they will be united in their desire for increases in the rate of profit at the expense of workers, will find themselves in conflict when they must share surplus value. More specifically, the division of the profits between interests and normal profits of enterprise would depend on the struggle between financial and productive capital (see Panico 1980; 1988b). Hence, it would justify the Marxian assumption that normal profits of enterprise are inversely proportional to the rate of money interest.[22] Indeed, as Marx (1894, 379) tells us, 'assuming the average profit to be given, the rate of the profit of enterprise is ... determined ... by the rate of the interest. It is high or low in inverse proportion to it'.

---

[18]See Pivetti (1991, 8).

[19]For the sake of clarity, it should be specified that we are assessing the neutrality of monetary policy solely with respect to the effect on income distribution. In the classical authors, the determination of output is separate from that of income distribution, and therefore there could be different influences of financial conditions depending on the aspect being analyzed. For instance, Smith, while rejecting an impact of interest rates on the profitability of capital and the distribution of income, analyzed the English and Scottish banking system and, in the same way as Marx, pointed out the influence of financial conditions on capital accumulation at the time and therefore the non-neutrality of money.

[20]The idea of a conventional interest rate is also present in Keynes (1937), in which the influence of monetary policy on the profitability of capital is accepted. However, the presence in his analysis of some traditional elements, including the notion of the marginal efficiency of capital based on an inverse relationship between the interest rate and investment demand, weakened this monetary view of the interest rate by allowing the reabsorption of Keynesian theses into the neoclassical synthesis (see Modigliani 1944). See on this point Pivetti (1991, 95–97).

[21]In line with Marx, there are also the contributions of Thomas Tooke (1826, section I) and John Stuart Mill (1844, 305). For further discussion of Tooke's thinking on this issue, see Pivetti (1998) and M. Smith (2006).

[22]Even for Mill (1844, 301) the normal profits of enterprise 'are regulated by the rate of interest, or equal to profits minus interest'. However, it should be noted that according to Pivetti (1987, 80), the assumed inverse relationship between the normal profits of enterprise and the interest rate would be unclear and incompatible with their normal level.

Thus, restrictive monetary policies will lead to a decrease in normal profits of enterprise, redistributing income in favor of financial capitalists at the expense of productive capitalists. But does this imply, in Marx, that monetary policy is not neutral to income distribution? To answer this, it should be noted that Marx does not depart from Smith and Ricardo in terms of explaining the determinants of the profit rate, which remain nonmonetary variables, such as the real wage rate and technical conditions of production. Therefore, the inability of interest rates to influence the profit rate has two important implications for the influence of monetary policy on income distribution. The first relates to the fact that central banks may not have much room to maneuver in setting interest rates, having the profit rate as an upper bound.[23] The second concerns the impossibility for monetary policy to be able to affect the distribution of income between wages and profits, thus between workers and capitalists (See Pivetti 1991, 66–69). As we have seen, monetary policy can only affect the distribution of income within the class of capitalists, and therefore even in Marx[24] we would not have a fully nonneutral monetary policy.

The above discussion of classical authors and Marx has shown that, for these authors, the determinants of income distribution among social classes are different from neoclassical theory's natural laws. Moreover, once we investigate whether monetary policy can be among the determinants, we find in some cases its *partial distributive-neutrality* (as in Marx) and in others its *substantial distributive-neutrality* (as in Smith and Ricardo): this would be due to their failure to consider influences of the interest rate on the profit rate. However, as we shall see in the next few pages, Sraffa (1960), while sharing the same theoretical basis, introduced the monetary determination of the profit rate, later developed by Panico (1988a) and Pivetti (1991) with the *Monetary Theory of Distribution*. And indeed, on that basis, according to Classical-Keynesian theory the interest rate would be a conventional phenomenon capable of influencing the functional income distribution permanently, reaffirming the non-neutrality of monetary policy in line with the post-Keynesian approach.

Monetary Policy and Income Distribution After Sraffa's Work: Monetary Theories of Distribution

In the previous pages we have seen how in the theory of classical economists and Marx, based on a wage at the subsistence level, monetary policy would not have a primary influence in the distribution of income between workers and capitalists. Yet, Sraffa, reinterpreting the thinking of these authors managed to point out how interest rates could play a non-neutral role in income distribution. Indeed, in paragraph 44 of *Production of Commodities by Means of Commodities*, Sraffa pointed out that if one were to admit the possibility of a wage above subsistence, the rate of profit could become the independent variable of the analysis, 'being determined from outside the system of production, in particular by the level of the money rate of interest' (Sraffa 1960, 33). Thus, Sraffa[25]

[23]In addition, Hilferding ([1910] 1981) also considers the profit rate as the maximum possible value for the interest rate (see Zolea 2022, 124).

[24]However, it should be remembered that Marx, like Smith, pointed out that currency was not neutral in influencing the accumulation of capital in an economy.

[25]Further contributions that developed or simply supported this suggestion by Sraffa include Sylos-Labini (1971), Garegnani (1979), Vianello (1985, 1988), Roncaglia (1988), and Bonifati (1991). However, other Sraffian authors have raised critical points regarding the monetary nature of the profit rate. For instance, according to Schefold (1985, 144–45) such a theory would be valid only in 'a situation of slow accumulation'. Moreover, a few years later, reviewing Pivetti's (1991)

opened the door to a monetary determination of income distribution, later taken up by various Classical-Keynesian authors such as Panico (1983, 1985, 1988a) and Pivetti (1985, 1991, 2023), with the *Monetary Theory of Distribution*.

Indeed, at the same time as in the post-Keynesian field, even Classical-Keynesian authors couldn't ignore the significant impact of the substantial interest rate hikes during the Volcker era, primarily due to their effects on income distribution. One such author, Pivetti (2023, 251), argues that the three decades preceding the Volcker era saw a golden age of capitalism, partly attributable to policies of maintaining low interest rates. This monetary policy direction was based on the Employment Act of 1946, which mandated the central bank to moderate long-term interest rates to ensure the objective of full employment. Consequently, during those years, monetary authorities kept long-term rates below the rate of GDP growth to sustain the fiscal deficits required to promote growth in the long run. Pivetti (2023, 251) states that:

> 'moderate' long-term interest rates and comparatively low public debts to GDP ratios also contributed to containing, over those three decades, the share of interest payments in national incomes, thereby facilitating overall distributive conditions conducive to long-run growth.

However, with the advent of the Volcker period, and the administrations of Reagan in the United States and Thatcher in the United Kingdom, the goal of full employment was sacrificed in favor of price stability. Consequently, monetary policy was no longer coordinated with fiscal policy to ensure stable long-term economic growth. This shift was also driven by the increasing influence of the financial sector in the power dynamics between social classes, leading to structural implications for income distribution. In fact, what occurred in the subsequent decades was an increase in the share of corporate profits in total value added, accompanied by a corresponding decline in workers' wages (Pivetti 2023, 247). Additionally, according to De Cecco (1987, 8–9), the end of the Bretton Woods agreements implied a greater centrality of financial power in social and political dynamics. Consequently, for De Cecco's analysis, the Volcker era represented an attempt by the United States to regain its financial hegemony, as it was no longer as dominant on the production front. The growing importance of financial aspects during the 1980s is also emphasized by classical-Keynesian economist Vianello (2013). Similar to De Cecco, Vianello argues that with the oil shocks of the 1970s, the golden era for the U.S. economy came to an end, while the banking sector flourished due to the substantial influx of petrodollars from oil-producing nations. Subsequently, as the U.S. financial sector realized the necessity of a strong dollar to maintain its global financial leadership, it exerted pressure against the Carter government in favor of restrictive central bank policies that opened the doors to the Volcker era — a period characterized by a dominant U.S. dollar and the seemingly unquestionable supremacy of Wall Street (De Cecco 1987).

---

book, Schefold (1993, 480) mentions how an additional difficulty in this framework "concerns his so-called profit of enterprise, for he [Pivetti] completely neglects the quasi-rents which it contains'. Then, even more profound is Pasinetti's (1990, p.460) critique, which points out how 'Sraffa's attitude in Production of Commodities (Sraffa 1960) is that he is concerned with the foundations of a theory of income distribution, not with any specific theory that may be laid on those foundations', as would have been the case with the *Monetary Theory of Distribution*.

These heterodox interpretations of the Volcker era perfectly represent what this theoretical approach considers the conduct of monetary policy: a process that is far from neutral, depending instead on various external monetary and distributional constraints and objectives (Pivetti 1991, 70). Consequently, it is precisely due to this non-neutrality that Pivetti (1985, 94) highlights the need for a more active consideration of the role of monetary policy in income distribution, given the change in the channels through which social class relations would manifest themselves in modern capitalism.

In that case, monetary policy and wage bargaining would be the main channels that would determine the distribution of income. Hence, following Sraffa's insight, according to Pivetti the new configuration of these power relations would no longer allow the wage rate to be viewed as an independent variable, but rather as the result of a process that begins with the monetary determination of the rate of profit. Then, an important player in this process would be the central bank, which, through its control of interest rates, would persistently influence the distribution of income between capitalists and workers. Thus, in the next few pages we will investigate the ways in which according to the *Monetary Theory of Distribution* monetary policy would be non-neutral, in line with the post-Keynesian theory already analyzed.

One aspect in common between *Monetary Distribution Theory* and the post-Keynesian approach studied in the previous section concerns the acceptance of the conventional nature of interest rates, being controlled directly by the central bank[26] (Lavoie 1992b, 65). However, this endogenous view of money would concern the entire structure of interest rates,[27] highlighting how the monetary authority could also control long-term rates (government or corporate securities with high creditworthiness such as AAA-rated bonds for the U.S.), which are likely to play an important role in income distribution (see Lavoie 2022, ch. 4). As postulated by Pivetti (1991, 22), long-term interest rates would be an *autonomous* component of normal production costs, since firms will have to repay such interest on amounts borrowed to finance investment in new capital goods.[28] Of particular significance[29] will be the role of real interest rates, which will matter more for the

[26]In defining the notion of endogenous money, Pivetti (1985, 96) refers directly to Kaldor's horizontalist view. For Lavoie (1992b, 64), too, the Sraffian position would be close to the post-Keynesian position on this aspect: 'It may seem ironic to note that Moore's views on endogenous money appear closer to those of the neo-Ricardians on the same subject, than to the views of fundamentalist post-Keynesians defending Keynes's liquidity preference.' See also Lavoie (1992a).

[27]Such elements appear clear in Pivetti (1991, 47): 'Money interest is considered to be under direct official control — that is, monetary policy is viewed as exerting itself primarily on the level of interest rates, rather than on the quantity of money ... One may suppose ... that the market opinion about the future course of long-term rates depends upon the present course of short rates which are under direct official control. Under these conditions, the direct operation of the monetary authorities on the short-term rates will cause the long-term rates to move in the same direction'. Also, see Deleidi and Levrero (2021) for empirical work that supports such theoretical assumptions.

[28]However, this argument would also apply if such investments were financed with equity or own capital. In this case, firms will aim for a return on such investments at least equal to the long-term interest rate, which would be an opportunity cost (see Pivetti 1991, 23).

[29]Pivetti (1991, ch.6) explicitly stresses this point. The influence of real rates on markups is also discussed in Godley and Cripps (1983), Lavoie (1995), and Godley and Lavoie (2007). From a Sraffian perspective, Ciccone (1990) emphasized the need for the central bank to control real interest rates in order to influence the distribution of income. For other classical-Keynesian contributions on this specific point, see also Serrano (1993), Podkaminer (1998) and Stirati (2001). For example, Serrano (1993) proposes several mechanisms through which real rates could be determined: "it is always a rate of increase in money wages that would produce enough inflation to reduce the real interest rate, and hence profits, enough to allow workers to obtain their desired real wage" (Serrano 1993, 122). Pivetti (2007, 145), while not rejecting this hypothesis, points out that it is easier for central banks to have control over nominal interest rates than it is for workers to have control over nominal wages, and thus over real interest rates. However, see Amico and Fiorito (2013) for the application of these different mechanisms for Argentina and Brazil.

financial situation of firms and exert a more substantial impact on the profit rate compared to nominal rates (Lavoie 1995, 157). Consequently, according to Pivetti, whenever there are changes in the determinants of normal production costs, such as monetary wages and real interest rates, the action of competition will adjust prices to the new cost levels.[30]

From here, by reconstructing the various steps we are now able to schematize the transmission mechanism of monetary policy on the income distribution for the Sraffian theory. A persistent increase in long-term real interest rates ($\uparrow i_L$), caused by a restrictive monetary policy ($\uparrow i_S$), will lead to an increase in the normal costs of production ($\uparrow$NC) and, therefore, in the price level ($\uparrow$P). Then, given the monetary wage ($\bar{W}$), such an increase in the price level will result in a change in the distribution of income that would consist of a lower real wage rate ($\downarrow \frac{W}{P}$) and a higher normal profit rate ($\uparrow$r):

$$\uparrow i_{S\rightarrow} \uparrow i_{L\rightarrow} \uparrow NC_{\rightarrow} \uparrow P_{\rightarrow} \downarrow \frac{W}{P} \rightarrow \uparrow r$$

Therefore, monetary policy would affect the distribution of income between wages and profits, thereby not being neutral in the conflict among workers and capitalists. In the well-known words of Pivetti (1991, 22):

> A lasting change in interest rates causes a change in the same direction in the level of prices in relation to the level of money wages, hereby generating changes in income distribution [such that] a prolonged fall in interest rates causes a fall in prices relative to the wage level, and thereby brings about a lower rate of profit and a higher real wage; whilst a prolonged rise in interest rates will raise the rate of profits, and thus reduce the real wage.

From here, the rate of interest would be a monetary phenomenon that, by regulating the ratio between prices and money wages, would govern distribution, constituting a channel through which the normal profit rate may be 'susceptible of being determined from outside the system of production' (Sraffa 1960, 33). Moreover, once the monetary nature of the interest rate is accepted, it would thus be 'given'. Hence, according to this theory, even normal profits of enterprise would be an independent component of the profit rate, provided it is 'independent of the rate of interest and is a sufficiently stable magnitude'[31] (Pivetti 1991, 24). Compared to classical authors and Marx, the profit rate ((Δr) will thus be the variable that must adjust whenever there is a change in the two autonomous components, ($\bar{i}$) and ($\overline{npe}$). In symbols:

$$\Delta r = \bar{i} + \overline{npe}$$

Thus summarizes Pivetti (1991, 69–70, italics added): 'As in Smith and Ricardo, profit and interest will move in sympathy over the long-run but the causal relationship connecting them goes in the opposite direction: *lasting changes in the rate of profit are the effect, not the cause, of lasting changes in the money rate of interest*, the latter being the variable which governs the ratio of prices to money wages'.

---

[30]Discussing the case of an open economy, Ginzburg and Simonazzi (1999) find that the interest rate could also influence production costs through an indirect channel based on the effects that monetary policies would have on the prices of imported commodities.

[31]Schefold (1993) raises critical aspects of Pivetti's interpretation of normal profits of enterprise, especially the absence of consideration of quasi-rents.

With the *Monetary Theory of Distribution*, the view proposed by Tooke (1844) of an interest rate as the cost of production is thus reintroduced, offering a direct explanation for the historically observed correlation between interest rates and prices,[32] which Keynes defined as Gibson's Paradox,[33] considering it as: 'one of the most completely established empirical facts within the whole field of quantitative economics' (Keynes 1930, 198).

However, it should be noted that in the history of economic thought the idea that interest rates would be both passed on to prices and positively correlated with markup has also found support in several heterodox authors not belonging to the surplus approach. In fact, for many post-Keynesians, although it would not be the only one, the *real* interest rate appears to be among the determinants of the profit rate (Lavoie 1995; 2022, 183). So it may be interesting to list some of these contributions. For instance,[34] for Kaldor (1982, 63) 'interest costs are passed on in higher prices in much the same way as wage costs', while Harrod (1973), working with the Oxford Economists' Research Group, observed both that 'firms often have some standard rate of profit, which includes interest, that they add to the input costs' (Harrod 1973, 44) and 'sustained low interest will presumably in the long run reduce the normal rate of profit' (Harrod 1973, 111). In addition to these contributions, we can find further support for these theses in:[35] Sayers (1951, 7–8), at first in Robinson[36] (1952, 96), Galbraith (1957, 130–131; 1958, 177), Kalecki (1971), De Cecco (1979, 96–98), Minsky (1982, 107), Godley and Cripps (1983), Taylor (1983, 7; 2004, 88–90), Dutt (1990), Fitoussi (1995, 93–94), Smithin (1997), and more recently in Hein (2007). In a different field than academia, a similar idea was expressed by Nancy Teeters, a member of the Federal Open Market Committee (FOMC) during the Volcker era: 'Interest rates may be [low] after tax, or in real terms, but they are still contributing to cost and are creating, I think, some of the upward pressure on prices.' (Teeters, FOMC meeting, May 1981).

The idea of a relationship between the interest rate and the profit rate, and of a relevant effect of monetary policy on income distribution, is also in another Sraffian approach that, unlike Pivetti's, introduces the banking industry into the analysis, considering the financial sector as a *basic one* (see Panico 1983, 1985, 1988a). This literature takes inspiration from what Marx indicated in Book III of *Capital* (1894), where, as we have seen, the relationships that link financial capitalists and industrialists are analyzed. Thus, Panico (1988a) identifies two channels through which the credit system could influence income distribution: on the one hand, it will facilitate the movement

[32]The literature has provided various empirical works supporting Gibson's Paradox or price puzzle. Among some of these, see: Sims (1992), Barth and Ramey (2001), Gaiotti and Secchi (2006), Cucciniello, Deleidi, and Levrero (2022), Di Bucchianico and Lofaro (2023). In addition, see Seccareccia and Lavoie (2004) and more recently Gahn (2022) for an econometric test of the relationship between interest rate and profit rate.

[33]In the Treatise on Money (1930), Keynes called this Gibson's Paradox — so named after the article in *Banker's Magazine* by Gibson (1923) that introduced this relationship.

[34]As cited by Lavoie (1995, 155; 2022, p.183).

[35]For these references see Lavoie (1995, 155; 2022, p.183), Stirati (2001, 429), and Lima and Setterfield (2010, 26).

[36]As reported by Lavoie (1995, 155), Joan Robinson (1979, 180), after initially endorsing the link between interest rates and the profit rate, criticized this idea, calling it "an inexplicable suggestion" ((Bhaduri and Robinson 1980, 103). Other post-Keynesians who did not support this relationship were Nell (1988) and Pasinetti (1990). In contrast, Wray's view had the opposite development to Robinson's: although he was critical at first (Wray 1988), he later noted that 'interest is also a cost, most importantly, an addition to working capital expenses. Much as rising energy costs are passed along in higher prices, interest costs are incorporated in sales prices. While higher costs and prices might negatively affect economic growth, no one has proposed policy to push up the price of oil — or other production costs, such as wages — as an inflation-fighting tactic' (Wray 2007, 17).

of finance capital to the most profitable sectors;[37] on the other hand, the difference between the interest rate on loans for productive investment and the interest rate on bank deposits, representing the cost in terms of interest to capitalists, will influence prices (Panico 1988a, 92).

This difference will also represent the profit of banks, which must be remunerated at the same rate as the industrial sector (Panico 1988a, 93). Hence, also for Panico (1988a), as in Pivetti, the increase in real interest rates will cause an increase in both prices and profit rates and a decrease in real wages. However, restrictive monetary policies will affect two distinct relationships between social classes: financial and industrial capitalists and capitalists and workers. In fact, an increase in interest rates, causing an increase in the costs to firms, will result, as in Marx, in a shift of income from the productive sector to the financial sector; subsequently, the industrial sector will pass on the increase in production costs to prices (Panico 1988a, 189). However, unlike Marx, the increase in prices, Panico notes, will decrease the purchasing power of workers, again defining an inverse relationship between interest rates and real wages. Again, for the *Monetary Theory of Distribution*, restrictive monetary policies will not be distribution-neutral, being able to be unfavorable for workers and favorable for capitalists. Considering this, a role for wage bargaining would also be accepted. Indeed, an inflation process will be triggered, if workers do not accept such a decrease in real wages, calling for increases in nominal wages[38] (see Panico 1988a, 98–99; but also, Serrano 1993; Pivetti 1991, ch.6; Stirati 2001).

In conclusion, as noted by Maurice Dobb (1973, 271), Sraffa's analysis showed the possibility that the interest rate and, therefore, the profit rate are 'somehow fixed by some kind of quasi-political or institutional decision-mechanism'. Starting from an endogenous view of money, according to Classical-Keynesian economists, restrictive monetary policies, contrary to 'traditional theory', would generate an increase in prices and a change in the distribution of income among social classes, leading to a decrease in the real wage and an increase in the profit rate. From this, also follows the rejection of the neutrality of monetary policy: interest rates would influence capital profitability, rather than being constrained to it in both the short and long run, thus maintaining a 'political' nature. Therefore, in line with post-Keynesian theory, the central bank's target real interest rate will not be influenced by an abstract variable such as the natural interest rate but will depend on various objectives and constraints related to fiscal, foreign, and distributional issues.[39] Specifically, wage bargaining, having a direct and indirect influence on income distribution, may have effects on prices and, therefore, on real interest rates.

[37]The inclusion of this factor comes from Marx's analysis (see Panico 1988a, 83–84 and p.183).

[38]Panico, Pinto, and Anyul (2012) and Panico and Pinto (2018), apply this analysis to understand how the evolution of the financial system in recent decades has affected distributional shares. Increasing financial deregulation, fostered by political institutions, would have led to a change in power relations between social classes. This would have resulted in a more unequal income distribution and significant household indebtedness to finance aggregate consumption. Other works have tried to develop some aspects of the '*Monetary Theory of Distribution*' (see the comprehensive literature review by Gahn 2022). Ciccarone (1998) does not consider interest as an opportunity cost and models a system in which only the banking sector is 'base' and banks exogenously set the spread on interest rates. Dvoskin and Feldman (2021), in addition to considering the spread on bank rates, also include the leverage ratio in their pricing system (following Franke 1988). Finally, Di Bucchianico (2021, 2022) points out that in recent decades both institutional factors, which compressed real wages, and household debt accumulation have had a significant influence on income distribution.

[39]See Pivetti (1991, ch.6), Serrano (1993), and Levrero (2023) to explore the effects of wage bargaining on the real interest rate.

Hence, within this framework, the complex interaction between monetary policy and wage bargaining is what determines the dynamics of income distribution.

Conclusions: Similarities and Differences Between PK and Sraffian Approaches

Our goal in this paper was to describe the views of the PK and the Sraffian approaches regarding the relationship between monetary policy and income distribution. Even if some differences still exist between the two approaches, we figured out that both approaches have several important common points on this issue. To make clearer our point of view we have tried to summarize these similarities and differences in Table 1.

To begin our discussion, it is worth noting, as portrayed in Table 1 point S1, that both post-Keynesian and Sraffian economists dismiss the quantitative theory of money. They propose that the creation of money is endogenous and demand-led and the authority to set interest rates rests with central banks. From this foundation, these heterodox approaches suggest that interest rates are a conventional occurrence, and central banks possess the capability to influence the structure of these rates. This resonates with the widespread long-term bond buying programs across major advanced economies. The flow of cause and effect from both these heterodox perspectives differs from the neoclassical viewpoint, proceeding from short to long-term interest rates.

Moreover, point S2 of Table 1 highlights that the interest rate, from the revolutionary contributions of the 1980s, is treated as a political or administered variable by both the maverick post-Keynesians and the Sraffians, like Pivetti and Panico. This perspective fundamentally contradicts any concept of a 'natural' interest rate. It is no coincidence that both these groups emphasized the distributive nature of monetary policy around the same time in the 1980s, asserting that the Volcker policies were less about inflation — which they do not believe to be demand-driven — but more a strategy to squeeze the income share of the working class and non-rentier groups.

This denial of a neutral interest rate leads to the third shared aspect (outlined in point S3 of Table 1) between these two schools of thought, which is a refusal to accept the neutrality of monetary policy. Monetary policy would alter the functional distribution of income, thereby inherently making it non-neutral. Consequently, the choices made by central banks will invariably create winners and losers among social classes. This redistribution of income could also have implications on aggregate demand, as the spending propensity of the working class notably differs from that of the rentier class. Hence, monetary policy could indirectly influence output through its impact on income distribution, while both post-Keynesians and Sraffians consider the responsiveness of output to interest rate changes as relatively low. This perspective subsequently led to a common rejection of fine-tuning policies and Taylor rules from the 1990s onwards.

Point S4 concludes that both heterodox schools primarily advocated the use of fiscal and monetary policies to drive full employment and redistribution policies.

Turning to the differences between the two theories, point D1 in Table 1 emphasizes the observation made by Marc Lavoie about the role of the interest rate in determining profit for each approach:

Table 1. Post-Keynesian and Sraffian Approaches on Monetary Policy and Distribution.

Similarities	Differences
S1. Money is endogenous from a horizontalist perspective. By controlling short interest rates, the central bank can influence long interest rates.	D1. The interest rate is the main determinant of the profit rate in the Sraffian approach while it is only one of various determinants in the PK approach.
S2. Interest rate is a political and distributive variable, whereas there is no 'natural' interest rate and fine-tuning policies, and Taylor rules are not useful.	D2. Post-Keynesians concentrate on the impact of monetary policy on the rentier versus the non-rentier classes, whereas Sraffians underscore the workers versus non-workers classes.
S3. Monetary policy has long-run effects on income distribution through which it can have indirect effects on output (low elasticity of output to interest rate change).	D3. Even if they are not activists, post-Keynesians propose monetary policy rules (parking-it approach), but Sraffians don't formulate a precise interest rate rule.
S4. Full-employment and redistribution policies are the focus through the coordination of fiscal and monetary policies.	D4. The focus is on functional income distribution, but post-Keynesians deal also with personal income distribution.

> [...] the rate of interest, in monetary or real terms, is not so much a variable designed to control the level of investment and that of aggregate demand, but rather it is a distributive variable, as it has been argued emphatically by some neo-Ricardians (Pivetti 1985; Roncaglia 1988) and also by some post-Keynesians (Eichner 1987, 860). Making such an admission does not necessarily imply that the rate of interest is the main determinant of the macroeconomic rate of profit, as the same neo-Ricardians would have it; it simply means that the rate of interest is an important determinant of the distribution of income between social classes and presumably between individuals. (Lavoie 1996, 536)

Additionally, point D2 from Table 1 mentions that, broadly speaking, post-Keynesians focus on the effects of monetary policy on the income share of rentiers vs. non-rentier classes, whereas Sraffians underline the impact of monetary policy on wage earners vs. non-wage earners. Moreover, point D3 indicates that while post-Keynesians favor the adoption of monetary policy rules as an alternative to mainstream Taylor rules (adopting a 'parking it' approach), Sraffians avoid proposing a specific rule, arguing instead that monetary policy should be conducted discretionally based on the unique institutional framework of each economy. In line with this, Levrero (2023, 17) states:

> Following the classification by Rochon and Setterfield (2007) between an activist and a parking-it approach to monetary policy; this view departs from any 'short run' monetary policy rule that mechanically aims to 'lean against the wind.' However, while sharing the emphasis on the distributive effects of the monetary policy with the parking-it approach, it also departs from the latter because no attempt is made to define the 'proper' value of the long-run rate of interest to be set by the central banks. The rate of interest is assumed to be the result of their objectives and constraints as influenced by institutional and social economic factors.

Lastly, point D4 observes that while both heterodox views traditionally concentrate on functional income distribution when studying the effects of monetary policy, some post-Keynesians, like Basil Moore and Chris Niggle, also explore impacts on personal income distribution.

In conclusion, the post-Keynesian and Sraffian perspectives share significant commonalities, which could potentially justify a collaborative effort towards further developing heterodox theories of monetary policy and income distribution. Even though differences exist, these should not hinder the continuation of deepening the collaboration between the two viewpoints.

Acknowledgements

We are specially grateful to Sylvio Kappes, Marc Lavoie, Sergio Levrero, and Mario Seccareccia for their insightful comments. We also thank two anonymous referees for their constructive comments. Of course, all remaining errors in this paper are the responsibility of the authors.

Disclosure Statement

No potential conflict of interest was reported by the author(s).

ORCID

Guillermo Matamoros http://orcid.org/0000-0001-7137-4710
Louis-Philippe Rochon http://orcid.org/0000-0002-8542-7497

References

Amico, F., and A. Fiorito. 2013. 'Exchange Rate Policy, Distributive Conflict and Structural Heterogeneity: The Argentinean and Brazilian Cases.' In *Sraffa and the Reconstruction of Economic Theory: Volume One: Theories of Value and Distribution*, edited by E. S. Levrero, A. Palumbo, and A. Stirati, 284–308. London: Palgrave Macmillan UK.

Arestis, P., and P. Howells. 1991. 'Financial Innovations and the Distributional Effects of Interest Rate Changes in the UK.' *Eastern Economic Journal* 17 (3): 263–271.

Arestis, P., and P. Howells. 1994. 'Monetary Policy and Distribution in the UK.' *Review of Radical Political Economics* 26 (3): 56–65.

Argitis, G. 2001. 'Intra-capitalist Conflicts.' *Monetary Policy and Income Distribution. Review of Political Economy* 13 (4): 453–470.

Argitis, G., and S. Michopoulou. 2010. 'Monetary Policy, Interest Payments, Income Distribution and the Macroeconomy.' *Review of Applied Economics* 6 (1-2), January-December, 29-39.

Argitis, G., and C. Pitelis. 2001. 'Monetary Policy and the Distribution of Income: Evidence for the United States and the United Kingdom.' *Journal of Post-Keynesian Economics* 23 (4): 617–638.

Barth III, M. J., and V. a. Ramey. 2001. 'The Cost Channel of Monetary Transmission.' *NBER Macroeconomics Annual* 16: 199–240.

Bhaduri, A., and J. Robinson. 1980. 'Accumulation and Exploitation: An Analysis in the Tradition of Marx, Sraffa and Kalecki.' *Cambridge Journal of Economics* 4 (2): 103–115.

Bonifati, G. 1991. *Saggio Dell'interesse e Distribuzione del Reddito*. Torino: Rosenberg & Sellier (pp. 1-196).

Ciccarone, G. 1998. 'Prices and Distribution in a Sraffian Credit Economy.' *Review of Political Economy* 10 (4): 399–413.

Ciccone, R. 1990. 'Comment on Pivetti.' In *Essays on Piero Sraffa: Critical Perspectives on the Revival of Political Economy*, edited by K. Bharadwaj and B. Schefold, 454–456. London: Unwin Hyman.

Cucciniello, M. C., M. Deleidi, and E. S. Levrero. 2022. 'The Cost Channel of Monetary Policy: The Case of the United States in the Period 1959–2018.' *Structural Change and Economic Dynamics* 61: 409–433.

Davidson, L. 1999. "In Defence of Post Keynesian Economics: A Response to Mongiovi." Uncertainty, International Money, Employment and Theory: Volume 3: The Collected Writings of Paul Davidson, 361-378.

De Cecco, M. 1979. 'Inflazione Italiana e Svalutazione.' In *Lezioni di Economia L'inflazione*, edited by F. Targetti. Milano: Feltrinelli.

De Cecco, M. 1987. 'La liberalizzazione valutaria: riflessioni di un economista.' *La Comunità Internazionale* 4.

Deleidi, M., and E. S. Levrero. 2021. 'Monetary Policy and Long-Term Interest Rates: Evidence from the US Economy.' *Metroeconomica* 72 (1): 121–147.
Di Bucchianico, S. 2021. 'The Impact of Financialization on the Rate of Profit.' *Review of Political Economy* 33 (2): 303–326.
Di Bucchianico, S. 2022. 'The Role of Commodity Speculation and Household Debt Accumulation During Financialization: A Classical-Keynesian Analysis.' *Cambridge Journal of Economics* 46 (2): 317–340.
Di Bucchianico, S., and A. Lofaro. 2023. The impact of monetary policy on functional income distribution: a panel SVAR analysis (1970-2019) (No. 900). *Department of Economics, University of Siena.*
Dobb, M. 1973. *Theories of Value and Distribution Since Adam Smith. Ideology and Economic Theory.* Cambridge: Cambridge University Press.
Dutt, A. K. 1990. 'Interest Rate Policy in LDCs: A Post Keynesian View.' *Journal of Post Keynesian Economics* 13 (2): 210–232.
Dvoskin, A., and G. D. Feldman. 2021. 'On the Role of Finance in the Sraffian System.' *Review of Political Economy* 33 (2): 261–277.
Eichner, A. S. 1987. *The Macrodynamics of Advanced Market Economies.* Armonk, New York: ME Sharpe.
Fitoussi, J. P. 1995. *Le débat interdit: monnaie, Europe, pauvreté (p. 00).* Paris: Editions Arléa.
Franke, R. 1988. 'Integrating the Financing of Production and a Rate of Interest Into Production Price Models.' *Cambridge Journal of Economics* 12 (2): 257–271.
Gahn, S. J. 2022. 'Interest and Profit: An Empirical Assessment of the Monetary Theory of Distribution for the Euro Area.' *Review of Political Economy*, 1–17.
Gaiotti, E., and A. Secchi. 2006. 'Is There a Cost Channel of Monetary Policy Transmission? An Investigation Into the Pricing Behavior of 2,000 Firms.' *Journal of Money, Credit and Banking*, 2013–2037.
Galbraith, J. K. 1957. 'Market Structure and Stabilization Policy.' *The Review of Economics and Statistics*, 124–133.
Galbraith, J. K. 1958. *The Affluent Society.* London: Hamish Hamilton.
Galbraith, J. K. 1998. *Created Unequal. The Crisis in American Pay.* Chicago: The University of Chicago Press.
Garegnani, P. 1970. 'Heterogeneous Capital, the Production Function and the Theory of Distribution.' *The Review of Economic Studies* 37 (3): 407–436.
Garegnani, P. 1978. 'Notes on Consumption, Investment and Effective Demand: I.' *Cambridge Journal of Economics* 2 (4): 335–353.
Garegnani, P. 1979. 'Notes on Consumption, Investment and Effective Demand: Ii.' *Cambridge Journal of Economics* 3 (1): 63–82.
Garegnani, P. 1984. 'Value and Distribution in the Classical Economists and Marx.' *Oxford Economic Papers* 36 (2): 291–325.
Gibson, A. H. 1923. 'The Future Course of High Class Investment Values.' *Banker's Magazine (London)* 115: 15–34.
Ginzburg, A., and A. Simonazzi. 1999. Foreign Debt Cycles and the "Gibson Paradox": an Interpretative Hypothesis. *Universita degli studi di Modena.*
Godley, W., and F. Cripps. 1983. *Macroeconomics.* London: Fontana.
Godley, W., and M. Lavoie. 2007. *Monetary Economics: An Integrated Approach to Credit, Money, Income, Production and Wealth.* Basingstoke: Palgrave Macmillan.
Harrod, R. 1973. *Economic Dynamics.* Basingstoke: Palgrave Macmillan.
Hein, E. 2007. *Money, Distribution Conflict and Capital Accumulation.* Basingstoke: Palgrave Macmillan.
Henry, J. 1982. 'Les méthodes « post-keynésiennes » et l'approche post-classique.' *L'Actualité économique* 58 (1-2): 17–60.
Hilferding, R. 1910[1981]. *Finance Capital a Study of the Latest Phase of Capitalist Development.* London: Routledge & Kegan Paul.
Kaldor, N. 1982. *The Scourge of Monetarism.* New York: Oxford University Press.

Kalecki, M. 1971. *Selected Essays on the Dynamics of the Capitalist Economy 1933-1970*. Cambridge Univesrity Pess: Cambridge.

Kappes, S. A. 2023. 'Monetary Policy and Personal Income Distribution: A Survey of the Empirical Literature.' *Review of Political Economy* 35 (1): 211–230.

Keynes, J. M. 1923. *A tract on monetary reform*, vol. 4 in Robinson, EAG and Moggridge, D. The Collected Writings of John Maynard Keynes, 1971-89.

Keynes, J. M. 1930. *A Treatise on Money: In 2 Volumes*. Basingstoke: Palgrave Macmillan.

Keynes, J. M. 1936. *The General Theory of Interest, Employment and Money*. Basingstoke: Palgrave Macmillan, 2018.

Keynes, J. M. 1937. 'The General Theory of Employment.' *The Quarterly Journal of Economics* 51 (2): 209–223.

Lavoie, M. 1992a. 'A moeda em um programa de pesquisa comum para o pós-keynesianismo e o neo-ricardianismo.' *Brazilian Journal of Political Economy* 12 (3): 425–447.

Lavoie, M. 1992b. 'Towards a new Research Programme for Post-Keynesianism and neo-Ricardianism.' *Review of Political Economy* 4 (1): 37–78.

Lavoie, M. 1995. 'Interest Rates in Post-Keynesian Models of Growth and Distribution.' *Metroeconomica* 46 (2): 146–177.

Lavoie, M. 1996. 'Monetary Policy in an Economy with Endogenous Credit Money.' *Money in Motion: The Post Keynesian and Circulation Approaches*, 532–545.

Lavoie, M. 2013. 'Sraffians, Other Post-Keynesians, and the Controversy Over Centres of Gravitation.' *Sraffa and the Reconstruction of Economic Theory: Volume Three: Sraffa's Legacy: Interpretations and Historical Perspectives*, 34–54.

Lavoie, M. 2022. *Post-Keynesian Economics: New Foundations*. Cheltenham: Edward Elgar Publishing.

Lavoie, M., and M. Seccareccia. 1988. 'Money, Interest and Rentiers: The Twilight of Rentier Capitalism in *Keynes's General Theory*.' *Keynes and Public Policy After Fifty Years* 2: 145–158.

Lavoie, M., and M. Seccareccia. 1999. 'Fair Interest Rates.' In *Encyclopedia of Political Economy, vol. 1*, edited by P. A. O'Hara, 543–545. London: Routledge.

Lavoie, M., and M. Seccareccia. 2019. 'Macroeconomics and Natural Rates: Some Reflections on Pasinetti's Fair Rate of Interest.' *Bulletin of Political Economy* 13 (2): 139–165.

Lavoie, M., and M. Seccareccia. 2020. *Going Beyond the Inflation-Targeting Mantra: A Dual Mandate. Max Bell School of Public Policy*. Montreal: McGill University. www.mcgill.ca/maxbellschool/files/maxbellschool/7_lavoie.pdf.

Levrero, E. S. 2011. 'Some Notes on Wages and Competition in the Labour Market.' In *Sraffa and Modern Economics*, Vol. 1, edited by R. Ciccone, C. Gehrke, and G. Mongiovi, 361–384. New York: Routledge.

Levrero, E. S. 2012. *Four lectures on wages and competition*. Roma, Aracne.

Levrero, E. S. 2023. 'The Taylor Rule and its Aftermath: An Interpretation Along Classical-Keynesian Lines.' *Review of Political Economy*, 1–19.

Lima, G. T., and M. Setterfield. 2010. 'Pricing Behaviour and the Cost-Push Channel of Monetary Policy.' *Review of Political Economy* 22 (1): 19–40.

Lofaro, A., and L.-P. Rochon. 2023. The Pasinetti Interest Rate Rule: what should central banks do? *Monetary Policy Institute Blog*, March 13, 2023. Retrieved on June 5, 2023 at: https://medium.com/@monetarypolicyinstitute/the-pasinetti-interest-rate-rule-what-should-central-banks-do-875804fa435f.

Marx, K. 1894. *Capital: A Critique of Political Economy, Vol. III*. London: Lawrence & Wishart, 1977.

McKay, A., and C. K. Wolf. 2023. 'Monetary Policy and Inequality.' *Journal of Economic Perspectives* 37 (1): 121–144.

Mill, J. S. 1844. 'On Profits and Interest, Essays on Some Unsettled Questions of Political Economy.' In *The Collected Works of John Stuart Mill: Vol. IV*. Toronto: University of Toronto Press, 1967.

Minsky, H. 1982. *Can it Happen Again?: Essays on Instability and Finance*. London: M.E. Sharpe.

Modigliani, F. 1944. 'Liquidity Preference and the Theory of Interest and Money.' *Econometrica, Journal of the Econometric Society*, 45–88.

Moore, B. J. 1989. *The Effects of Monetary Policy on Income Distribution in Macroeconomic Problems and Policies of Income Distribution*. Aldershot: Edward Elgar.

Morris, J. 1982. 'The Revenge of the Rentier or the Interest-Rate Crisis in the United States.' *Monthly Review* 38 (8): 28–34.

Nell, E. J. 1988. 'Does the Rate of Interest Determine the Rate of Profit?' *Political Economy* 4 (2): 263–267.

Niggle, C. J. 1989. 'Monetary Policy and Changes in Income Distribution.' *Journal of Economic Issues* 23 (3): 809–822.

Panico, C. 1980. 'Marx's Analysis of the Relationship Between the Rate of Interest and the Rate of Profits.' *Cambridge Journal of Economics* 4 (4): 363–378.

Panico, C. 1983. *Politiche monetarie, prezzi e distribuzione*. Italy: Liguori.

Panico, C. 1985. 'Market Forces and the Relation Between the Rates of Interest and Profits.' *Contributions to Political Economy* 4 (1): 37–60.

Panico, C. 1988a. *Interest and Profit in the Theories of Value and Distribution*. London: Springer.

Panico, C. 1988b. 'Marx on the Banking Sector and the Interest Rate: Some Notes for a Discussion.' *Science & Society*, 310–325.

Panico, C., and A. Pinto. 2018. 'Income Inequality and the Financial Industry.' *Metroeconomica* 69 (1): 39–59.

Panico, C., A. Pinto, and M. P. Anyul. 2012. 'Income Distribution and the Size of the Financial Sector: A Sraffian Analysis.' *Cambridge Journal of Economics* 36 (6): 1455–1477.

Pasinetti, L. L. 1980. 'The Rate of Interest and the Distribution of Income in a Pure Labor Economy.' *Journal of Post Keynesian Economics* 3 (2): 170–182.

Pasinetti, L. L. 1981. *Structural Change and Economic Growth*. Cambridge: Cambridge University Press.

Pasinetti, L. L. 1990. 'Comment on: Massimo Pivetti's "On the Monetary Explanation of Distribution".' In *Essays on Piero Sraffa-Critical Perspectives on the Revival of Classical Theory*, edited by B. Schefold, and K. Bharadwaj, 460–462. London: Taylor & Francis.

Pasinetti, L. L. 2002. 'An «analytical» approach to the «just» rate of interest: the priority of labour over capital.' *Rivista internazionale di scienze sociali*, 323–329.

Piketty, T. 2014. *Capital in the Twenty-First Century*. Cambridge, MA: Harvard University Press.

Pivetti, M. 1985. 'On the Monetary Explanation of Distribution.' *Political Economy* 1 (2): 73–103.

Pivetti, M. 1987. 'Interest and Profit in Smith.' *Ricardo and Marx. Political Economy* 3 (1): 63–74.

Pivetti, M. 1991. *An Essay on Money and Distribution*. London: Macmillan.

Pivetti, M. 1998. 'Thomas Tooke and the Influence of the Rate of Interest on Prices: Implications for Distribution Theory.' *Contributions to Political Economy* 17 (1): 39–52.

Pivetti, M. 2007. 'Distribution, Inflation and Policy Analysis.' *Review of Political Economy* 19 (2): 243–247.

Pivetti, M. 2023. 'On Interest and Interest-Rate Policy.' In *Central Banking, Monetary Policy and Income Distribution. Chapter 10*, edited by S. Kappes, L.-P. Rochon, and G. Vallet, 242–260. Cheltenham, UK: Edward Elgar Publishing.

Podkaminer, L. 1998. 'Inflationary Effects of High Nominal Interest Rates.' *Journal of Post Keynesian Economics* 20 (4): 583–596.

Ricardo, D. 1821. *On the Principles of Political Economy*. London: J. Murray.

Robertson, D. H. 1940. *Essays in Monetary Theory*. London: PS King & son, Limited.

Robinson, J. 1952. *The Interest Rate and Other Essays*. London: Macmillan.

Robinson, J. 1956. *The Accumulation of Capital*. (3rd Ed.). Hampshire, UK: Palgrave Macmillan, 2013.

Robinson, J. 1979. 'Garegnani on Effective Demand.' *Cambridge Journal of Economics* 3 (2): 179–180.

Rochon, L. P. 1999. *Credit, Money, and Production: An Alternative Post-Keynesian Approach*. Cheltenham, UK: Edward Elgar.

Rochon, L. P. 2020. 'The Economics of Basil Moore: Slow Progress Toward Horizontalism.' *European Journal of Economics and Economic Policies: Intervention* 17 (3): 313–324.

Rochon, L. P., and M. Setterfield. 2007. 'Interest Rates, Income Distribution, and Monetary Policy Dominance: Post Keynesians and the" Fair Rate" of Interest.' *Journal of Post Keynesian Economics* 30 (1): 13–42.

Rochon, L. P., and M. Setterfield. 2008. 'The Political Economy of Interest-Rate Setting, Inflation, and Income Distribution.' *International Journal of Political Economy* 37 (2): 5–25.

Rochon, L. P., and M. Setterfield. 2012. 'A Kaleckian Model of Growth and Distribution with Conflict-Inflation and Post Keynesian Nominal Interest Rate Rules.' *Journal of Post Keynesian Economics* 34 (3): 497–520.

Rochon, L. P. 2022. 'The General Ineffectiveness of Monetary Policy or the Weaponization of Inflation.' In *The Future of Central Banking*, edited by S. Kappes, L.-P. Rochon, and G. Vallet. Cheltenham, UK: Edward Elgar Publishing.

Rochon, L. P., and M. Seccareccia. 2023. 'A Primer on Monetary Policy and its Effect on Income Distribution: A Heterodox Perspective.' In *Central Banking, Monetary Policy and Income Distribution*, edited by S. Kappes, L.-P. Rochon, and G. Vallet. Cheltenham, UK: Edward Elgar Publishing.

Roncaglia, A. 1988. 'The neo-Ricardian Approach and the Distribution of Income.' In *Theories of Income Distribution*, edited by A. Asimakopulos, 159–180. Dordrecht: Springer Netherlands.

Sayers, R. S. 1951. 'The Rate of Interest as a Weapon of Economic Policy.' In *Oxford Studies in the Price Mechanism*, edited by T. Wilson, 1–16. London: Clarendon Press.

Schefold, B. 1985. 'Cambridge Price Theory: Special Model or General Theory of Value?' *The American Economic Review* 75 (2): 140–145.

Schefold, B. 1993. '[Review of An Essay on Money and Distribution, by M. Pivetti].' *Journal of Institutional and Theoretical Economics (JITE) / Zeitschrift Für Die Gesamte Staatswissenschaft* 149 (2): 478–480. http://www.jstor.org/stable/40751620.

Seccareccia, M. 1988. 'Systemic Viability and Credit Crunches: An Examination of Recent Canadian Cyclical Fluctuations.' *Journal of Economic Issues* 22 (1): 49–77.

Seccareccia, M., and M. Lavoie. 2004. 'Long-term Interest Rates, Liquidity Preference and the Limits of Central Banking.' In *Central Banking in the Modern World: Alternative Perspectives*, edited by M. Lavoie and M. Seccareccia, 164–182. Cheltenham: Edward Elgar.

Seccareccia, M., and M. Lavoie. 2010. 'Inflation Targeting in Canada: Myth Versus Reality.' In *Macroeconomics, Finance and Money: Essays in Honour of Philip Arestis*, edited by G. Fontana, J. McCombie, and M. Sawyer, 35–53. Basingstoke: Palgrave Macmillan.

Seccareccia, M., and M. Lavoie. 2016. 'Income Distribution, Rentiers, and Their Role in a Capitalist Economy: A Keynes–Pasinetti Perspective.' *International Journal of Political Economy* 45 (3): 200–223.

Seccareccia, M., and G. Matamoros. 2022. 'Is There an Appropriate Monetary Policy Framework to Achieve a More Equitable Income Distribution or Do Central Bank Mandates Really Matter? Interest-Rate Rules Versus a Full-Employment Policy.' *Journal of Economic Issues* 56 (2): 498–507.

Seccareccia, M., and G. Matamoros. 2023. 'Why Central Bank Policy is not Income-Distribution 'Neutral': History, Theory and Practice.' In *Central Banking, Monetary Policy and Income Distribution*, edited by S. Kappes, L.-P. Rochon, and G. Vallet. London: Edward Elgar.

Seccareccia, M., and G. Matamoros. 2023b. 'Is 'Inflation First' Really 'Rentiers First'? The Taylor Rule and Rentier Income in Industri-Alized Countries.' *INET Working Paper* 209, July 10: 1–51.

Serrano, F. 1993. "Review of Pivetti's Essay on Money and Distribution'.' *Contributions to Political Economy*, 117–124.

Sims, C. A. 1992. 'Interpreting the Macroeconomic Time Series Facts: The Effects of Monetary Policy.' *European Economic Review* 36 (5): 975–1000.

Smith, A. 1776. *An Inquiry Into the Nature and Causes of the Wealth of Nations: Volume One*. London: printed for W. Strahan; and T. Cadell, 1776.

Smith, M. 2006. 'On Interest and Profit: Thomas Tooke's Major Legacy to Economics.' *Contributions to Political Economy* 25 (1): 1–34.

Smithin, J. N. 1996. *Macroeconomic Policy and the Future of Capitalism: The Revenge of the Rentiers and the Threat to Prosperity*. Cheltenham: Edward Elgar Pub.

Smithin, J. 1997. 'An Alternative Monetary Model of Inflation and Growth.' *Review of Political Economy* 9 (4): 395–409.

Sraffa, P. 1960. *Production of Commodities by Means of Commodities*. London: Cambridge University Press.

Stirati, A. 1994. *The Theory of Wages in Classical Economics: A Study of Adam Smith, David Ricardo, and Their Contemporaries*. Cheltenham: Edward Elgar Publishing.

Stirati, A. 2001. 'Inflation, Unemployment and Hysteresis: An Alternative View.' *Review of Political Economy* 13 (4): 427–451.

Stirati, A., and G. Zezza. 2022. "The Core Idea is That Income Distribution is Always the Result of a Conflict of Powers among Social Classes': Interview with Antonella Stirati.' *European Journal of Economics and Economic Policies* 19 (3): 299–306.

Sylos-Labini, P. 1971. 'La theorie des prix en regime d'oligopole et la theorie du developpement.' *Revue d'economie politique*, 244–272.

Taylor, L. 1983. *Structuralist Macroeconomics. Applicable Models for the Third World*. Berlin: Basic Books.

Taylor, L. 2004. *Reconstructing Macroeconomics*. Cambridge: Harvard University Press.

Tobin, J. 1974. "There are Three Types of Inflation", *New York Times*, September 6, p. 33.

Tooke, T. 1826. *Considerations on the State of the Currency*. UK: John Murray.

Tooke, T. 1844. *An Inquiry into the Currency Principle: the Connection of the Currency with Prices, and the Expediency of a Separation of Issue from Banking* (No. 33834). UK: Longman, Brown, Green, and Longmans.

Vianello, F. 1985. 'The Pace of Accumulation.' *Political Economy: Studies in the Surplus Approach* 1 (1): 69–87.

Vianello, F. 1988. 'A Critique of Professor Goodwin's "Critique of Sraffa".' In *Growth Cycles and Multisectoral Economics: The Goodwin Tradition: Proceedings of the Workshop in Honour of RM Goodwin*, edited by G. Ricci, K. Velupillai, and R. M. Goodwin, 112–119. Berlin, Heidelberg: Springer Berlin Heidelberg.

Vianello, F. 2013. 'La moneta unica europea.' *Economia & lavoro* 47 (1): 17–46.

Wicksell, K. 1898. *Geldzins und Güterpreise: Eine Studie über die den Tauschwert des Geldes Bestimmenden Ursachen*. Germany: Verlag Wirtschaft und Finanzen.

Wray, L. R. 1988. 'The Monetary Explanation of Distribution: A Critique of Pivetti.' *Political Economy* 4 (2): 269–273.

Wray, L. R. 2007. 'A Post Keynesian View of Central Bank Independence, Policy Targets, and the Rules Versus Discretion Debate.' *Journal of Post Keynesian Economics* 30 (1): 119–141.

Zolea, R. 2022. 'A History of the Relationship Between Interest Rate and Profit Rate in Heterodox Approaches.' *International Journal of Political Economy* 51 (2): 121–136.

OPEN ACCESS

The Distributive Monetary Analysis of a (un)Sustainable Economy

Samuele Bibi

ABSTRACT

This article is a post-Keynesian stock flow consistent (PK-SFC) model that analyses the dynamics of an economy characterised by several — often individually studied — features of PK-SFC studies together with some innovative aspects. In particular, we investigate the income and wealth distribution between two social classes, capitalists and workers, after a period of a crisis subject to different policy scenarios. Non-financial firms but also government can undertake investments decisions and both accumulate capital. Finally, we consider the workers' and capitalists' consumption behaviour that contributes to produce (un)sustainable paths. Our model is built upon Bibi (2020, 2021) within an endogenous money framework and is calibrated using available data for major advanced economies. Simulations are conducted to question the different government fiscal policies to reduce unemployment boosting the economic activity, to obtain a more equitable distribution between social classes while obtaining those goals in a sustainable way.

1. Introduction

In the years after the 2007 crisis, the recovery and distribution issues revamped interest both in economic theories and political discussions. Together with these, particular attention was paid to the ecological problems associated with the ambitious, but nonetheless necessary, objective of achieving the first two goals in an ecologically sustainable way.

Despite many contributions focused on some of the previous topics, few of them tried to tackle them all in a comprehensive way and considering one of the most important breakthroughs in recent decades, namely, the rediscovery of the endogenous money phenomena. Here, we argue that the endogenous money feature is precisely the essential *fil rouge* to better understand and connect those three importantly related aspects.

Our work is strongly based on Sawyer (2010), Arestis and Sawyer (2005), Zambelli (2007, 2014), and Bibi (2020, 2021). It is also inspired by Sawyer and Passarella Veronese (2017) and Fontana and Sawyer (2016), who examined environmental aspects within a monetary circuit model, and Dafermos et al. (2017), who integrated thoroughly

This is an Open Access article distributed under the terms of the Creative Commons Attribution License (http://creativecommons.org/licenses/by/4.0/), which permits unrestricted use, distribution, and reproduction in any medium, provided the original work is properly cited. The terms on which this article has been published allow the posting of the Accepted Manuscript in a repository by the author(s) or with their consent.

monetary and physical variables in a coherent ecological stock-flow consistent (SFC) macroeconomic model. The basis of endogenous money and the structure of the economy in what has been known as the post-Keynesian stock-flow consistent approach relies mainly on the work of Graziani (2003), Godley and Lavoie (2007), Fontana and Setterfield (2009), and Rochon et al. (2020).

The structure of our model is an extension of Bibi (2021) but also borrows some key features from Godley and Lavoie (2007). In particular, even if the model described in Godley and Lavoie's (2007) Chapter 11 is a growth model, our scenario differs from that since it considers a stationary level of output as a starting point but still retains the possibility of capacity output growth. We do that mainly to highlight a more immediate contrast between the policy scenarios simulations and implications contained here and those of Bibi (2021) where capacity output growth is not allowed. In line with Bibi, we take into account that production takes time and that banks create credit money and consider the lack of market clearing conditions. The mismatching between aggregate demand and aggregate production in consumption goods creates inventories.

Different features characterize our model and also distinguish it from Bibi.

- First, households comprise two social groups: workers and capitalists. These households differ not only in terms of their consumption behaviour but also in terms of their initial endowment, of the different conditions of loan repayment required by banks and in terms of how they can use their financeable wealth.
- Second, we consider the a-synchronized Kaleckian investment production process. In line with that, we consider the three different investment stages proposed by Kalecki himself (1971) and developed by Zambelli (2014) and borrowed by Bibi (2021).
- Third, we consider the investments and capital held by both non-financial firms and the government; this distinction is relevant because we want to explore how different drivers of investment can affect the formation of capital and the economic and ecological sustainability of our economy.
- Fourth, and finally, we consider the ecological impacts of workers' and capitalists' consumption processes. In particular, their dissimilar consumption level — based on different incomes and wealth — is assumed to have different impacts on the ecological balance and resources needed to obtain the consumption goods required. This seems in line with the conclusions of most studies about environmental pressure related to levels of income (Mackenzie et al. 2008). It is important to highlight here that our work is based on intuition regarding the impact of consumption on ecological variables. Dafermos et al. (2017) consider ecosystem-related variables to a much greater degree; for example, they differentiate between conventional and green investment and discuss how the degradation of ecosystem services has feedback effects on the economy.

This article proceeds as follows. Section Two describes the overall model through its balance sheet and transaction flow matrices. Section Three provides a sketch of the model and underlines the main behavioural rules of its actors. Section Four presents the main simulations based on our key question: how does the government manoeuvre to achieve an economic, social and ecologically sustainable recovery. Section Five offers conclusions.

2. Balance Sheet and Transaction-Flow Matrix

Following Kaleckian features and Bibi (2020, 2021), we describe an economy characterized by two different types of socioeconomic class, namely, workers' and capitalists' households. They are different because of their consumption capacity, which is linked to their different purchasing power resulting from both the wealth they are endowed with and the different loan repayment conditions required of them by commercial banks. Finally, even if production firms are described as a separate sector in the economy, these are legally owned by capitalists' households while workers' households have no claim on firms beyond the wages they receive from them in return for their labour.

Workers' and capitalists' households are allowed to take loans from commercial banks (hereafter, CBs) and they have access to cash and deposits. Workers maintain their wealth in the form of deposits while capitalists maintain their wealth also in the form of bills and long-term bonds. Capitalists are the owners of both financial and non-financial firms and therefore they hold bank funds (OFs), too. In our economy, production firms own both fixed capital and inventories and they are allowed to take loans to finance their productive activity.

The government is supposed to own capital, reflected, for example, in the value of transport and educational infrastructure, while emitting bills and bonds. The country central bank (CCB[1]) holds part of the bills emitted by the government and emits cash (H). CBs make loans to firms and households while having treasury bills (B_b) and cash balances (H_b). The net worth of the CBs calculated as the difference between assets and liabilities constitutes their own funds (OF_b) and is also reflected in the balance sheets of their owners, the capitalists (see Table A1).

The transaction-flow matrix (hereafter, TFM) describes how the flows of different sectors of the economy are connected within a certain unit of time, using a positive sign for the source of funds and a negative sign for the use of funds (see Table A2).

Workers' households receive wages and interest on deposits and use their income to consume final goods, pay taxes and interest on loans and, finally, save the residual in the form of cash, deposits or to pay back the loans that they previously took. While capitalists' households do not receive any wages, they do receive part of the non-financial and financial firms' profits. Capitalists' households also use their income on consumption of final goods and payment of taxes and interests on loans. In addition, they receive positive interest on financial assets while they are supposed to hold their savings in bills and bonds.

Non-financial firms sell consumption goods to households and hold inventories. Furthermore, they produce investment goods and sell part of them to the government. The resources generated by productive activities are used to pay workers employed for their supply of labour and the interest on loans used to activate the production process; finally, after retaining part of the profits, they are used to distribute the remaining profits to capitalists.

[1]To avoid any confusion between commercial banks and the central bank, we call CBs the former and CCB (country central bank) the latter.

The government undertakes an investment by purchasing investment goods from firms[2] contributing to increase physical and social capital. The government pays interest on the bills and bonds it emitted while collecting taxes from households and obtaining the profits received by the central bank. The CCB obtains interest from the bills but, since we suppose a CCB with nil profit goals, it redistributes all profit to the government.

Finally, CBs obtain the interest on the loans provided to non-financial firms and on the bills emitted by the government while paying the those on deposits to households. CBs are supposed to distribute their entire profits to the owners of the banks, the capitalists.

3. A Sketch of the Economy

Here, we analyse a demand-driven economy in which the consumption behaviour of the two different social classes influences the ecological scenario. We use the ecological footprint (EF) as an indicator of the resources depleted by consumption activity and, in this way, capture the effects of consumption on the ecological sustainability of an economy.[3]

We borrow one of the main aspects of Mackenzie et al. (2008), that is, considering how different socioeconomic classes have different impacts on the ecological footprint. In particular, the consumption of capitalists has a larger EF than that of workers. This supposition is in line with Mackenzie et al., who highlight how the richest 10 per cent of Canadian households create an ecological footprint nearly two-and-a-half times that of the poorest households.[4]

3.1. Analysis of Firms, Employment, and Wage–Profit Determination

Our analysis of firms, households, and the wage–employment relationship is based on Bibi (2020, 2021). In line with the Kaleckian tradition, we recognize that investment production takes time and effort. Like Bibi (2021), we follow the three different investment stages considered by Kalecki (1971).

Equations (1–27)[5] describe firms' behaviour in both the production of consumption goods and the investment decision-making process. Firms produce consumption goods based on their expectation of consumption demand and considering a variety of inventories and they make investments based on their most important explanatory

[2]For simplicity, we will often call the investment goods that firms sell to the government 'public investments'.

[3]The ecological footprint is a 'measure of how much area of biologically productive land and water an individual, population or activity requires to produce all the resources it consumes and to absorb the waste it generates, using prevailing technology and resource management practices' (Global Footprint Network 2015). This simple approach to ecological sustainability is intended to give just an idea of the effects that different consumption structures have in relation to the depletion of resources. A much deeper and more comprehensive consideration of ecosystem-related variables is contained in Dafermos et al. (2017), where, for example, there is a differentiation between conventional and green investments and where the degradation of ecosystem services has feedback effects on the economy.

[4]Mackenzie et al. (2008) also show how, while in general the size of an individual ecological footprint increases as household income increases, the real jump is at the top 10 per cent level. In housing and transportation, in particular, the ecological footprint of the richest 10 per cent of Canadian households is several times the size of the footprint of lower — and lower-middle-income Canadians and significantly greater than that of the next highest-income 10 per cent of households. According to collected data, the richest decile consumes more than nine times that of the poorest decile.

[5]Equations 1–4, 9–10 and 23–25 are taken from the analysis presented in the Macroeconomics and Monetary System module at Trento University (Zambelli 2014).

variables: the rate of capacity utilization (or sales) and cash flow (or cash flow profits), as suggested by Lavoie (2014).

In the spirit of Lavoie (2014) and following the collective wage bargaining approach, we consider that workers claim higher wages based on their labour productivity and on the pressure of the demand for labour (28–31). Following Sawyer and Passarella Veronese (2017), we also assume that firms are able to set long-term strategic prices.[6] In this way, and assuming that they are in equal units, nominal and real values are the same.

Part of entrepreneurial profit is considered to be undistributed while the distributed portion will be shared among capitalists as soon as it is obtained by firms. Finally, firms take out loans. The amount of loans requested by firms in a particular period is the sum of the loans requested in the previous period, of investments and of variations in inventory value, with the deduction of undistributed profits partly offsetting firms' need of loans.

3.2. Consumption and Household Relations

Here, we describe the relations between the households of workers and capitalists in our model. While workers' personal income comprises only wages and the interest they obtain from deposits, that of capitalists is composed of firm and bank profits and the interest on deposits, bills, and bonds. The disposable income of the latter households is obtained by deducing taxes and interest payments on banks loans from personal incomes.

In line with Godley and Lavoie (2007), in our model we assume that taxes are paid on households' personal income and that households' consumption is based partly on disposable income increased by new loans and partly on accumulated wealth. Equations (61) and (62) assume that marginal propensities of both classes tend to grow, even if at different magnitudes, when tax rates decrease. Symmetrically, the former tend to decrease and the latter to increase. This idea of a variable marginal propensity to consume is not new, having first been considered by Samuelson (1939).

Finally, (64–66) estimate the ecological impact of workers, capitalists and overall consumption in terms of EF. The parameters φ_w and φ_π reflect the respective green consumption weight of workers and capitalists and are based on Mackenzie et al. (2008).

In line with Godley and Lavoie (2007), (67–74) model an economy in which households are able to access loans. However, we take a different approach by supposing the existence of two different social classes and commercial banks applying higher repayment requirements on workers' households than on capitalists' households. This could be because workers are less able to offer loan guarantees, making CBs desire quicker repayment.

Equations (78–85) now consider the possibility of households allocating their wealth to different financial activities, based mainly on their relative remuneration. We model an economy in which workers' families use their savings mainly for precautionary purposes, keeping them in the form of deposits or cash for consumption. Capitalists' households, instead, are supposed to save enough to maintain part of their wealth for precautionary reasons and, at the same time, to invest in financial activities. In this way, beyond keeping

[6]This assumption is in line with the idea that firms are not willing to change their prices unless their unit costs change significantly.

their resources in deposits and cash, they keep part of them also in bonds and bills. Equations (AC1–AC8) define Tobin's vertical and Godley's horizontal constraints, which ensure consistency of the asset demand functions. Following Godley and Lavoie (2007), we also assume — for both capitalists and workers — that expected investible wealth is the financial asset wealth of the previous period. With respect to the allocation of households' wealth, we assume that the demands for financial assets are always realized, with the exception of the demand for money. In fact, we consider the buffering role of bank deposits in the allocation of resources (80–81).

3.3. Public Sector Relations

Now we consider an active public sector formed by government and central bank (CCB). The former collects resources through taxation and makes long-term public investments for the economy[7] (86–104) while the latter is in charge of monetary policy.

As was the case for private investments, we adopt the same distinction between demanded, produced and concluded public investments that eventually form public capital (93–96). Public investment demand is studied via three different scenarios. In the baseline scenario (BL), the government passively maintains public expenditure and tax rates at a constant level through time, independent of variations in aggregate demand (93). In the second scenario the government tries to achieve a zero-budget deficit (0BD), with the final purpose of not letting public debt increase (93A). In both previous scenarios the government does not manipulate tax rates — that remain constant — and therefore (87–92) and (99–101) are not activated. Rather, those equations are activated in the case of a proactive government trying to manage all available fiscal tools to create a sustainable recovery path (proactive policy scenario). More specifically, the government will increase its demand of public investments (93B) whenever the growth of aggregate demand is lower than a determined minimum threshold and it will decrease its level whenever the growth of aggregate demand exceeds a particular maximum established threshold (99–101). At the same time, the government implements a fiscal policy so that capitalists' and workers' tax rates decrease whenever their personal incomes fall behind a certain negative growth threshold and increase whenever those exceed a certain positive growth threshold (87–92). The aim of such a fiscal policy is to stimulate (calm) household consumption — and therefore overall aggregate demand — whenever economic activity is facing an excessive negative slowdown (or a boom).[8] Finally, (102) describes the government deficit while (104) represents the government debt and (103) the amount of new bills issued by the government.

Following Godley and Lavoie's (2007, Chapter 11) model, here we consider a simplified central bank that holds treasury bills as assets and bank reserves and banknotes

[7]The main reason for this assumption is to stress the goal divergence of the investment projects demanded by the private sector (driven mainly by the desire to increase production capacity and ultimately profit) and those demanded by the public sector (driven by a functional finance approach, increasing the capital of the overall economy and also using public expenditure as a tool to support demand in periods of recession). This is just a simplification hypothesis, which might be altered in future research projects in line with this work. It is assumed that the government spends only by purchasing investment goods and not on current expenditure. This too is a simplification that may be modified in future.

[8]These policy scenario simulations are based on Bibi (2021) and this work intends to expand that by analysing the same policies and their implications through a comprehensive analysis within the features of an SFC model.

as liabilities. Government securities and central bank liabilities are supposed to be supplied on demand (106–112) thus allowing interest rates on treasury bills and government bonds (113–114) to be treated as exogenous variables in line with the horizontalist approach in endogenous money (EM) theory. In the EM framework, commercial banks — through making loans — simultaneously create deposits and then demand a monetary base from the central bank (Bibi and Canelli 2022). Commercial banks must accumulate reserves in proportion to their deposits and these are supplied on demand by the central bank (Godley and Lavoie 2007).

3.4. Banking Sector Relations

Equations (116–126) in this section express the endogenous monetary approach followed by the majority of horizontalist economists, according to whom money is mainly an endogenous phenomenon created on demand. More precisely, we follow here the Godley and Lavoie (2007) approach on the main CCB and government relationships. Bank deposits, loans to firms and personal loans are all supplied on demand. Banks holdings of bills (120) are considered as the buffer absorbing the mismatching mechanism between bank assets and liabilities while bank demand of bills (121) is determined as a part of their balance-sheet constraint. Equations (122–126) describe the mechanism through which CBs decide on the deposit interest rate variation based on their aim of maintaining the bank liquidity ratio (BLR) within certain boundaries. Finally, (127–130) describe bank mark-up policy in determining the bank loan interest rate. This structure is a simplified version of the one considered in our reference model since the determination of bank profits is not the main focus of this work.

4. Effects of a Crisis on Socioeconomic and Ecological Distribution

In recent decades, many activists and also researchers have claimed that consumption (and indirectly growth) reduction is necessary, and in some scenarios even sufficient, to address ecological imbalances in our economies. That is so, since the reduction of consumer consumption would directly reduce our ecological footprint and production of greenhouse gases (Tamburino and Bravo 2021; WWF 2019). According to Bowen and Stern (2010), even a demand-induced downturn (crisis) might be helpful in achieving this goal because it would provide a good opportunity to take a necessary step toward an environmental policy shift able to shrink the consumption level and contribute to a more balanced ecological path.

Our analysis focuses on the effects of a crisis at the economic, social, and ecological distributional levels. Through simulation exercises,[9] we analyse the impact of a negative demand for investments shock by considering the three different scenarios previously analyzed in Section Three, namely, a passive government scenario, a zero-budget deficit scenario (0BD), and, finally, a proactive government scenario.

[9]The model is calibrated using available data for major advanced economies (for example, the different marginal propensities to consume of workers and capitalists, different coefficients for their ecological footprints, coefficients of wage reactions to changes in unemployment levels) and reasonable values (such as proportions of *C*, *I*, *G*, and the wage bill upon GD together with parameters adopted by previous literature). The initial values of the variables and parameters used in the simulation analysis are reported in the appendices and Table A3.

4.1. Passive Government Scenario

In this first scenario we consider a passive government, which, despite the crisis, does not change its expenditure. The reduction of investments has a negative impact both on the demand side, further causing a reduction in expected and actual consumption, and the production side, through a reduction in consumption and investment goods produced (Figure 1a–e). The following fall in employment, together with a wage reduction (linked to weaker worker bargaining power), makes the wage bill fall further (Figures 1b–3c), thus depressing demand to an even greater extent.

However, while profits are initially reduced by the negative impact of the economic crisis, the reduction in wages and costs allows profits to stop falling and once more increase (Figure 1c). Such a reversed trend in profits stimulates economic activity expectations and, in that way, both demanded and produced private investments, too (Figure 1e). The partial recovery of investments stimulates overall demand and production, together with a slight increase in the wage bill. Such a recovery, however, is not strong enough to restore the pre-crisis wage bill and activity levels. In that way, while the wage bill level remains much lower, total and distributed profits remain higher than the pre-crisis level, thanks to the reduced cost of production (Figure 1c).

Despite the initial volatile periods that occur, mainly due to incorrect expectations,[10] such volatility is increasingly reduced and the resultant dynamics of the previous scenario have a clear impact on overall social distribution between workers and capitalists. In fact, the lower wage bill reduces the workers' personal income (Figure 1f), which also affects their overall wealth and ability to make financial investments. In the same way, the increased distributed profits obtained by capitalists contribute to their persistently growing higher personal income and, consequently, their higher level of overall and financially investible wealth (Figure 1g). The increase in financially investible wealth stimulates the capitalists' demand for bills and bonds that are supplied on demand. The increase in government debt — due to the fall in income, which will generate smaller tax payments and therefore a larger government deficit — and a simultaneous reduction in GDP are the main reason for an increased and increasing government debt to GDP ratio (Figure 1h).

Although the crisis did generate a much lower level of economic activity and demand for consumption goods at aggregate level (Figure 1i), it reduced only the consumption levels of workers while increasing that of capitalists, reflecting the distributional effect on disposable income and wealth.

In this way, the EF reduction caused by lower workers consumption is compensated by the increase in the consumption of capitalists. The final effect is a substantially unchanged level of EF (Figure 1j) and more polarized social classes. The economy faced a shift both in the distribution of social classes and the burden of their EF.

[10]The main source of volatility derives from the larger values allowed to be taken from η'. With smaller values of η', volatility would be reduced even if the main results are maintained. Bibi (2020) provides a deeper explanation of the volatility of the main variables in the model, which is related to the expectations of firms (η'), the interaction between the sensitivity of wages to the variation of EPL (γ_z), the sensitivity of wages to the variation of the unemployment level (γ_u), and the sensitivity of workers' productivity to variations in wages (γ_w). Despite the volatility in the production of consumption goods initially affecting all other variables, such volatility is reduced with time and the main variable trends are clearly visible.

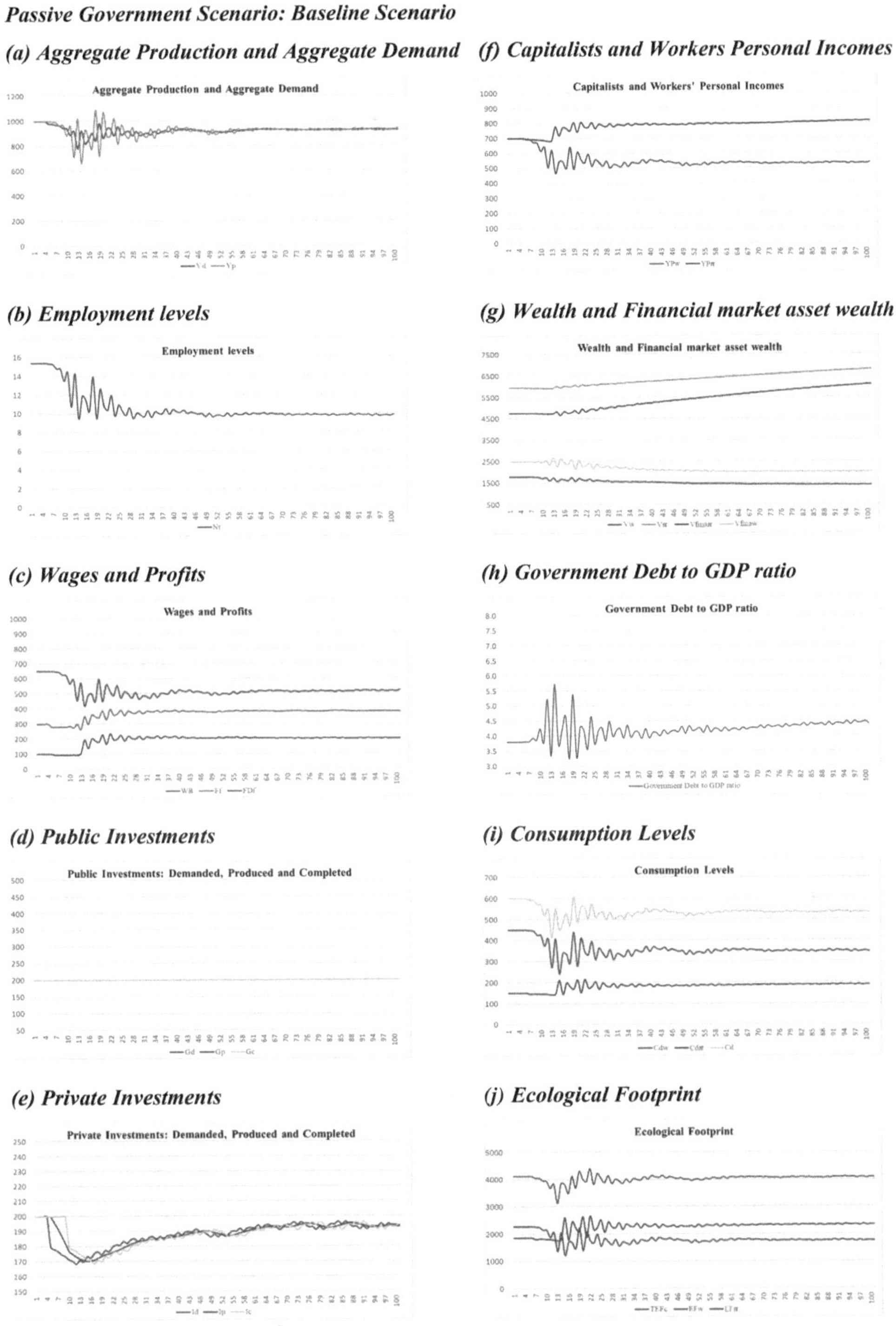

Figure 1. Evolution of macroeconomic, financial, and ecological variables of the baseline scenario.

Note: The initial values of the variables and parameters used in the simulation analysis are reported in Appendices A–C and Table A3.

A sensitivity test is conducted (Figure 2) considering weaker (stronger) reactions of the economic agents in response to the exogenous drop in investments compared to the baseline scenario. The values used in the simulation analysis are reported in Table A3.

4.2. 0BD Government Policy Scenario

In our second scenario, we consider a zero-budget deficit (0BD) policy framework, in which the government tries to achieve constant parity between outlays (pure expenditure plus interest payments on both kinds of debt) and all revenues (tax receipts and central bank profits, F_{cb}, which are returned to the government). This policy might be due to the government's final aim of not letting the public debt/GDP ratio increase above current levels.

However, as Sawyer (2010) clearly pointed out, the budget deficit cannot be controlled exactly by government, potentially persistently frustrating such a policy goal if we consider that, in the end, the budget deficit is actually an endogenous variable:

> In effect the budget deficit can be viewed as endogenous and indeed something of a residual … whilst a government can set tax rates and its intentions for public expenditure, the resulting budget deficit arises as a result of decisions made by the private sector and the resulting level of economic activity. (p. 37)

Because it is impossible for the government to calculate the exact amount of public expenditure that would satisfy a constant zero-budget deficit, its best approximation is probably to spend an amount of resources on public investments that would allow a parity of budget if such an amount had been spent in the previous period, according to (93).

In this scenario, the starting dynamics are similar to those in the previous scenario. In fact, as soon as the economy faces the external negative shock in demand for investment, it suffers a decrease in aggregate demand and therefore a decrease in production too (Figure 3a). Such a decrease in production leads to a drop in the employment rate (Figure 3b), which has a further negative impact on aggregate demand. In that way, at first, both the workers' wage bill and capitalists' profits drop (Figure 3c), which also decreases their personal incomes (Figure 3f). These decreased personal incomes produce a reduction in taxes collected by the government. In attempting to achieve a zero-budget deficit, the government decreases the amount of public investments available (Figure 3d), which is the biggest difference from the previous scenario. In fact, such a decrease in government expenditure affects the production level (Figure 3d) and, in so doing, decreases the need for employment, lowering the overall employment level even further with respect to the BL (Figure 3b) where the government was not decreasing public expenditure.

The larger decline in employment makes the wage bill shrink further with respect to the BL (Figure 3c). The lower main cost of production — wages — allows profits finally to increase, stimulating private investment (Figure 3e). Meanwhile, the decreased wage bill and the increased profits affect the personal incomes of the two social classes, contributing to the lowering of the overall and financially investible wealth of the workers, on one side, and increasing the overall and financially investible wealth of the capitalists, on the other (Figure 3f–g).

Sensitivity Analysis of the Baseline Scenario

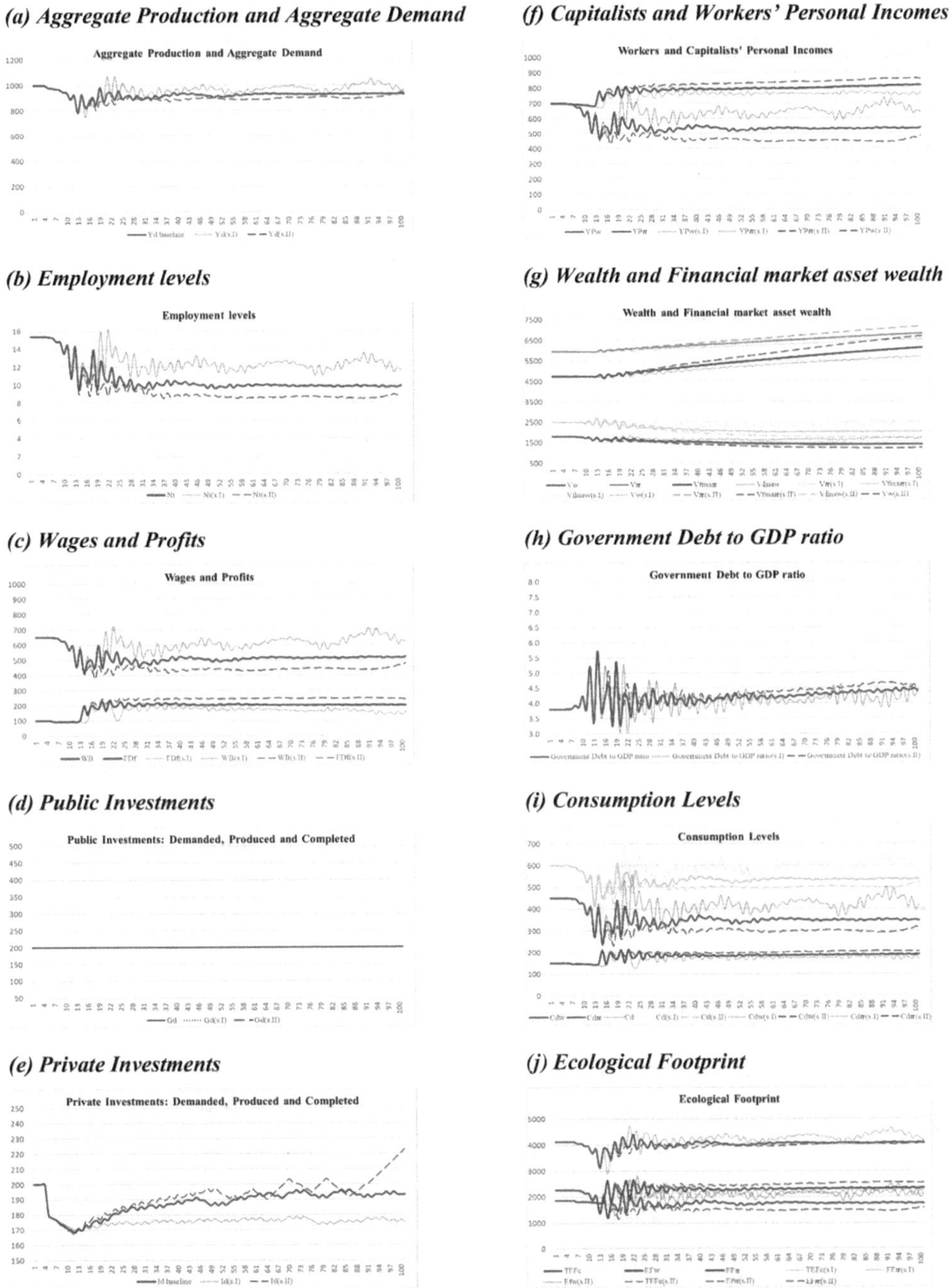

Figure 2. Sensitivity test of the baseline scenario related to the evolution of macroeconomic, financial, and ecological variables.

Note: The initial values of the variables and parameters used in the simulation analysis are reported in Appendices A–C and Table A3.

Even if the recovery of private investment partially attenuates the fall in aggregate demand, its level remains much lower than that in the pre-crisis period, with no significant prospect of increasing again. This situation makes private investments stagnate and slightly decrease (Figure 3e) until the dissociation between demanded, produced and concluded investments becomes relevant again. In fact, although the demand for public investments almost recovered after its first strong decline, concluded public investments also start to fall because of the previous continuously lowered levels of demanded and produced public investments (Figure 3d). Such a fall in concluded public investments decreases public, and thus overall level of, capital stock in the economy.[11] The reduced level of capital per worker in the economy leads to a decrease in labour productivity too (via 43), producing two direct effects, namely, reduction of potential output (via 22) and increase in workers needed for production activities (via 34–36). The previous situation puts pressure on capacity utilization and therefore provides a positive stimulus to private investment (Figure 3e). The reactivation of demanded and produced investments mildly supports the employment level, together with wage bill (Figure 3c).

The halting of the declining wage bill together with increased demand for investments finally leads to a light recovery trend for the overall economy. However, there are several differences with respect to the BL scenario. While both the BL and the 0BD aggregate demand and aggregate production levels remain lower than those pre-crisis, in the 0BD scenario those levels stay considerably lower than those of the BL until the end.

The prolonged levels of reduced demand and production cause a consistently lower level of employment that remains significantly lower than the BL scenario too (Figure 3b). The decreased level of employment affects the wage bill, which remains at a lower level with respect to the BL, while it allows firms to reduce their main production costs and thus obtain higher profits. The resultant effect is an even greater polarization of the social classes with respect to both the BL and the pre-crisis situation. In fact, while the higher profit levels produce higher personal incomes for capitalists, thus building up higher levels of overall and financially investible wealth, lower wage bill levels negatively affect workers' personal income (Figure 3c, f, g).

The 0BD policy did not contribute to reducing the public debt to GDP ratio below the pre-crisis level, while its value remains consistently even higher than the BL (Figure 3h). At the same time, the final aggregate consumption level remains inferior to that achieved in the BL scenario. However, the composition of the demand for consumption goods is quite different. In fact, we can highlight a shift between the consumption of workers and capitalists (Figure 3i) corresponding to their polarized income and disposable wealth. The workers consume less while the capitalists consume more in comparison to the pre-crisis situation and with respect to the BL. This shift in their consumption patterns produces a correspondent shift in their ecological footprint (Figure 3j). As a matter of fact, while the EF of workers is reduced, that of capitalists is higher with respect to the BL. The final overall EF level is higher than the pre-crisis situation and ultimately it is even slightly higher than the BL, with a projection to increase further in future.

[11] In fact, the simulated data show that, while total capital levels were slowly increasing again after the crisis up to period 56 (thanks to the recovery of private capital), period 57 demarks the reduction of public capital that — due to its magnitude — negatively affects the level of total capital (values not represented in the charts).

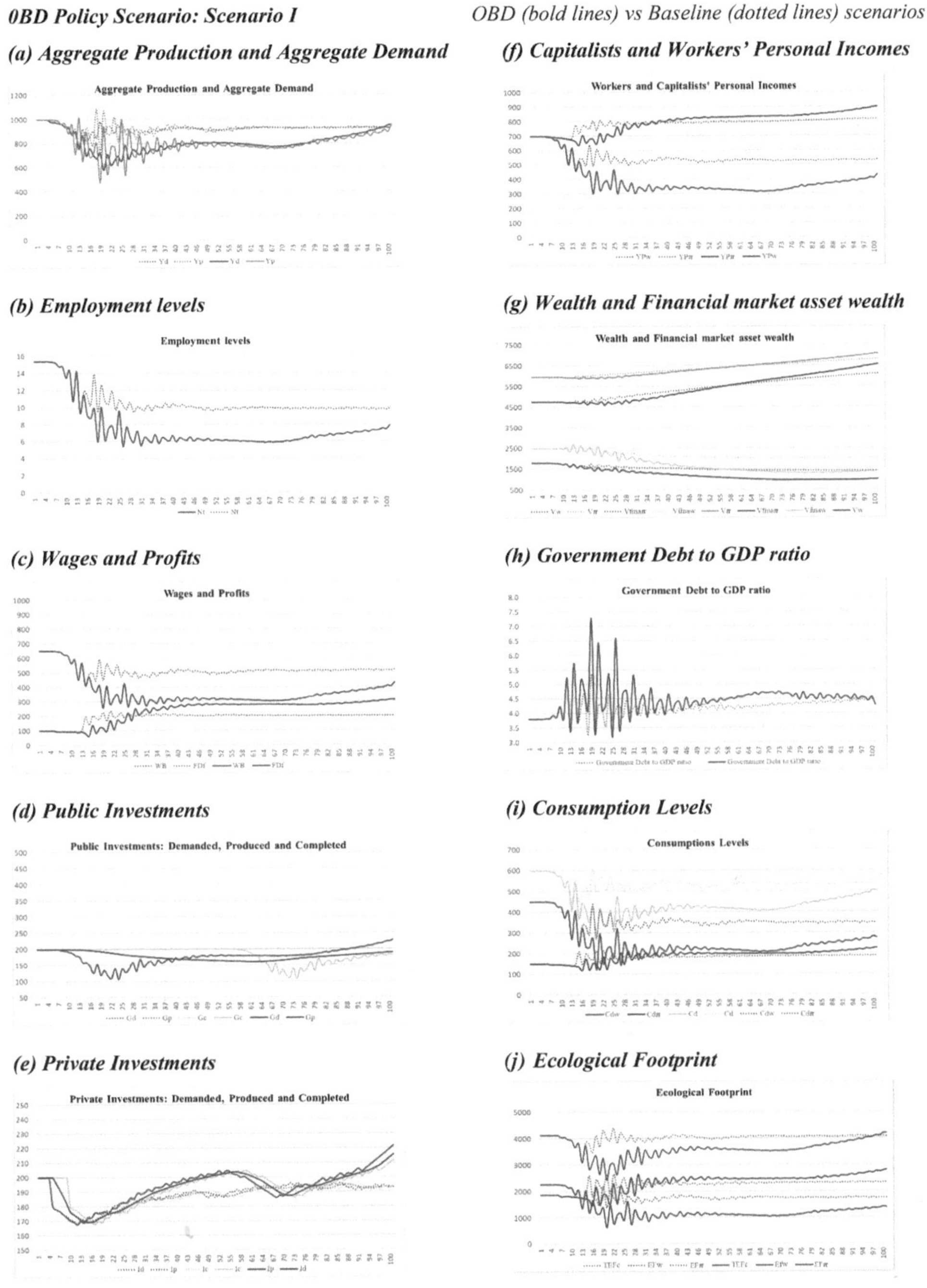

Figure 3. Evolution of macroeconomic, financial, and ecological variables. 0BD (bold lines) versus baseline (dotted lines) scenarios.

Note: The initial values of the variables and parameters used in the simulation analysis are reported in Appendices A–C and Table A3.

4.3. Proactive Government Scenario

In our final scenario we consider a 'proactive' government, the final aim of which is to secure a high level of economic activity supporting the aggregated demand level through public social investment. According to this scenario, the government increases its demand for public investment whenever the growth of aggregate demand is lower than a determined minimum threshold, while it decreases demand whenever the growth of aggregate demand exceeds a particular maximum established threshold. Such a government spending policy will be tackled together with a fiscal policy based on taxation. Keynes (1936) perfectly suggested this means of supporting aggregate demand and fighting unemployment by stating that

> the remedy would lie in various measures designed to increase the propensity to consume by the redistribution of incomes or otherwise. (p. 324)

> The State will have to exercise a guiding influence on the propensity to consume partly through its scheme of taxation, partly by fixing the rate of interest, and partly, perhaps, in other ways. (p. 378)

As previously mentioned (Section 3.6), in such a scenario the government implements a fiscal policy rule so that the tax rates of capitalists and workers decrease whenever their personal incomes fall behind a certain negative growth threshold and increase whenever they exceed a certain positive growth threshold. The aim of such a fiscal policy is to stimulate (calm) their consumption — and therefore overall aggregate demand — whenever economic activity is facing an excessive negative slowdown (or boom). The theoretical background for such a coordinated fiscal policy, that is, to steer the economy whilst simultaneously reducing income inequality, has been suggested and developed by several post-Keynesians, such as Sawyer (2010). The simulation exercises in Figure 4 explore those ideas.

In this scenario, as soon as the exogenous investment shock induces a crisis, the government reacts rapidly by increasing its demand for public investment (Figure 4d), which stimulates overall aggregate demand, thus containing downward instability. Such an idea was previously explored by Fazzari et al. (2013), who argued that, 'autonomous demand has a profound effect on the model dynamics. It induces a floor that turns around negative dynamics toward growth' (p. 18). In effect, that demand support directly stimulates the demand for private investments and, consequently, the production of both public and private investments (Figure 4d, e). The overall trend to increase both public and private investment after the crisis leads to a reversed trend in employment required (Figure 4b, period 15), pushing it above the pre-crisis level. Such an effect causes wage levels and therefore the wage bill to increase. At first (see period 20), such a strong increase in wage levels causes a drop in profits, reducing capitalists' consumption and therefore aggregate demand slightly too. Such a slight drop calls for a further government intervention (see period 22), which again stimulates overall aggregate demand, aggregate production, and level of profits too. The restoration of economic activity continues, also boosting private demanded and produced investments (Figure 4e).

The economic cyclicality characterizing the moment after the exogenous negative shock is reduced by the immediate support of government demand and production but economic trends are quite clear. In fact, the strong intervention of the government via higher demanded and produced public investments generate a positive impact on

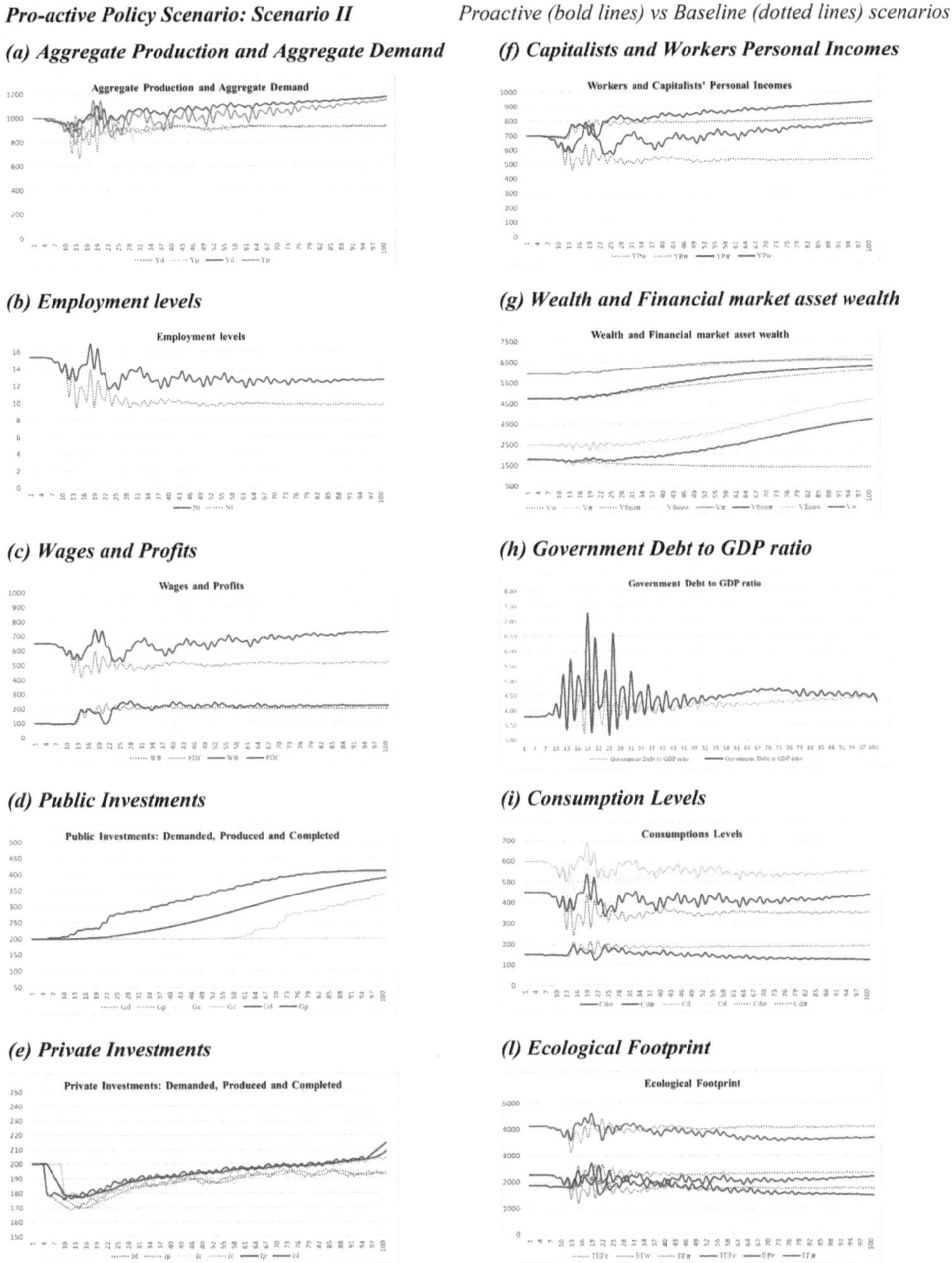

Figure 4. Evolution of macroeconomic, financial, and ecological variables. Proactive (bold lines) versus baseline (dotted lines) scenarios.

Note: The initial values of the variables and parameters used in the simulation analysis are reported in Appendices A–C and Table A3.

the overall levels and trajectory of aggregate demand. Increased production stimulates the employment levels that, together with the wage increase, generate an overall positive trend in the wage bill, thus supporting aggregate consumption and overall aggregate demand.

The increase in both capitalist' profits and workers' wages induce their personal income to constantly rise. However, following a proactive spending policy, as long as their personal incomes vary, the government manages to change the disposable income patterns of both capitalists and workers by affecting their tax rates. By so doing, the government is able to steer higher levels of the overall and financially investible wealth of both social classes. While the personal incomes of both classes are finally higher than the pre-crisis levels, and projected to increase, their differences in wealth are very much reduced with respect to the pre-crisis, the BL, and the passive government scenarios. The government debt to GDP ratio volatility is much lower with respect to the BL during all the periods under consideration, finally stabilizing its value with a decreasing trend projection.

Overall consumption is finally slightly lower with respect to the pre-crisis levels — such as in the BL scenario — but that alone does not assure a decrease in EF too. In fact, what seems to be relevant for reducing the total EF is also the composition of consumption related to the EF weight of the different social classes. Since the workers have a lower EF weight than the capitalists, even a relevant reduction in workers' consumption together with an increase in capitalists' consumption might not assure that an overall decrease in aggregate consumption will lead to an overall reduction in total EF. In fact, in this scenario, the greatest contribution to the reduction of the total EF — with respect to both the pre-crisis and to the BL — comes mainly from the slight reduction in capitalists' EF.

5. Conclusions

This work developed a post-Keynesian SFC macroeconomic model analysing the dynamics of key socioeconomic variables after a period of a crisis. Our model is built upon Bibi (2020, 2021) within an endogenous money framework and is calibrated using available data for major advanced economies. The model's framework is characterized by several post-Keynesian features. First, the presence of two social classes, capitalists and workers, with different consumption behaviours and different endowments. Second, the differing consumption behaviours of workers and capitalists have an impact on resources needed and affect ecological balance. Third, non-financial firms and also government can undertake investment decisions and both accumulate capital. Through simulations, different policy scenarios are investigated in which the government might use different fiscal policy rules and tools to achieve recovery in a sustainable way. Socioeconomic sustainability is here interpreted in terms of reduced unemployment, a less polarized society and ecological sustainability proxied by the ecological footprint.

In particular, three different policy scenarios were investigated as a reaction to an exogenous fall in private investment. First, we considered a situation in which the government does not change its expenditure despite the negative exogenous shock (our baseline scenario). We then analysed a policy scenario whereby the government pursued a zero-budget deficit (OBD) policy rule with the final aim of not letting the public debt to GDP ratio increase. Finally, the third situation was represented by a proactive policy scenario whereby the government implemented its main fiscal policies — spending and taxation — to support economic activity following a functional finance approach.

The analysis was carried out using an SFC model that takes into account all monetary connections within the economy among the different sectors and between the two social classes, too. This work contains some interesting novelties with respect to the existing literature. While few SFC models explicitly consider an economy formed by two social classes, no one — to our knowledge — considers the impacts of the Kaleckian temporal lags among demanded, produced and concluded private investments in such a framework. Second, while SFC models generally consider the government sector, rarely do any consider its role in demanding and producing social public investments that, together with private investments, form the overall capital endowment of an economy. Such analysis is relevant to stress the divergence in outcomes sought for engagement in investment projects: for the private sector, it is driven mainly by the desire to increase production capacity and ultimately profit; for the public sector, it is motivated by a functional finance approach, increasing the capital of the overall economy and using public expenditure as a tool to support demand in periods of recession too. Finally, combining those Kaleckian ideas with those of Keynesians regarding the ways in which a government can restore the economy through government spending and taxes, we highlighted how investment decisions such as consumption patterns might be steered to ensure economic and social recovery in a sustainable ecological way. Our model draws some relevant conclusions in terms of the key indicators of an economy after an exogenous drop in demand. Fiscal policies adopted by the government were studied, together with the recovery path followed by the economy, the employment level, and wage and wealth distribution between social classes, and some simple ecological inferences made. In the passive government policy scenario (BL), the lack of reactiveness in terms of fiscal expenditure meant it was unable to restore the economy to its pre-crisis situation regarding aggregate production and employment, with a further polarization of the social classes in terms of income and wealth. Overall economic consumption falls but, as a result of the redistribution in consumption and because of the different EF weights of the social classes, an overall reduction in ecological impact is not necessarily guaranteed. In the 0BD scenario, the austerity measures cause a worse outcome in terms of restoration of economic activity and employment with respect to the BL, with even more polarized distribution between the social classes in terms of both income and wealth. In fact, the policy rule — that the government pursues here — leads the government to contract its expenditure, inducing aggregate demand, production, and employment to contract even further. For the whole period considered, the indicators of the real side of the economy remain much lower than in both the pre-crisis situation and the BL scenario. If the total EF remains inferior to that in the BL scenario during most of the simulated period, its value finally reaches the BL level with a clear tendency to surpass it. As in the BL scenario, in the 0BD scenario the government is not able to avoid increasing the debt/GDP ratio even if this was the ultimate goal of its policy. Finally, in the proactive government policy scenario, the countercyclical reaction of government expenditure enables economic activity to be supported and to reverse the fall of the main real macroeconomic variables. A further polarization of the social classes is avoided and, in fact, even reduced. However, such a result is obtained without imposing a cut on the income or wealth of either social classes. The personal incomes and wealth of both workers and capitalists increase while reduced consumption allows the total EF to be reduced. Increased production contributes to stabilizing the government debt/GDP ratio.

Our model can be expanded in several ways. First, further features of the ecological balance might be incorporated to also include the effects of damage functions. Second, future investigations could research the space for monetary or combined policies able to achieve a similar social, economic, and ecological sustainable scenario. Third, country-specific analysis might further consider this work by applying specificities of developed or developing countries.

Acknowledgements

I would like to use this opportunity to acknowledge and thank the reviewers who reviewed this article and aided in its publication. I am grateful to Malcolm Sawyer and Stefano Zambelli who accompanied me during the journey of my PhD, as well as to the Editor and the two anonymous referees for their suggestions and comments to the present work that allowed me to deeply shape and improve it. I am also grateful to Diego Guevara, Marco Veronese Passarella and Gennaro Zezza for the support they provide at the beginning of this work. Any remaining errors or omissions are strictly my own.

Disclosure Statement

No potential conflict of interest was reported by the author.

ORCID

Samuele Bibi http://orcid.org/0000-0002-9010-0368

References

Arestis, P., and M. Sawyer. 2005. 'Aggregate Demand, Conflict and Capacity in the Inflationary Process.' *Cambridge Journal of Economics*, 959–974. doi:10.1093/cje/bei079

Banca d'Italia. 2015. 'I bilanci delle famiglie italiane nell'anno 2014 in *Supplementi al Bollettino Statistico*.' https://www.bancaditalia.it/pubblicazioni/indagine-famiglie/bil-fam2014/suppl_64_15.pdf.

Bibi, S. 2020. 'Keynes, Kalecki and Metzler in a Dynamic Distribution Model.' *Cambridge Journal of Economics* 44 (1): 73–104.

Bibi, S. 2021. 'The Stabilising Role of the Government in a Dynamic Distribution Growth Model.' *Journal of Post-Keynesian Economics* 44 (1): 112–142. doi:10.1080/01603477.2020.1835495

Bibi, S., and R. Canelli. 2022. *The interpretation of CBDC within an endogenous money framework.* Manuscript submitted for publication.

Bowen, A., and N. Stern. 2010. 'Environmental Policy and the Economic Downturn.' *Oxford Review of Economic Policy* 26 (2). https://www.jstor.org/stable/43664557. doi:10.1093/oxrep/grq007

Dafermos, Y., M. Nikolaidi, and G. Galanis. 2017. 'A Stock-Flow-Fund Ecological Macroeconomic Model.' *Ecological Economics* 131: 191–207. doi:10.1016/j.ecolecon.2016.08.013.

Fazzari, S. M., P. E. Ferri, E. G. Greenberg, and A. M. Variato. 2013. 'Aggregate Demand, Instability, and Growth*.' *Review of Keynesian Economics* 1 (1): 1–21. doi:10.4337/roke.2013.01.01.

Font, P., M. Izquierdo, and S. Puente. 2015. 'Real Wage Responsiveness to Unemployment in Spain: Asymmetries Along the Business Cycle.' *IZA Journal of European Labor Studies* 4 (13). doi:10.1186/s40174-015-0038-x.

Fontana, G., and M. Sawyer. 2016. 'Towards Post-Keynesian Ecological Macroeconomics.' *Ecololgical Economics*, 186–195. doi:10.1016/j.ecolecon.2015.03.017

Fontana, G., and M. Setterfield. 2009. *Macroeconomic Theory and Macroeconomic Pedagogy*. s.l.: Palgrave Macmillan.

Global Footprint Network. 2015. *The Footprint and Biocapacity Accounting: Methodology Background for State of the States 2015*. Oakland.

Godley, W. 1996. Money, Finance, and National Income Determination. *Working Paper No. 167*, Issue Annandale-on-Hudson, NY: Levy Economics Institute of Bard College.

Godley, W., and M. Lavoie. 2007. *Monetary Economics: An Integrated Approach to Credit, Money, Income, Production and Wealth*. Basingstoke: Palgrave Macmillan.

Grasselli, M., and A. Nguyen-Huu. 2018. 'Inventory Growth Cycles with Debt-Financed Investment.' In *Structural Change and Economic Dynamics*, 1–13.

Graziani, A. 2003. *The Monetary Theory of Production*. Cambridge: Cambridge university press.

IMF Working Paper. 2011. *Who's Going Green and Why? Trends and Determinants of Green Investment*. s.l.: Fiscal Affairs Department.

Islam, S. N. 2015. Inequality and Environmental Sustainability. *DESA Working Paper n.145*.

Kalecki, M. 1933. 'Outline of a Theory of the Business Cycle.' In *Essays in the Theory of Economic Fluctuations*, 1–14. London: Allen and Unwin.

Kalecki, M. 1971. *Selected Essays on the Dynamics of the Capitalist Economy: 1933–1970*. London; New York: Cambridge university press.

Kenner, D. 2015. Inequality of overconsumption: the ecological footprint of the richest. *(Working Paper)*.

Keynes, J. M. 1936. *The General Theory of Employment, Money and Interest Rate*. s.l.: Palgrave Macmillan.

Keynes, J. M. 1937. 'The General Theory of Employment.' *The Quarterly Journal of Economics*, 209–223. doi:10.2307/1882087

Lavoie, M. 2014. *Post-Keynesian Economics_ New Foundations*. s.l.: Edward Elgar.

Mackenzie, H., H. Messinger, and R. Smith. 2008. *SIZE MATTERS: Canada's Ecological Footprint, by Income*. Toronto, Ontario: Canadian Centre for Policy Alternatives.

McLeay, M., A. Radia, and T. Ryland. 2014. *Money Creation in the Modern*. London: Bank of England.

Metzler, L. A. 1941. 'The Nature and Stability of Inventory Cycles.' *The Review of Economic Statistics*, 113–129. doi:10.2307/1927555

Minam. 2013. *Cálculo de la Huella Ecológica Departamental y por Estratos Socioeconómicos*. Lima: Minam-Ministerio del Ambiente del Peru.

Pasinetti, L. 1981. *Structural Change and Economic Growth: A Theoretical Essay on the Dynamics of the Wealth of Nations*. Cambridge: Cambridge University Press.

Pasinetti, L. 1993. *Structural Economic Dynamics: A Theory of the Economic Consequences of Human Learning*. Cambridge University Press.

Peattie, K. 2010. 'Green Consumption: Behaviours and Norms.' *Annual Review of Environment and Resources*, 195–228. doi:10.1146/annurev-environ-032609-094328

Rochon, L. P., M. Czachor, and G. Bachurewicz. 2020. 'Introduction: Kalecki and Kaleckian Economics.' *Review of Political Economy* 32: 487–491. doi:10.1080/09538259.2020.1844963

Samuelson, P. A. 1939. 'Interection Between the Multiplier Analysis and the Principle of Acceleration.' *The Review of Economics and Statistics*, 75–78. doi:10.2307/1927758

Sawyer, M. 2010. Budget deficits and reductions in inequality for economic prosperity: a Kaleckian analysis. *Lebret*.

Sawyer, M., and M. Passarella Veronese. 2017. 'The Monetary Circuit in the age of Financialisation: A Stock-Flow Consistent Model with a Twofold Banking Sector.' *Metroeconomica*, 321–353. doi:10.1111/meca.12103

Tamburino, L., and G. Bravo. 2021. 'Reconciling a Positive Ecological Balance with Human Development: A Quantitative Assessment.' *Ecological Indicators* 129: 107973. doi:10.1016/j.ecolind.2021.107973.

Taylor, L., A. K. Rezai, and D. Foley. 2016. 'An Integrated Approach to Climate Change, Income Distribution, Employment and Economic Growth.' *Ecological Economics* 121: 196–205. doi:10.1016/j.ecolecon.2015.05.015

WWF. 2010. *Living Planet. Biodiversity, Biocapacity and Development*. London: WWF.

WWF. 2019. The ecological footprint and biocapacity explained the impact of our ecological footprint on biodiversity. https://wwfeu.awsassets.panda.org/downloads/wwf_eu_overshoot_day___living_beyond_nature_s_limits_web.pdf.

Zambelli, S. 2007. 'A Rocking Horse That Never Rocked: Frisch's Propagation Problems and Impulse Problems.' *History of Political Economy* 39 (1): 99–120. doi:10.1215/00182702-2006-027

Zambelli, S. 2014. Slides from the Macroeconomics and Monetary System module of professor Stefano Zambelli at Trento University, Italy.

Appendix A. Balance Sheet Matrix, Transaction-Flow Matrix, Equations list and values of key parameters.

Table A1. Balance sheet matrix.

	Households						
	Workers	Capitalists	Production firms	Government	Central bank	Banks	Σ
Inventories			$+IN$				$+IN$
Fixed capital			$+K^{I}$	$+K^{G}$			$+K^{T}$
HPM (cash)	$+H_w$	$+H_\pi$			$-H$	$+H_b$	0
Money (deposit)	$+M_w$	$+M_\pi$				$-M$	0
Bills		$+B_\pi$		$-B$	$+B_{cb}$	$+B_b$	0
Bonds		$+BL_\pi \cdot p_{bL}$		$-BL_\pi \cdot p_{bL}$			0
Loans	$-L_w$	$-L_\pi$	$-L_f$			$+L$	0
Bank capital		$+OF_b$				$-OF_b$	0
Balance (net worth)	$-V_w$	$-V_\pi$	$-V_f$	$-V_g$	0	0	$-(IN+K)$
Σ	0	0	0	0	0	0	0

Equations used in the model.

$$Y^D = C^D + I^D + G^D \tag{1}$$

$$Y^P = C^P + I^P + G^P \tag{2}$$

$$C^P = E_{-1}(C^D) + s^* \tag{3}$$

$$E_{-1}(C^D) = C^D_{-1} + \eta'(C^D_{-1} - C^D_{-2}) \tag{4}$$

$$\eta' = \frac{C^D_{-1} - C^D_{-2}}{C^D_{-2} - C^D_{-3}} \tag{5}$$

$$\eta' = 0 \textit{ if } C^D_{-2} = C^D_{-3} \tag{6}$$

$$\eta' = \eta'_L \textit{ if } \frac{C^D_{-1} - C^D_{-2}}{C^D_{-2} - C^D_{-3}} < \eta'_L \tag{7}$$

$$\eta' = \eta'_U \textit{ if } \frac{C^D_{-1} - C^D_{-2}}{C^D_{-2} - C^D_{-3}} \geq \eta'_U \tag{8}$$

$$s^* = \alpha E_{-1}(C^D) - Q_{-1} \tag{9}$$

$$Q = s + Q_{-1} = C^P - C^D + Q_{-1} \tag{10}$$

$$IN = Q \cdot UC \tag{11}$$

$$I^D = I^D_{-1} + a_1 \cdot \pi^e_{(t+1)} \cdot I^D_{-1} + a_2 \cdot cu_{-1} \cdot I^D_{-1} \tag{12}$$

Table A2. Transaction-flow matrix.

	Households		Firms		Government	Central bank		Banks		Σ
	Workers (1)	Capitalists (2)	Current (3)	Capital (4)	Current (5)	Capital (6)	Current (7)	Capital (8)	Current (9)	
Consumption	$-C_w^D$	$-C_\pi^D$	$+C^D$							0
Government expenditure					$-G^D$					0
Government Expenditure			$+G^D$							0
Fixed investment			$+I^D$	$-I^D$						0
Inventory accumulation										0
Taxes	$-T_w$	$-T_\pi$			$+T$					0
Wages	$+WB$		$-WB$							0
Inventory financing cost			$-r_{l-1} \cdot IN_{-1}$					$+r_{l-1} \cdot IN_{-1}$		0
Entrepreneurial profits		$+FD_f$	$-F_f$	$+FU_f$				$+r_{l-1} \cdot (L_{f-1} - IN_{-1})$		0
Bank profits		$+F_b$						$-F_b$		0
Central bank profits					$+F_{cb}$	$-F_{cb}$				0
Loan interest	$-r_{l-1} \cdot L_{w-1}$	$-r_{l-1} \cdot L_{\pi-1}$						$+r_{l-1} \cdot L_{h-1}$		0
Deposit interest	$+r_{m-1} \cdot M_{w-1}$	$+r_{m-1} \cdot M_{\pi-1}$						$-r_{m-1} \cdot M_{-1}$		0
Bill interest		$+r_{b-1} \cdot B_{\pi-1}$			$-r_{b-1} \cdot B_{-1}$	$+r_{b-1} \cdot B_{cb-1}$		$+r_{b-1} \cdot B_{b-1}$		0
Bond interest		$+BL_{-1}$			$-BL_{-1}$					0
Flows of funds (changes in stocks) Change in loans	$+\Delta L_w$	$+\Delta L_\pi$		$+\Delta L_f$					$-\Delta L$	0
Change in HPM (cash)	$-\Delta H_w$	$-\Delta H_\pi$					$+\Delta H$		$-\Delta H_b$	0
Change in money (deposits)	$-\Delta M_w$	$-\Delta M_\pi$							$+\Delta M$	0
Change in bills		$-\Delta B_\pi$			$+\Delta B$		$-\Delta B_{cb}$		$-\Delta M_b$	0
Change in bonds		$-\Delta BL \cdot p_{bL}$			$+\Delta BL \cdot p_{bL}$					0
Σ	0	0	0	0	0 0	0	0	0	0	0

$$\pi^e_{(t+1)} = \frac{\pi^e_{(t+1)}}{Y^D} \tag{13}$$

$$\pi^e_{(t+1)} = a_3 \cdot \ F_f - 1 + a_4 \cdot (\ F_f - 1 - \ F_f - 2) \tag{14}$$

$$a_1 = +|a_1| \ if \ (\ F_f - 1 - \ F_f - 2) > 0 \tag{15}$$

$$a_1 = -|a_1| \ if \ (\ F_f - 1 - \ F_f - 2) < 0 \tag{16}$$

$$a_1 = 0 \ if \ (\ F_f - 1 - \ F_f - 2) = 0 \tag{17}$$

$$a_2 = +|a_2| \ if \ (Y^D_{-1} - Y^D_{-2}) > 0 \tag{18}$$

$$a_2 = -|a_2| \ if \ (Y^D_{-1} - Y^D_{-2}) < 0 \tag{19}$$

$$a_2 = 0 \ if \ (Y^D_{-1} - Y^D_{-2}) = 0 \tag{20}$$

$$cu = \frac{Y^D}{Y^*} \tag{21}$$

$$Y^* = Y^*_{-1} + \psi_L \cdot \left(\frac{L^T - L^T_{-1}}{L^T_{-1}}\right) \cdot Y^*_{-1} + \psi_A \cdot \left(\frac{A - A_{-1}}{A_{-1}}\right) \cdot Y^*_{-1} \tag{22}$$

$$I^P = \frac{1}{\theta_I} \sum_{j=1}^{\theta} I^D_{(-1-\theta+j)} \tag{23}$$

$$I^C = I^D_{-\theta_I} \tag{24}$$

$$K^I = K^I_{-1} - \delta_{KI} \cdot K^I_{-1} + I^C \tag{25}$$

$$C^P = AN^C \tag{26}$$

$$I^P = AN^I \tag{27}$$

$$w = w_{-1} + \gamma_z \cdot \frac{z - z_{-1}}{z_{t-1}} \cdot w_{-1} - \gamma_u \cdot (u_{-1} - u_{-2}) \cdot w_{-1} \tag{28}$$

$$\gamma_u = \gamma_{u-} \ if \ (u_{-1} - u_{-2}) > 0 \tag{29}$$

$$\gamma_u = \gamma_{u+} \ if \ (u_{-1} - u_{-2}) < 0 \tag{30}$$

$$\gamma_u = 0 \ if \ u_{-1} = u_{-2} \tag{31}$$

$$WB = w \ \cdot N^T \tag{32}$$

$$p_y = (1 + \rho)\left(\frac{w}{A}\right) \tag{33}$$

$$\rho = \left(\frac{Y^D}{WB}\right) - 1 \tag{34}$$

$$N^C = \frac{C^P}{A} \tag{35}$$

$$N^I = \frac{I^P}{A} \tag{36}$$

Table A3. Values of the key parameters in the baseline scenario, in the sensitivity test, in scenario I and in scenario II.

Values of key parameters in the sensitivity and policy analysis							
Parameter		Baseline scenario	Sensitivity test I	Sensitivity test II	OBD Ggvernment (scenario I)	Proactive government (scenario II)	Notes
Adjustment workers *mpcW* parameter	$\gamma_{c\pi 1}$	0.800	0.600	1.000	0.800	0.80	In Sensitivity test I (Sensitivity test II) weaker (stronger) reaction parameters respect to the Baseline scenario are considered.
Adjustment capitalists *mpcW* parameter	γ_{cw2}	1.500	1.200	1.800	1.500	1.50	
Coefficient of *w* reaction to change in *z*	γ_z	0.200	0.100	0.300	0.200	0.20	
Coefficient of (+)*w* reaction to change in (−)$\underline{u}$	γ_{u-}	0.500	0.200	0.800	0.500	0.50	
Coefficient of (−)*w* reaction to change in (+)*u*	γ_{u+}	0.250	0.100	0.400	0.250	0.25	In the 0 Budget Deficit policy (0BD, scenario I), the Government try to achieve a 0 Budget Deficit demanding an amount of Government expenditure such that the Budget Deficit of the previous period could have been nil.
Coefficient of *A* reaction to change in *w*	γ_w	0.500	0.080	0.700	0.500	0.50	
Coefficient of *A* reaction to change in (*K/N*)	γ_{L+}	0.300	0.275	0.325	0.300	0.30	
Labour force reaction to change in (+)*Yd*	γ_{L-}	0.250	0.200	0.300	0.250	0.25	
Labour force reaction to change in (−)*Yd*	a_1	0.250	0.200	0.300	0.250	0.25	
Expected investment parameter	a_2	0.100	0.080	0.120	0.100	0.10	
cu parameter related to investment	a_3	0.012	0.010	0.014	0.012	0.012	In the Proactive policy (scenario II) the government implements a fiscal policy such that capitalists and workers' tax rates decrease (increase) when their personal incomes fall behind (exceed) a certain degrowth (growth) threshold with the aim of stimulate (calm) their consumption and in this way the economic activity. With the same intention, Government expenditure increase (decrease) when the aggregate demand fall behind (exceed) a certain degrowth (growth) threshold.
Weight to previous level of profits	a_4	0.100	0.040	0.160	0.100	0.10	
Weight to previous change in profits	ψ_L	1.000	0.200	1.800	1.000	1.00	
Capacity output growth *wrt L*		2.000	1.000	3.000	2.000	2.00	
Capacity output growth *wrt A*	ψ_A ζ_m	2.000	1.000	3.000	2.000	2.00	
Change in deposit rate reaction parameter		0.00020	0.00020	0.00025	0.00020	0.0002	
Adjustment workers tax parameter	$\gamma_{\tau w}$ $\gamma_{\tau\pi}$	0	0	0	0	0.5	
Adjustment capitalists tax parameter		0	0	0	0	0.3	
Threshold of (+)*w* to let *w* tax increase	$\varphi_{\tau wh\ (high)}$	0.0%	0.0%	0.0%	0.0%	0.5%	
	$\varphi_{\tau\pi h\ (high)}$						
Threshold of (+)π to let π tax increase	$\varphi_{\tau whl\ (low)}$	0.0%	0.0%	0.0%	0.0%	0.5%	
Threshold of (−)w to let w tax decrease	$\varphi_{\tau\pi l\ (low)}$	0.0%	0.0%	0.0%	0.0%	−6.0%	
Threshold of (−)π to let π tax decrease	$\gamma_{g(-)}$	0.0%	0.0%	0.0%	0.0%	−7.0%	
Variation of (−)government intervention	$\gamma_{g(+)}$	0	0	0	0	0	
Variation of (+)government intervention	$\varphi_{Gl\ (low)}$	0	0	0	0	0.75	
Threshold of (−)*Yd* to let government +*G*	$\varphi_{Gh\ (high)}$	0.0%	0.0%	0.0%	0.0%	0.0%	
Threshold of (+)*Yd* to let government −G		0.0%	0.0%	0.0%	0.0%	5.0%	

$$N^G = \frac{G^P}{A} \tag{37}$$

$$N^T = N^C + N^I + N^G \tag{38}$$

$$u = \frac{U}{LF} = \frac{LF - N^T}{LF} = 1 - \frac{N^T}{LF} \tag{39}$$

$$LF = LF_{-1} + \gamma_L \cdot \frac{Y^D_{-1} - Y^D_{-2}}{Y^D_{-2}} \cdot LF_{-1} \tag{40}$$

$$\gamma_L = \gamma_{L-} \; if \; \frac{Y^D_{-1} - Y^D_{-2}}{Y^D_{-2}} < 0 \tag{41}$$

$$\gamma_L = \gamma_{L+} \; if \; \frac{Y^D_{-1} - Y^D_{-2}}{Y^D_{-2}} > 0 \tag{42}$$

$$\gamma_L = 0 \; if \; \frac{Y^D_{-1} - Y^D_{-2}}{Y^D_{-2}} = 0 \tag{43}$$

$$A = A_{-1} + \gamma_\omega \cdot \left(\frac{w - w_{-1}}{w_{-1}}\right) \cdot A_{-1} + \gamma_k \cdot \left(\frac{\frac{K^T_{-1}}{N^T_{-1}} - \frac{K^T_{-2}}{N^T_{-2}}}{\frac{K^T_{-1}}{N^T_{-1}}}\right) \cdot A_{-1} \tag{44}$$

$$UC = \frac{WB}{A} \tag{45}$$

$$F_f = Y^D - WB + \Delta IN - r_l \cdot IN_{-1} \tag{46}$$

$$FD_f = \psi_D \cdot F_{f-1} \;\; if \; L_{fd-1} > \psi_{IN} \cdot IN_{-1} \tag{47}$$

$$FD_f = F_f - FU_f - r_l \cdot (L_{fd-1} - IN_{-1}) \; if \; L_{fd-1} \leq \psi_{IN} \cdot IN_{-1} \tag{48}$$

$$FU_f = F_f - FD_f - r_l \cdot (L_{fd-1} - IN_{-1}) \;\; if \; L_{fd-1} > \psi_{IN} \cdot IN_{-1} \tag{49}$$

$$FU_f = I^D \;\; if \; L_{fd-1} \leq \psi_{IN} \cdot IN_{-1} \tag{50}$$

$$L_{fd} = L_{fd-1} + I^D + \Delta IN - FU_f \tag{51}$$

$$YP_w = WB + r_{m-1} \cdot M_{w-1} \tag{52}$$

$$YP_\pi = FD_f + FD_b + r_{m-1} \cdot M_{\pi-1} + r_{b-1} \cdot B_{\pi d-1} + BL_{\pi d-1} \tag{53}$$

$$YD_w = YP_w - T_w - r_{l-1} \cdot L_{w-1} \tag{54}$$

$$YD_\pi = YP_\pi - T_\pi - r_{l-1} \cdot L_{\pi-1} \tag{55}$$

$$T_w = \tau_w \cdot YP_{w-1} \tag{56}$$

$$T_\pi = \tau_\pi \cdot YP_{\pi-1} \tag{57}$$

$$V_w = V_{w-1} + YD_w - C_w^D \tag{58}$$

$$V_\pi = V_{\pi-1} + YD_\pi - C_\pi^D \tag{59}$$

$$C_w^D = c_{w1} \cdot (YD_{w-1} + NL_{sw-1}) + c_{w2} \cdot V_{w-1} \tag{60}$$

$$C_\pi^D = c_{\pi 1} \cdot (YD_{\pi-1} + NL_{\pi-1}) + c_{\pi 2} \cdot V_{\pi-1} \tag{61}$$

$$c_{w1} = c_{w1-1} - \gamma_{cw1} \frac{\tau_{w-1} - \tau_{w-2}}{\tau_{w-2}} \cdot c_{w1-1} \tag{62}$$

$$c_{\pi 1} = c_{\pi 1-1} - \gamma_{c\pi 1} \frac{\tau_{\pi-1} - \tau_{\pi-2}}{\tau_{\pi-2}} \cdot c_{\pi 1-1} \tag{63}$$

$$C^D = C_w^D + C_\pi^D \tag{64}$$

$$EF_w = \varphi_w \cdot C_w^D \tag{65}$$

$$EF_\pi = \varphi_\pi \cdot C_\pi^D \tag{66}$$

$$TEF = EF_w + EF_\pi \tag{67}$$

$$GL_T = GL_\pi + GL_w \tag{68}$$

$$GL_\pi = \beta \cdot YP_\pi \tag{69}$$

$$GL_w = \beta \cdot YP_w \tag{70}$$

$$\beta = \beta_0 - \beta_r \cdot r_l \tag{71}$$

$$NL_\pi = GL_\pi - REP_\pi \tag{72}$$

$$NL_w = GL_w - REP_w \tag{73}$$

$$REP_\pi = \xi_\pi \cdot L_{h\pi d-1} \tag{74}$$

$$REP_w = \xi_w \cdot L_{hwd-1} \tag{75}$$

$$L_{hd} = L_{h\pi d} + L_{hwd} \tag{76}$$

$$L_{h\pi d} = L_{h\pi d-1} + NL_\pi \tag{77}$$

$$L_{hwd} = L_{hwd-1} + NL_w \tag{78}$$

$$\begin{bmatrix} \dfrac{M_{\pi d}}{V_{fma\pi-1}} \\ \dfrac{B_{\pi d}}{V_{fma\pi-1}} \\ \dfrac{(p_{bL} \cdot BL_{\pi d})}{V_{fma\pi-1}} \end{bmatrix} = \begin{bmatrix} \lambda\pi_{10} \\ \lambda\pi_{20} \\ \lambda\pi_{30} \end{bmatrix} + \begin{bmatrix} \lambda_{\pi 11} & \lambda_{\pi 12} & \lambda_{\pi 13} \\ \lambda_{\pi 21} & \lambda_{\pi 22} & \lambda_{\pi 23} \\ \lambda_{\pi 31} & \lambda_{\pi 32} & \lambda_{\pi 33} \end{bmatrix} \begin{bmatrix} r_m \\ r_b \\ r_{bL} \end{bmatrix} + \begin{bmatrix} \lambda_{\pi 14} \\ \lambda_{\pi 24} \\ \lambda_{\pi 34} \end{bmatrix} YP_\pi \tag{79}$$

$$\lambda\pi_{10} + \lambda\pi_{20} + \lambda\pi_{30} = 1 \tag{AC1}$$

$$\lambda\pi_{11} + \lambda\pi_{21} + \lambda\pi_{31} = 0 \tag{AC2}$$

$$\lambda\pi_{12} + \lambda\pi_{22} + \lambda\pi_{32} = 0 \tag{AC3}$$

$$\lambda\pi_{13} + \lambda\pi_{23} + \lambda\pi_{33} = 0 \tag{AC4}$$

$$\lambda\pi_{14} + \lambda\pi_{24} + \lambda\pi_{34} = 0 \tag{AC5}$$

$$\lambda\pi_{11} = -(\lambda\pi_{12} + \lambda\pi_{13}) = 0 \tag{AC6}$$

$$\lambda\pi_{22} = -(\lambda\pi_{21} + \lambda\pi_{23}) = 0 \tag{AC7}$$

$$\lambda\pi_{33} = -(\lambda\pi_{31} + \lambda\pi_{32}) = 0 \tag{AC8}$$

$$M_{wd} = V_{fmaw-1} \tag{79}$$

$$M_{\pi h} = V_{fma\pi} - B_{\pi d} - p_{bL} \cdot BL_{\pi d} \tag{80}$$

$$M_{wh} = V_{fmaw} \tag{81}$$

$$V_{fma\pi} = M_{\pi d} + B_{\pi d} + p_{bL} \cdot BL_{\pi d} \tag{82A}$$

$$V_{fma\pi} = V_{\pi} + L_{\pi d} - H_{\pi d} - OF \tag{82}$$

$$V_{fmaw} = M_{wd} \tag{83A}$$

$$V_{fmaw} = V_w + L_{wd} - H_{wd} \tag{83}$$

$$H_{\pi d} = \lambda_{c\pi} \cdot C_{\pi}^{D} \tag{84}$$

$$H_{wd} = \lambda_{cw} \cdot C_{w}^{D} \tag{85}$$

$$T_T = T_w + T_{\pi} \tag{86}$$

$$T_w = \tau_w \cdot YP_{w-1} \tag{55}$$

$$T_{\pi} = \tau_{\pi} \cdot YP_{\pi-1} \tag{56}$$

$$\tau_w = \tau_{w-1} + \gamma_{\tau w} \cdot \left(\left| \frac{YP_{w-1} - YP_{w-2}}{YP_{w-1}} \right| \right) \cdot \tau_{w-1} \tag{87}$$

$$\tau_{\pi} = \tau_{\pi-1} + \gamma_{\tau\pi} \cdot \left(\left| \frac{YP_{\pi-1} - YP_{\pi-2}}{YP_{\pi-1}} \right| \right) \cdot \tau_{\pi-1} \tag{88}$$

$$\gamma_{\tau w} = +|\gamma_{\tau w}| \text{ } if \text{ } \frac{YP_{w-1} - YP_{w-2}}{YP_{w-1}} > \varphi_{\tau wh} \tag{89}$$

$$\gamma_{\tau\pi} = +|\gamma_{\tau\pi}| \text{ } if \text{ } \frac{YP_{\pi-1} - YP_{\pi-2}}{YP_{\pi-1}} > \varphi_{\tau\pi h} \tag{90}$$

$$\gamma_{\tau w} = -|\gamma_{\tau w}| \text{ } if \text{ } \frac{YP_{w-1} - YP_{w-2}}{YP_{w-1}} \leq \varphi_{\tau wl} \tag{91}$$

$$\gamma_{\tau\pi} = -|\gamma_{\tau\pi}| \text{ } if \text{ } \frac{YP_{\pi-1} - YP_{\pi-2}}{YP_{\pi-1}} \leq \varphi_{\tau\pi l} \tag{92}$$

$$G^D = G_{-1}^D \tag{93}$$

$$G^D = G_{-1}^D - PSBR_{-1},\ G^D \geq 0 \tag{93A}$$

$$G^D = G_{-1}^D + \gamma_g \cdot \left(\left| \frac{Y_{-1}^D - Y_{-2}^D}{Y_{-2}^D} \right| \right) \cdot G_{-1}^D,\ G^D \geq 0 \tag{93B}$$

$$G^P = \frac{1}{\theta_G}\sum_{j=1}^{\theta} G^D_{(-1-\theta+j)} \tag{94}$$

$$G^C = G^D_{(-\theta_G)} \tag{95}$$

$$K^G = K^G_{-1} - \delta_{KG} \cdot K^G_{-1} + G^C \tag{96}$$

$$K^T = K^I + K^G \tag{97}$$

$$G^P = AN^G \tag{98}$$

$$\gamma_g = +|\gamma_g|\ if\ \frac{Y^D_{t-1} - Y^D_{t-2}}{Y^D_{t-2}} \leq \varphi_{Gl} \tag{99}$$

$$\gamma_g = -|\gamma_g|\ if\ \frac{Y^D_{t-1} - Y^D_{t-2}}{Y^D_{t-2}} > \varphi_{Gh} \tag{100}$$

$$\gamma_g = 0\ else\ if \tag{101}$$

$$PSBR = G^D + r_{b-1} \cdot (B_{\pi s-1} + B_{bs-1}) + BL_{\pi s-1} - T_T \tag{102}$$

$$B_s = B_{s-1} + PSBR - \Delta BL_{\pi s} \cdot p_{bL} \tag{103}$$

$$GD = B_{\pi s} + BL_{\pi s} + H_s \tag{104}$$

$$F_{cb} = r_{b-1} \cdot B_{cbd-1} \tag{105}$$

$$BL_{\pi s} = BL_{\pi d} \tag{106}$$

$$B_{\pi s} = B_{\pi d} \tag{107}$$

$$H_{hs} = H_{\pi d} + H_{wd} \tag{108}$$

$$H_{bs} = H_{bd} \tag{109}$$

$$H_s = H_{bs} + H_{hs} \tag{110}$$

$$B_{cbd} = H_s \tag{111}$$

$$B_{cbs} = B_{cbd} \tag{112}$$

$$r_b = \bar{r}_b \tag{113}$$

$$r_{bL} = r_b + add_{BL} \tag{114}$$

$$p_{bL} = \frac{1}{r_{bL}} \tag{115}$$

$$M_s = M_h \tag{116}$$

$$L_{fs} = L_{fd} \tag{117}$$

$$L_{hs} = L_{hd} \tag{118}$$

$$H_{bd} = \rho_b \cdot M_s \tag{119}$$

$$B_{bs} = B_s - B_{hs} - B_{cbs} \tag{120}$$

$$B_{bd} = M_s - L_{fs} - L_{hs} - H_{bd} + OF_b \tag{121}$$

$$BLR = \frac{B_{bd}}{M_s} \tag{122}$$

$$r_m = r_{m-1} + \Delta r_m \tag{123}$$

$$\Delta r_m = \zeta_m \cdot (z_1 - z_2) \tag{124}$$

$$z_1 = 1 \text{ iff } BLR < bot \tag{125}$$

$$z_2 = 1 \text{ iff } BLR > top \tag{126}$$

$$r_l = r_m + add_1 \tag{127}$$

$$F_b = r_{l-1} \cdot (L_{fs-1} + L_{hs-1}) + r_{b-1} \cdot B_{bd-1} - r_{m-1} \cdot M_{s-1} \tag{128}$$

$$OF = OF_{-1} \tag{129}$$

$$B_{bd} = B_{bs} \tag{130}$$

Appendix B. Initial values of endogenous variables

Symbol	Description	Value	Remarks/sources
A	Labour productivity	65	Calibrated such that the model generates the baseline scenario described in Section Four
B_{bd}	Bills demanded by banks (balance-sheet constraint of banks)	2,500	Calculated from Equation (121) using the initial values of M_s, L_{fs}, L_{hs}, H_{bd} and OF_b
B_{bs}	Household bills supplied on demand	2,500	Calculated from Equation (120) using the initial values of B_s, B_{hs} and B_{cbs}
B_{cbd}	Demand of central bank bills	2,500	Calculated from Equation (111) using the initial values of H_s
B_{cbs}	Supply of central bank bills	2,500	Calculated from Equation (112) using the initial values of B_{cbd}
B_s	Government bills	6,250	Calibrated such that the model generates the baseline scenario described in Section Four
$B_{\pi d}$	Bills demanded by capitalists	1,250	Selected from a reasonable range of values in relation to $V_{fma\pi}$ and respecting the condition of Equation (78)
$B_{\pi s}$	Bills supplied to capitalists on demand	1,250	Calculated from Equation (107) using the initial values of $B_{\pi d}$
BLR	Bank liquidity ratio	0.50	Calculated from Equation (122) using the initial values of B_{bd} and M_s
$BL_{\pi d}$	Long-term bonds demanded by capitalists	1,000	Selected from a reasonable range of values in relation to $V_{fma\pi}$ and respecting the condition of Equation (78)
$BL_{\pi s}$	Bond supplied to capitalists	50	Calculated from Equation (106) using the initial values of $BL_{\pi d}$
C^D	Total demand for consumption goods	600	Calculated from Equation (63) using the initial values of C^D_w and C^D_π
C^D_w	Demand for consumption goods by workers	450	Calculated from Equation (59) using the initial values of c_{w1}, YD_w, NL_w, c_{w2} and V_w
C^D_π	demand for consumption goods by capitalists	150	Calculated from Equation (60) using the initial values of $c_{\pi 1}$, YD_π, NL_π, $c_{\pi 2}$ and V_π
C^P	Consumption goods produced	600	Calculated from Equation (3) using the initial values of $E_{-1}(C^D)$ and s^*
cu	Capacity utilization	0.83	Calculated from Equation (21) using the initial values of $Y^D$and Y^*
$E_{-1}(C^D)$	Expected sales	600	Calculated from Equation (4) using the initial values of C^D and η'_t

(Continued)

Continued.

Symbol	Description	Value	Remarks/sources
EF_w	Ecological footprint generated by workers	2,264	Calculated from Equation (64) using the initial values of φ_w and C^D_w
EF_π	Ecological footprint generated by capitalists	1,863	Calculated from Equation (65) using the initial values of φ_π and C^D_π
F_b	'Payment from commercial banks'	450	Calculated from Equation (128) using the initial values of r_L, L_{fs}, L_{hs}, r_b, B_{bd}, r_m and M_s
F_{cb}	Realized central bank profits	100	Calculated from Equation (105) using the initial values of r_b and B_{cbd}
F_f	Realized entrepreneurial profits	300	Calculated from Equation (45) using the initial values of Y^D, WB, IN and r_l
FD_f	Distributed entrepreneurial profits	100	Calculated from Equation (46) using the initial values of F_f and ψ_D
FU_f	Undistributed entrepreneurial profits	200	Calculated from Equation (48) using the initial values of F_f, FD_f, r_l, L_{fd} and IN
G^C	Completion of public investments	200	Calculated from Equation (95) using the initial values of $G^D$and θ
G^D	Demand for public investments	200	Calculated from Equation (93A/93B) using the initial values of γ_g, Y^D and $PSBR$ in Scenario I/II
G^P	Production of public investments	200	Calculated from Equation (94) using the initial values of $G^D$and θ
GD	Government debt	3,800	Calculated from Equation (104) using the initial values of $B_{\pi s}$, $BL_{\pi s}$ and H_s
GL_T	Total gross amount of new personal loans	210	Calculated from Equation (67) using the initial values of $GL_\pi$and GL_w
GL_w	Gross amount of new personal loans taken by workers	105	Calculated from Equation (69) using the initial values of β and YP_w
GL_π	Gross amount of new personal loans taken by capitalists	105	Calculated from Equation (68) using the initial values of β and YP_π
H_{bd}	Reserve requirements of banks	1,450	Calculated from Equation (119) using the initial values of ρ_b and M_s
H_{bs}	Reserves supplied on demand	1,450	Calculated from Equation (109) using the initial values of H_{bd}
H_{hs}	Total households' cash supplied on demand	1,050	Calculated from Equation (108) using the initial values of $H_{\pi d}$ and H_{wd}
H_s	Total supply of high-powered money	2,500	Calculated from Equation (110) using the initial values of H_{bs} and H_{hs}
H_{wd}	Workers' demand for cash	800	Calculated from Equation (85) using the initial values of λ_{cw} and C^D_w
$H_{\pi d}$	Capitalists' demand for cash	250	Calculated from Equation (84) using the initial values of $\lambda_{c\pi}$ and C^D_π
I^C	Private investments concluded	200	Calculated from Equation (24) using the initial values of I^D
I^D	Demand for private investments	200	Selected from a reasonable range of values with respect to Y^D and considering Bibi (2020) and Bibi (2021)
I^P	Private investments produced	200	Calculated from Equation (23) using the initial values of $I^D$and θ
IN	Inventories valued at current cost	500	Calculated from Equation (11) using the initial values of UC and Q
K^G	Public capital	10,000	Calibrated such that the model generates the baseline scenario described in Section Four
K^I	Private capital	1,000	Calibrated such that the model generates the baseline scenario described in Section Four
K^T	Total capital	11,000	Calculated from Equation (97) using the initial values of K^I and K^G
L_{fd}	Demand for loans by firms	500	Calibrated such that the model generates the baseline scenario described in Section Four
L_{fs}	Supply of loans to firms	500	Calculated from Equation (117) using the initial values of L_{fd}
L_{hd}	Total demand for personal loans	4,000	Calculated from Equation (75) using the initial values of $L_{h\pi d}$ and L_{hwd}
L_{hs}	Total supply of personal loans	4,000	Calculated from Equation (118) using the initial values of L_{hd}
L_{hwd}	Demand for personal loans by workers	1,500	Calibrated such that the model generates the baseline scenario described in Section Four

(*Continued*)

Continued.

Symbol	Description	Value	Remarks/sources
$L_{h\pi d}$	Demand for personal loans by capitalists	2,500	Calibrated such that the model generates the baseline scenario described in Section Four
LF	Labour force	16.5	Selected from a reasonable range of values with respect to N^T
M_s	Money bank deposits	5,000	Calculated from Equation (116) using the initial values of M_s
M_{wd}	Money deposits demanded by workers	2,500	Calculated from Equation (79) using the initial values of V_{fmaw}
M_{wh}	Money deposits held by workers	2,500	Calculated from Equation (81) using the initial values of V_{fmaw}
$M_{\pi d}$	Money deposits demanded by capitalists	2,500	Selected from a reasonable range of values in relation to $V_{fma\pi}$ and respecting the condition of Equation (78)
$M_{\pi h}$	Money deposits held by capitalists	2,500	Calculated from Equation (80) using the initial values of $V_{fma\pi}$, $B_{\pi d}$, p_{bL} and $BL_{\pi d}$
N^C	Employment level related to production of consumption goods	9.23	Calculated from Equation (34) using the initial values of A and C^P
N^I	Employment level related to production of private investments	3.08	Calculated from Equation (35) using the initial values of A and I^P
N^G	Employment level related to production of public investments	3.08	Calculated from Equation (36) using the initial values of A and G^P
N^T	Total employment level	15.38	Calculated from Equation (37) using the initial values of N^C, N^I and N^G
NL_w	Net amount of new personal loans taken by workers	0	Calculated from Equation (72) using the initial values of GL_w and REP_w
NL_π	Net amount of new personal loans taken by capitalists	0	Calculated from Equation (71) using the initial values of GL_π and REP_π
OF_b	Own Funds (retained profits) of commercial banks	3,450	Calibrated such that the model generates the baseline scenario described in Section Four
p_{bL}	Price of long-term bonds	20	Calculated from Equation (115) using the initial values of r_{bL}
$PSBR$	Government deficit	0	Calculated from Equation (102) using the initial values of G^D, r_b, $B_{\pi s}$, B_{bs}, $BL_{\pi s}$ and T_T
Q	Stock of inventories	769.23	Calculated from Equation (10) using the initial values of C^P, C^D and Q
r_{bL}	Rate of interest on long-term bonds	0.05	Calculated from Equation (114) using the initial values of r_b and add_{BL}
r_l	Rate of interest on loan	0.10	Calculated from Equation (127) using the initial values of r_m and add_1
r_m	Deposit interest rate	0.02	Selected from a reasonable range of values
REP_w	Personal loan repayments by workers	105	Calculated from Equation (74) using the initial values of ξ_w and L_{hwd}
REP_π	Personal loan repayments by capitalists	105	Calculated from Equation (73) using the initial values of ξ_π and $L_{h\pi d}$
s^*	Desired proportion of inventories	0	Calculated from Equation (9) using the initial values of α, $E_{-1}(C^D)$ and Q
T_T	Total income taxes	400	Calculated from Equation (86) using the initial values of T_w and T_π
T_w	Income taxes raised by workers	100	Calculated from Equation (55) using the initial values of τ_w and YP_w
T_π	Income taxes raised by capitalists	300	Calculated from Equation (56) using the initial values of τ_π and YP_π
TEF^C	Total ecological footprint generated	4,127	Calculated from Equation (66) using the initial values of EF_w and EF_π
u	Unemployment rate	0.07	Calculated from Equation (38) using the initial values of N^T and LF
UC	Actual unit cost	0.65	Calculated from Equation (44) using the initial values of A and WB
V_{fmaw}	Financial market asset (investible) wealth of workers	4,750	Calculated from Equation (83) using the initial values of V_w, L_{wd} and H_{wd}
$V_{fma\pi}$	Financial market asset (investible) wealth of capitalists	2,500	Calculated from Equation (82) using the initial values of V_π, $L_{\pi d}$, $H_{\pi d}$ and OF
V_w	Wealth of workers	1,800	Calibrated such that the model generates the baseline scenario described in Section Four

(Continued)

Continued.

Symbol	Description	Value	Remarks/sources
V_π	Wealth of capitalists	5,950	Calibrated such that the model generates the baseline scenario described in Section Four
w	Real wage obtained by worker	42.25	Calculated from Equation (32) using the initial values of N^T and WB
WB	Wage bill	650	Selected from a reasonable range of values with respect to Y^P and considering Bibi (2020) and Bibi (2021)
Y^*	Potential output	1,200	Selected from a reasonable range of values with respect to Y^P
Y^D	Aggregate demand	1,000	Calculated from Equation (1) using the initial values of C^D, I^D and G^D
Y^P	Aggregate production	1,000	Calculated from Equation (2) using the initial values of C^P, I^P and G^P
YD_w	Aggregate demand by workers	450	Calculated from Equation (53) using the initial values of YP_w, T_w, r_l and L_w
YD_π	Aggregate demand by capitalists	150	Calculated from Equation (54) using the initial values of YP_π, T_π, r_l and L_π
YP_w	Personal workers' income	700	Calculated from Equation (51) using the initial values of WB, r_m and M_w
YP_π	Personal capitalists' income	700	Calculated from Equation (52) using the initial values of FD_f, FD_b, r_m, $\cdot M_\pi$, r_b, $B_{\pi d}$ and $BL_{\pi d}$
π^e	Expected profit share	0.03	Calculated from Equation (13) using the initial values of Π^e, and Y^D
Π^e	Expected profit level	30	Calculated from Equation (14) using the initial values of a_3, a_4 and F_f
z_1	Logical functions dependent on whether the bank liquidity	1	Since the initial situation is stationary there is no activation of this parameter at the beginning
z_2	ratio is within its bottom *(bot)* and top *(top)* range	1	Since the initial situation is stationary there is no activation of this parameter at the beginning
Δr_m	Variation of deposit interest rate	0	Since the initial situation is stationary there is no activation of this parameter at the beginning
ρ	Profit margin over labour cost	0.54	Calculated from Equation (33) using the initial values of Y^D and WB

Appendix C. Values for parameters and exogenous variables (baseline scenario)

Symbol	Description	Value	Remarks/sources
a_1	Coefficient of investment reaction to expected profit rate	0.10	Selected from a reasonable range of values considering Bibi (2021)
a_2	Coefficient of investment reaction to capacity utilization	0.01	Selected from a reasonable range of values considering Bibi (2021)
a_3	Coefficient of expected profit to previous realized profit level	0.10	Selected from a reasonable range of values considering Bibi (2021)
a_4	Coefficient of expected profit to previous change in realized profits	1	Taken from Bibi (2021)
add_1	Mark-up of loan interest rate on deposit interest rate	0.08	Calibrated such that the model generates the baseline scenario described in Section Four
add_{BL}	Mark-up of long-term bonds additional on bills	0.01	Calibrated such that the model generates the baseline scenario described in Section Four
bot	Bottom BLR limit below which r_m increases	0.49	Calibrated such that the model generates the baseline scenario described in Section Four
c_{w1}	Marginal propensity of consumption by workers on personal income	0.80	Based on Banca d'Italia (2015)—I bilanci delle famiglie italiane nell'anno 2014
c_{w2}	Marginal propensity of consumption by workers on wealth	0.05	Calibrated such that the model generates the baseline scenario described in Section Four
$c_{\pi 1}$	Marginal propensity of consumption by capitalists on personal income	0.60	Based on Banca d'Italia (2015)—I bilanci delle famiglie italiane nell'anno 2014

(*Continued*)

Continued.

Symbol	Description	Value	Remarks/sources
$c_{\pi 2}$	Marginal propensity of consumption by capitalists on wealth	0.01	Calibrated such that the model generates the baseline scenario described in Section Four
G^D	Demand of public investments	200	Selected from a reasonable range of values with respect to Y^D and considering Bibi (2020) and Bibi (2021)
p_y	Unit price of output	1	Considered exogenous and constant in the model
r_b	Rate of interest on bills	0.04	Selected from a reasonable range of values with respect to Y^P
top	Upper BLR limit below which r_m decreases	0.52	Calibrated such that the model generates the baseline scenario described in Section Four
α	Proportion of inventories/expected sales	1.28	Calibrated such that the model generates the baseline scenario described in Section Four
β	New loans to personal income ratio	0.15	Calculated from Equation (70) using the initial values of β_0, β_r and r_l
β_0	Autonomous coefficient of β	0.025	Calibrated such that the model generates the baseline scenario described in Section Four
β_r	Coefficient of β reaction to interest rate	1	Calibrated such that the model generates the baseline scenario described in Section Four
$\gamma_{c\pi 1}$	Adjustment workers *mpcW* parameter	0.80	Calibrated such that the model generates the baseline scenario described in Section Four
γ_{cw2}	Adjustment capitalists *mpcW* parameter	1.50	Calibrated such that the model generates the baseline scenario described in Section Four
γ_g	Coefficient of G adjustment to change in variation of GDP	0	There is no activation of this parameter in the baseline scenario with a passive government role
$\gamma_{g(-)}$	Variation of (−) government intervention	0	There is no activation of this parameter in the baseline scenario with a passive government role
$\gamma_{g(+)}$	Variation of (+) government intervention	0.75	There is no activation of this parameter in the baseline scenario with a passive government role
γ_k	Coefficient of *A* reaction to change in (*K*/*N*)	0.30	Based on Bibi (2021)
γ_L	Sensitivity of *LF* reaction to a variation in Y^D	0	Calculated from Equation (40–41) using the initial values of Y^D
γ_{L+}	Sensitivity of (+) *LF* reaction to (+) variation in Y^D	0.25	Calibrated such that the model generates the baseline scenario described in Section Four
γ_{L-}	Sensitivity of (−) LF reaction to (−) variation in Y^D	0.50	Taken from Bibi (2021)
γ_u	Coefficient of *W* reaction to change in *u*	0	Calculated from Equation (29–31) using the initial values of *u*
γ_{u+}	Coefficient of +*W* reaction to change in *u*	0.50	Taken from Font et al. (2015)
γ_{u-}	Coefficient of *W* reaction to change in *u*	0.25	Selected from a reasonable range of values considering Bibi (2020) and Bibi (2021)
γ_ω	Coefficient of A reaction to change in *w*	0.50	Selected from a reasonable range of values considering Bibi (2020) and Bibi (2021)
γ_z	Coefficient of *W* reaction to change in *z*	0.20	Taken from Bibi (2020) and Bibi (2021)
γ_{TW}	Coefficient reaction of workers' tax rate to personal income variation	0	There is no activation of this parameter in the baseline scenario with a passive government role
$\gamma_{T\pi}$	Coefficient reaction of capitalists' tax rate to personal income variation	0	There is no activation of this parameter in the baseline scenario with a passive government role
δ_{KI}	Coefficient of erosion of private capital stock	0.2	Taken from Bibi (2021)
δ_{KG}	Coefficient of erosion of public capital stock	0.02	Calibrated such that the model generates the baseline scenario described in Section 4
ζ_m	Coefficient reaction of deposit interest rate	0.0002	Calibrated such that the model generates the baseline scenario described in Section 4
η'	Coefficient reaction in expected consumption goods demanded	0	Calculated from Equation (5) using the initial values of C^D
η'_L	Lower boundary of η'_t	0.5	Selected from a reasonable range of values considering Metzler (1941), Bibi (2020) and Bibi (2021)
η'_U	Upper boundary of η'_t	0.5	Selected from a reasonable range of values considering Metzler (1941), Bibi (2020) and Bibi (2021)

(*Continued*)

Continued.

Symbol	Description	Value	Remarks/sources
θ_I	Period of construction of private investments	5	Based on Bibi (2021)
θ_G	Period of construction of public investments	50	Calibrated such that the model generates the baseline scenario described in Section Four
λ_{cw}	Proportion of workers' expenditures paid in cash	1.77	Calibrated such that the model generates the baseline scenario described in Section Four
$\lambda_{c\pi}$	Proportion of capitalists' expenditures paid in cash	1.66	Calibrated such that the model generates the baseline scenario described in Section Four
$\lambda\pi_{10}$	Autonomous coefficient of capitalists' demand for money	0.44	Calibrated such that the model generates the baseline scenario described in Section Four
$\lambda\pi_{11}$	Coefficient of capitalists' demand for money related to r_m	0.10	Calibrated such that the model generates the baseline scenario described in Section Four
$\lambda\pi_{12}$	Coefficient of capitalists' demand for money related to r_b	−0.05	Calibrated such that the model generates the baseline scenario described in Section Four
$\lambda\pi_{13}$	Coefficient of capitalists' demand for money related to r_{bL}	−0.05	Calibrated such that the model generates the baseline scenario described in Section Four
$\lambda\pi_{14}$	Coefficient of capitalists' demand for money related to personal income	0.60	Calibrated such that the model generates the baseline scenario described in Section Four
$\lambda\pi_{20}$	Autonomous coefficient of capitalists' demand for money	0.30	Calibrated such that the model generates the baseline scenario described in Section Four
$\lambda\pi_{21}$	Coefficient of capitalists' demand for bills related to r_m	−0.05	Calibrated such that the model generates the baseline scenario described in Section Four
$\lambda\pi_{22}$	Coefficient of capitalists' demand for bills related to r_b	0.15	Calibrated such that the model generates the baseline scenario described in Section Four
$\lambda\pi_{23}$	Coefficient of capitalists' demand for bills related to r_{bL}	0.15	Calibrated such that the model generates the baseline scenario described in Section Four
$\lambda\pi_{24}$	Coefficient of capitalists' demand for bills related to personal income	−0.30	Calibrated such that the model generates the baseline scenario described in Section Four
$\lambda\pi_{30}$	Autonomous coefficient of capitalists' long-term demand for bonds	0.25	Calibrated such that the model generates the baseline scenario described in Section Four
$\lambda\pi_{31}$	Coefficient of capitalists' long-term demand for bonds related to r_m	−0.05	Calibrated such that the model generates the baseline scenario described in Section Four
$\lambda\pi_{32}$	Coefficient of capitalists' long-term demand for bonds related to r_b	−0.10	Calibrated such that the model generates the baseline scenario described in Section Four
$\lambda\pi_{33}$	Coefficient of capitalists' long-term demand for bonds related to r_{bL}	0.15	Calibrated such that the model generates the baseline scenario described in Section Four
$\lambda\pi_{34}$	Coefficient of capitalists' long-term demand for bonds related to personal income	−0.30	Calibrated such that the model generates the baseline scenario described in Section Four
ξ_w	Proportion of personal loans repaid by workers	0.07	Calibrated such that the model generates the baseline scenario described in Section Four
ξ_π	Proportion of personal loans repaid by capitalists	0.04	Calibrated such that the model generates the baseline scenario described in Section Four
ρ_b	Proportion of banks reserves to their deposit	0.29	Calibrated such that the model generates the baseline scenario described in Section Four
τ_w	Workers' tax rate on their personal income	0.14	Selected from a reasonable range of values
τ_π	Capitalists' tax rate on their personal income	0.43	Selected from a reasonable range of values
φ_{Gh}	Upper limit above which government expenditure decreases	0.0%	There is no activation of this parameter in the baseline scenario with a passive government role
φ_{Gl}	Lower limit below which government expenditure increases	0.0%	There is no activation of this parameter in the baseline scenario with a passive government role
φ_w	Weight of workers' consumption ecological footprint	5.03	Taken from Mackenzie et al. (2008)
φ_π	Weight of capitalists' consumption ecological footprint	12.42	Taken from Mackenzie et al. (2008)
$\varphi_{\tau wh}$	Upper threshold above which workers' tax rate increases	0.0%	There is no activation of this parameter in the baseline scenario with a passive government role
$\varphi_{\tau\pi h}$	Upper threshold above which capitalists' tax rate increases	0.0%	There is no activation of this parameter in the baseline scenario with a passive government role
$\varphi_{\tau wl}$		0.0%	

(Continued)

Continued.

Symbol	Description	Value	Remarks/sources
	Lower threshold below which the workers' tax rate decreases		There is no activation of this parameter in the baseline scenario with a passive government role
$\varphi_{T\pi l}$	Upper threshold below which the capitalists' tax rate decreases	0.0%	There is no activation of this parameter in the baseline scenario with a passive government role
ψ_A	Coefficient of Y^* (capacity output) growth *wrt A*	2	Calibrated such that the model generates the baseline scenario described in Section Four
ψ_D	Proportion of entrepreneurial profits distributed	0.33	Selected from a reasonable range of values
ψ_L	Coefficient of Y^* (capacity output) growth *wrt LF*	2	Calibrated such that the model generates the baseline scenario described in Section Four

Note: The file with which the simulation exercises have been developed is available on request from the author.

Foreign Price Shocks and Inflation Targeting: Effects on Income and Inflation Inequality

Lilian Rolim and Nathalie Marins

ABSTRACT

Foreign price shocks have significant effects on functional income distribution and on inflation inequality. By increasing prices in domestic currency that are linked to foreign prices, they increase the profit share in some sectors and reduce real wages, in particular of workers whose consumption basket is more sensitive to the price of certain goods (e.g., food prices for low-wage workers). We propose a new extension to the conflicting-claims inflation model by incorporating workers heterogeneity (in terms of nominal income and consumption patterns) in an open economy model following an inflation-targeting regime. Then, we investigate the impacts of foreign price shocks on income and inflation inequality by increasing the foreign inflation rate and analyze how monetary policy influences these outcomes. Our simulation results indicate that a positive foreign price shock increases the profit share and the within-workers inequality (in real terms), since low-wage workers are more affected by these shocks. Yet, such effects are mediated by the strength of the monetary policy's transmission channels (domestic economic activity or nominal exchange rate), indicating that the monetary authority response may exacerbate or attenuate these distributive effects.

1. Introduction

The inflationary impact of foreign price shocks has long been a concern in emerging market and developing economies (EMDE), where the consumption basket and price indexes are more sensitive to the exchange rate and imported inflation (Ha et al. 2019), which can generate inflation inequality (i.e., a difference in inflation rates between income groups). This was the case of the Brazilian economy during the pandemic, for instance, when the inflation rate experienced by the bottom of the income distribution was almost double of the inflation rate experienced by the richest households (IPEA 2023). However, after the COVID-19 crisis and the Russia-Ukraine war, increases in food and energy prices have raised global concerns about inflation. In particular, inflation inequality became a key matter since lower-income households' consumption baskets present a higher portion of these goods (Hobijn and Lagakos 2005; Ari et al. 2022). Moreover, these price shocks are associated with an increase in the revenue of firms in specific sectors, leading to increases in their profit margins and to a redistribution of income (Weber 2022).

These concerns have sparked a heated debate about the appropriate monetary policy response, especially as many countries adopt the inflation targeting (IT) regime. While some emphasize that the increase in inflation rates for low-income groups is detrimental to their living standard (Beaudry 2023; Powell 2022), which would justify a strong response by the monetary policy authorities, others argue that increasing interest rates can have negative consequences in terms of unemployment and income distribution (Weber and Wasner 2023).

The effects of monetary policy on income distribution have been extensively studied by the post-Keynesian literature (Rochon and Setterfield 2007). In this perspective, the interest rate is considered an intrinsically distributional variable that can, directly and indirectly, distribute income between different groups and inflation is a result of the class conflict over the income distribution, following the models put forward by Dutt (1987) and Rowthorn (1977). Although most of the literature has focused on a closed economy perspective, contributions in the post-Keynesian literature recognize, both theoretically and empirically, that the exchange rate also has distributive effects (Blecker 1989; Ribeiro, McCombie, and Lima 2017, 2020). Moreover, since interest rate changes can exert a relevant impact on the exchange rate (Andrade and Prates 2013; Kaltenbrunner 2015), incorporating the exchange rate dynamics to the conflicting-claims inflation model suggests that monetary policy has multiple (and conflicting) partial effects on the functional income distribution (Rolim and Marins 2022).

In this context, our aim in this paper is to explore the distributive impacts of the monetary policy response to a foreign price shock in a conflicting-claims inflation model capturing a small open economy by considering two distributive dimensions:[1] functional income inequality and inflation inequality.[2] To do so, we incorporate the possibility of two conflicting partial effects of monetary policy and assume that households belonging to different income groups consume different goods and services, creating the potential for inflation inequality if changes in these prices differ substantially. This comprehensive approach suggests that monetary policy can either exacerbate or attenuate the distributive consequences of a foreign price shock depending on its transmission mechanisms. Therefore, our analysis provides a theoretical framework to understand the distributive effects of the IT regime in the current context wherein many countries are experiencing high inflation rates associated with foreign shocks.

In addition to this introduction, the article is organized as follows. In Section Two, we briefly discuss the transmission mechanisms of monetary policy on inflation and income distribution and how it can also affect inflation inequality. In Section Three, we develop a conflicting-claims inflation model with two classes of workers. In Section Four, we simulate the model with different values for the parameters that capture the strength of the transmission mechanisms of monetary policy and discuss the simulation results. Section Five concludes the article.

[1]Our work is closely related to other studies investigating the distributive effect of foreign shocks through the conflicting-claims framework, such as Morlin (2023), Rolim, Lima, and Baltar (2022), and Wildauer et al. (2023).

[2]Inflation inequality captures the discrepancies of inflation rates associated with class-specific consumption baskets.

2. Foreign Shocks and Monetary Policy: Interactions and Implications for Income Distribution and Inequality

In post-Keynesian conflicting-claims inflation models, changes in prices are explained by the class conflict between workers and capitalists over the distribution of income. A key contribution of this literature is to show that inflation dynamics are often associated with movements in income distribution. Since prices are mostly based on costs, this conflict materializes as adjustments in nominal wages and profit margins as each class tries to achieve its desired income. Moreover, in an open economy, imported materials must also be taken into account. Consequently, inflation in this context is explained mainly by rising mark-ups, growth in nominal wages above labor productivity, and changes in the relative prices of imported materials used as means of production (Hein and Vogel 2008; Hein and Mundt 2012; Lavoie 2022).

Since changes in foreign prices depend on external forces and not on domestic demand or other internal variables, monetary policy has '*no or little control over one of the main sources of price inflation in a country*' (Lavoie 2022, p. 596). However, since monetary policy can influence variables that affect workers' and firms' claims, it can affect both the inflation rate and the income distribution. That is, since changes in the interest rate can also affect the nominal exchange rate, it can alter the impact of foreign prices on the domestic inflation rate.

In this section we explore the main channels through which changes in the policy rate can affect the distribution of income and also exert some impact on inflation inequality after responding to a foreign shock. Although there are many transmission mechanisms through which changes in the policy rate operate, as discussed in Rolim and Marins (2022), here we focus on two main channels that act simultaneously on inflation and the wage share:[3] the economic activity channel and the exchange rate channel.

Through the economic activity channel, changes in the policy rate operate through changes in domestic costs. For example, suppose that a reduction in the interest rate leads to an increase in economic activity. This can reduce the unemployment rate and have a positive effect on the bargaining power of workers to negotiate better wages. Firms, in turn, adjust downward their profit margins in this context to preserve their competitiveness (Kalecki 1971), leading to a higher wage share, but they also try to protect their cost margins by passing on to prices (part of) the cost increases, which leads to higher inflation rates (Rowthorn 1977). This effect is illustrated in Figure 1(a), where, for simplicity, we assume no feedback from the wage share to economic activity.[4] However, an increase in economic activity can also affect the bargaining power of firms and their capacity to pass the increase of costs to prices as they approach full capacity utilization (Rowthorn 1977). This could lead to uncertain effects on income distribution.

[3]For instance, through the 'direct channel' monetary policy redistributes income from debtors to creditors. Yet, this channel does not have a clear effect on inflation. On the other hand, through the cost-channel changes in the policy rate that translate into high debt burdens can be incorporated into higher prices. This affects real wages negatively (Pivetti 1991; Lima and Setterfield 2010) and can exert temporary pressures on the inflation rate or a permanent effect depending on how these relations are modeled (for instance, in Hein and Stockhammer 2010).

[4]It is worth emphasizing that this channel depends on the interest rate affecting the economic activity, for instance, through investment or durable goods consumption based on credit. The evidence on the strength of this channel is debatable, but our analysis does not depend necessarily on the economic activity channel being the main channel.

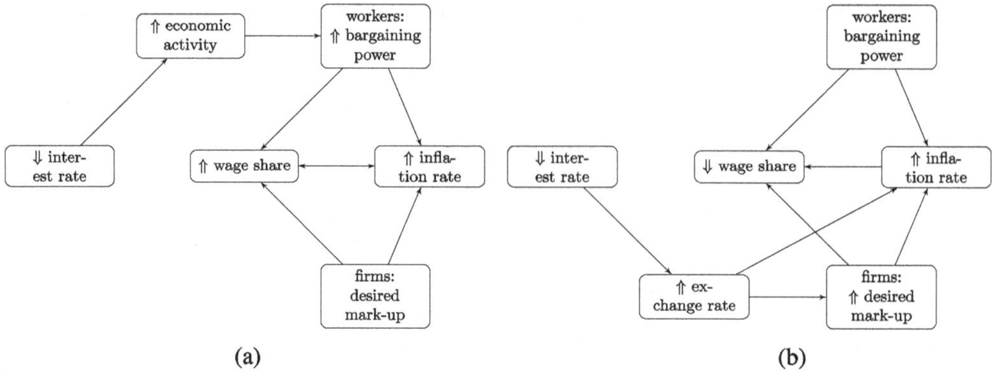

Figure 1. Transmission mechanisms of monetary policy. (a) Economic activity channel and (b) Exchange rate channel.

Note: In each subfigure, all variables that are not preceded by an arrow are assumed to remain constant.

We assume that firms are most likely to respond to higher capacity utilization by increasing output rather than raising prices (by increasing their profit margins). In this case, the effect of demand on nominal wage adjustments through higher workers' bargaining power outweighs the price increases, and a higher wage share is obtained.[5]

On the other hand, a lower interest rate may, *ceteris paribus*, have the opposite effect on the wage share while also increasing the inflation rate through the exchange rate channel. This channel operates through two mechanisms illustrated in Figure 1(b). The first is the impact on changes in the nominal domestic currency following risk-adjusted interest rate differential shocks.[6] That is, a reduction in the policy rate can lead to an exchange rate depreciation and have a positive effect on the price level since it makes imported (intermediate and final) goods and private external debt (denominated in foreign currency) more expensive. This increase in the price level, in turn, can have a persistent impact on the inflation rate (Bastian and Setterfield 2020). If this effect is not counteracted by nominal wage adjustments of the same magnitude, the real wage decreases. The second effect of a domestic currency depreciation is to increase domestic firms' mark-up rates as their international price competitiveness increases (Blecker 1989, 2011; Ribeiro, McCombie, and Lima 2020) and increase the exports sector's revenues - if we consider that prices (in foreign currency) in the tradables

[5]As a result, the wage share would be pro-cyclical. In reality, this positive stimulus to the wage share would interact with a tendency towards a counter-cyclical wage share due to overhead labor (Lavoie 2022), as obtained in many empirical data. Yet, as long as prices are based on normal unit labor costs and workers' bargaining power leads to reductions in the mark-up level, a higher real wage could be obtained even in this case. Since here we abstract from overhead labor, we are capturing only the positive effect of higher workers' bargaining power on the wage share.

[6]The strength of this channel depends on the sensitivity of the exchange rate to the domestic interest rate, which can vary depending on international conditions such as changes in the global risk aversion sentiment. Assuming that exchange rate movements are mostly driven by speculative financial flows, they will be mostly explained by changes in the expected return of international investors of assets denominated in the domestic currency. Besides interest rate differential, this includes expectations about the exchange rate, a country-risk variable and a risk aversion sentiment (Andrade and Prates 2013; Kaltenbrunner 2015; Conti, Prates, and Plihon 2014; Ramos 2016). Thus, a reduction of the domestic interest rate that leads to a negative interest rate differential relative to the external rate - assuming that expectation and risk variables do not change - will reduce the return on assets denominated in the domestic currency, attract fewer capital flows and depreciate the exchange rate. An increase in the interest rate, in turn - *ceteris paribus* - will have the opposite effect.

sector are determined by the international level (Rossi and Galbraith 2016). This is particularly evident for commodity goods. In the conflicting-claims inflation model, this effect can be considered by assuming that firms' target and realized mark-up rates (or income share) increase with increases in the real exchange rate, thus leading to a reduction in the wage share.

Therefore, the final outcome of changes in the policy rate on income distribution depends on the relative strength of the economic activity and the exchange rate channels, while there is always a negative relation between the inflation rate and interest rate if we consider solely these two transmission mechanisms. As discussed in Rolim and Marins (2022), in an inflation targeting regime the distributive outcome will also be mediated by two other layers related to institutional characteristics of the regime and the source of inflation that triggers a monetary policy reaction.

In the present study, we focus on the specific effects of a monetary policy response to a shock on foreign prices. Theoretically, in conflict-claims inflation models, foreign shocks can affect inflation and income distribution when the economy imports commodities and/or intermediate goods from abroad, that is, when external prices exert some influence on domestic prices. Changes in these exogenously determined prices can directly affect production costs and real wages (Hein and Vogel 2008; Hein and Mundt 2012; Lavoie 2022). Indirectly, through its effect on relative prices between domestic and external products that result in changes of the real exchange rate, foreign shocks can affect firms' desired mark-up (Blecker 1989, 2011). Thus, while an increase in the real exchange rate can increase domestic firms' profits and competitiveness, increasing their desired and realized mark-up rates, it can also trigger a response of workers as they try to protect their real wages. This relation is captured in an extended way in some models that assume that the real exchange rate also increases the workers' target real wage (Bastian and Setterfield 2020).

In an inflation targeting regime, when such shock occurs and spreads to the domestic inflation index, it triggers an interest rate increase as a central bank response. As discussed previously, after a foreign price shock, monetary policy can act through the economic activity and the exchange rate channel to fight this inflation pressure, while the final effect on the distribution of income is uncertain.

However, besides its impact on income distribution, the foreign shock and the subsequent monetary policy response can also influence inflation inequality, given that workers with different incomes have different consumption baskets. For example, Hobijn and Lagakos (2005) document that the inflation experienced by different household groups in the United States varies widely, with lower-income households being more affected by fluctuations in gasoline prices. In Europe, the rise in energy prices following the Ukraine war has - with few exceptions - led to regressive effects, as poorer households spend a relatively higher share of their consumption budget on electricity and natural gas (Ari et al. 2022). Moreover, in emerging markets, food prices account for a higher relative share in household consumption baskets than in industrialized countries, making EME price indexes more sensitive to the exchange rate and foreign prices (Farhi 2007), which is also reflected in inflation differentials between households within these countries, as documented for Brazil (Gouvêa 2022).

Thus, a shock on foreign prices will have a greater effect on countries with a higher import content and commodity prices in their consumption basket, but will also be more detrimental to low-wage workers who consume a higher share of their income on food and energy prices. These examples of inflation inequality provide important new insights into the relationship between monetary policy and income distribution. While there are different types of inflation, which will have different implications for the different income groups, monetary policy targets an average or representative index for the economy. In this context, monetary policy can attenuate some inequalities generated by foreign shocks, but depending on its transmission mechanisms, it may also create new ones. Thus, the claim that inflation hurts more the poor - and therefore, following many IT regime proponents, fighting inflationary pressures contributes to protecting the poor - can be critically discussed by evaluating its effects in specific contexts. We illustrate how this happens and discuss the policy implications through the simple simulation model built in the next section.

3. The Model

We build a conflicting-claims inflation model for a small open economy, wherein there is no productivity growth and workers are divided into two groups with heterogeneous nominal income levels and consumption baskets. In line with the conflicting-claims inflation model, nominal wage growth and price inflation are endogenously determined, and their interaction determines the functional income distribution. The latter is analyzed through the wage share, which is the ratio of nominal wages to the domestic price level ($\omega_t = w_t/p_{d,t}$). Conversely, the foreign interest rate and foreign price inflation are taken as exogenous. There is no government, except for a monetary authority that sets the nominal interest rate and does not intervene in the foreign exchange market. For simplicity, we do not consider any influence of the wage share or of the real exchange rate on economic activity.[7]

3.1. Workers' Heterogeneity

Workers are divided into two groups: low- and high-wage workers, which are represented by the subscripts L and H respectively. We assume that the ratio between their nominal wages is constant and equal to $\delta = w_{H,t}/w_{L,t} > 1$.[8] The share of high-wage workers in total employment is fixed and given by $n_H < 0.5$. Consequently, the share of low-wage workers is total employment is given by $n_L = 1 - n_H$.

In addition to heterogeneous nominal wages, workers also differ with respect to their consumption basket. Indeed, low-wage workers consume more commodity goods, whose price is determined by the foreign price level. Thus, the average price of the consumption basket for each group $w = L, H$ is given by:

$$p_{w,t} = \alpha_w p_{d,t} + (1 - \alpha_w) p_{f,t} e_t \tag{1}$$

[7]This is a relevant simplification relative to post-Keynesian models discussing the relationship between income distribution and economic growth (Dutt 1984; Blecker 1989; Bhaduri and Marglin 1990). Considering these dimensions would add multiple feedback effects that could have implications for the dynamics of the inflation rate and income distribution. While these effects could either strengthen or attenuate our results, our simplifying assumptions are enough to obtain the possibility of conflicting effects of monetary policy depending on the transmission mechanisms.

[8]By keeping δ fixed we can analyze the changes in the real income of each group of workers that arise exclusively from inflation inequality.

where $1 > \alpha_w > 0$ is the share of non-commodity goods in the consumption goods basket for group $w = H, L$, $p_{d,t}$ is the price in domestic currency of non-commodity goods, $p_{f,t}$ is the price in foreign currency of commodity goods, and e_t is the nominal exchange rate. We assume that $\alpha_H > \alpha_L$, since high-wage workers consume a larger share of non-commodity goods than low-wage workers.

Accordingly, the price level of the average consumption basket for workers is given by Equation 2. This is a democratic price index because the weight of each worker is equal to one.[9]

$$p_t = (n_H\alpha_H + n_L\alpha_L)p_{d,t} + (1 - (n_H\alpha_H + n_L\alpha_L))p_{f,t}e_t \tag{2}$$

3.2. Price and Wage Adjustments

The price of commodity goods follows the price set in the foreign market.[10] It is assumed that this price level grows at a rate given by $\hat{p}_{f,t} > 0$. Therefore, the foreign price level in foreign currency is given by:

$$p_{f,t} = p_{f,t-1}(1 + \hat{p}_{f,t}) \tag{3}$$

The foreign price inflation is subject to an exogenous shock at T_i, which lasts until T_f, as follows:

$$\hat{p}_{f,t} = \begin{cases} \hat{p}_f^* & \text{if } t < T_i \text{ and } t > T_f, \\ \hat{p}_f^* + \mu & \text{otherwise.} \end{cases} \tag{4}$$

where $\hat{p}_f^*$ is the foreign inflation rate in the absence of shocks and μ is the shock to the foreign inflation rate.

The domestic price component dynamics (Equation 5) depends on the domestic inflation rate (Equation 6), which is assumed to reflect the class conflict between workers and capitalists. In line with the post-Keynesian conflicting-claims inflation model, firms increase the price level in an effort to achieve their desired wage share and the adjustment speed depends on the difference between their desired wage share ($\omega_{f,t}$) and the actual wage share (ω_{t-1}):

$$p_{d,t} = p_{d,t-1}(1 + \hat{p}_{d,t}) \tag{5}$$

$$\hat{p}_{d,t} = \varphi(\omega_{t-1} - \omega_{f,t}) \tag{6}$$

where $\varphi > 0$ is a fixed parameter capturing the sensitivity of price adjustments to the difference between the desired and realized wage share.

[9]In other words, this is similar to how the consumer price index is calculated, but we weight the index by the number of workers in each group. In comparison, a plutocratic index is constructed as a weighted average of all household-specific inflation rates in which the weight given to each household is proportional to its total expenditure (Hobijn and Lagakos 2005).

[10]For simplicity, it is assumed that all commodity goods are imported goods and that all non-commodity goods are produced domestically. This means that we do not capture the automatic effect of nominal exchange rate depreciations or foreign prices on firms' revenue (Rossi and Galbraith 2016). Yet, there is a connection between the real exchange rate and firms' profits through their mark-up adjustments (see Equations 6 and 7).

Following Blecker (2011), the desired wage share by firms is assumed to be a decreasing function of the real exchange rate:

$$\omega_{f,t} = \omega_{\max} - \psi rer_{t-1} \tag{7}$$

where $1 > \omega_{\max} > 0$ is the maximum wage share desired by firms,[11] rer_{t-1} is the real exchange rate, and $\psi > 0$ is a parameter capturing the sensitivity of firms' desired wage share to the real exchange rate.[12] This equation creates a link between the real exchange rate and mark-up rates for which empirical support is provided in Berman, Martin, and Mayer (2012).

The nominal wage for each group of workers $w = H, L$ grows at the same rate $\hat{w}_t$, as shown in Equation 8.[13] Similarly to firms, workers demand nominal wage adjustments in order to try to achieve their desired wage share. Therefore, the nominal wage growth rate depends on the difference between the desired wage share by workers $(\omega_{w,t})$ and the actual wage share:

$$w_{w,t} = w_{w,t-1}(1 + \hat{w}_t) \tag{8}$$

$$\hat{w}_t = \Omega(\omega_{w,t} - \omega_{t-1}) \tag{9}$$

where $\Omega > 0$ is a fixed parameter capturing the sensitivity of wage adjustments to the difference between the desired and realized wage share.

The wage share desired by workers is also assumed to be an endogenous variable, which increases with capacity utilization rate (Sasaki, Sonoda, and Fujita 2013).[14]

$$\omega_{w,t} = \omega_{\min} + \lambda u_{t-1} \tag{10}$$

where $1 > \omega_{\min} > 0$ is the minimum wage share desired by workers and $\lambda > 0$ is a parameter capturing the sensitivity of workers' desired wage share to the capacity utilization rate u_{t-1}.[15]

Following Rochon and Setterfield (2007), it is assumed that capacity utilization is a decreasing function of the real interest rate, as follows:[16]

$$u_t = u_0 - \gamma r_t \tag{11}$$

where $1 > u_0 > 0$ is the capacity utilization rate when the real interest rate is equal to zero, $\gamma \geq 0$ is the sensitivity of capacity utilization to the real interest rate, and r_t is the real interest rate.[17]

[11]The maximum wage share is just the part of the desired wage share that is not related to the real exchange rate. It has to be a positive value, otherwise any positive value of the real exchange rate would mean a negative desired wage share by firms. A positive value of $\omega_{\max}$ prevents this issue (as long as ψ and *rer* are not too large).

[12]We assume that $\omega_{f,t}$ is insensitive to changes in capacity utilization because firms tend to respond to higher demand by increasing production (rather than increasing prices).

[13]Given the main purpose of this article, which is to analyze the effect of foreign shocks on inflation inequality, we assume that, albeit belonging to different groups, all workers have the same nominal wage adjustment.

[14]The capacity utilization rate is assumed to be a proxy to the employment rate and, consequently, to workers' bargaining power. Blecker (2011) and Sasaki, Sonoda, and Fujita (2013) also assume that the real exchange rate affects the workers' desired wage share. For simplicity, this effect is omitted in our equation.

[15]For simplicity, we abstract from the possibility of changes in workers' desired wage share being sensitive to business cycle fluctuations. The same applies for their bargaining power, which is assumed to be fixed throughout the cycle.

[16]Therefore we are not explicitly modeling the investment and consumption channels mentioned in the previous section, but implicitly capturing them through the reaction of the capacity utilization rate.

[17]Since our aim is to analyze the long-run impact of the shock, potential lags are relatively less important for our main results. Thus, we adopt the simplifying assumption of a contemporary impact of the interest rate on capacity utilization.

3.3. Monetary Policy

In line with the inflation targeting regime, the monetary authority is assumed to use a single instrument (nominal interest rate) to achieve a single target (inflation rate target). The price index is the democratic price index p_t from Equation 2. The nominal interest rate is determined by Equation 12, according to which the interest rate increases (decreases) if the average inflation rate in the last T_p periods is above (below) the target.

$$i_t = i_{t-1} + \rho\left(\frac{\sum_{i=1}^{T_p} \hat{p}_{t-i}}{T_p} - \hat{p}^T\right)\Bigg) \tag{12}$$

where $\rho > 0$ is the sensitivity of the nominal interest rate to the inflation gap, $T_p \geq 1$ is the number of periods considered by the monetary policy rule, $\hat{p}_t$ is the inflation rate considered by the monetary authority (growth rate of p_t), and $1 > \hat{p}^T > 0$ is the inflation rate target.

By definition, the real interest rate is given by Equation 13:

$$r_t = \frac{(1 + i_t)}{(1 + \hat{p}_{t-1})} - 1 \tag{13}$$

3.4. Exchange Rate

Following the post-Keynesian framework of exchange rate determination, we assume that changes in the interest rate differential lead to portfolio adjustments by investors that have implications for the international capital flows and, consequently, for the nominal exchange rate (Andrade and Prates 2013; Kaltenbrunner 2015; Ramos 2016).[18] Accordingly, the nominal exchange rate depends on the change in the interest rate differential — i.e., an increase (decrease) in the domestic interest rate results in a currency appreciation (depreciation) - as reported in Equation 14:

$$e_t = e_{t-1} + \xi \sum_{i=0}^{T_e} \Delta i_{t+1-i}^{dif} \tag{14}$$

where $\xi \geq 0$ is a fixed parameter capturing the sensitivity of the exchange rate to changes in the interest differential, $T_e \geq 1$ is the number of periods for exchange rate adjustment to changes in the interest rate differential, $i_t^{dif} = i_f - i_t$ is the interest rate differential, where $1 > i_f > 0$ is the fixed nominal interest rate in the foreign sector.

By definition, the real exchange rate is given by Equation 15:

$$rer_t = \frac{e_t p_{f,t}}{p_{d,t}} \tag{15}$$

[18]It is worthwhile mentioning that EMDE's currencies have a lower currency premium and, therefore, are demanded for speculative purposes in periods of low risk aversion, when the international liquidity preference is low (Ramos 2016). However, we omit this important component in our equation since the analysis of this dimension is beyond the scope of this article.

4. Simulation Results

The model described in the previous section is coded in R and three scenarios are computationally simulated to capture different transmission mechanisms of the monetary policy after a shock on the foreign inflation rate.[19]

The monetary policy rule, which is described in Equation 12, responds to the foreign price shock when it causes a deviation of the domestic inflation rate from the target pursued by the monetary authority. As a result, the interest rate is the intervening variable after the exogenous shock and acts through two transmission mechanisms: the exchange rate and economic activity. While only the nominal exchange rate channel is considered in the ER scenario and only the economic activity channel is considered in the UT scenario, both channels operate in the Baseline scenario. Thus, changes in the interest rate affect both the exchange rate and capacity utilization in the Baseline scenario. In each of the other two scenarios, only one of these mechanisms operate.

The parameters that change across the scenarios are reported in Table 1.[20]

All scenarios are simulated for 1000 periods and are subject to a temporary increase in the foreign price inflation rate at time $T_i = 500$,[21] which leads to an increase in the foreign inflation rate given by $\mu = 0.02$ for 20 periods. At $T_f = 520$, the foreign inflation rate returns to its initial value.

4.1. Inflation Rate Dynamics

Figure 2 reports the inflation rates for the foreign and domestic sectors. As described above, the positive shock to the foreign inflation rate leads to a higher foreign inflation rate from $t = 500$ to $t = 520$. This shock triggers an inflationary process in the domestic economy, leading to an inflation rate larger than the targeted inflation rate ($\hat{p}^T = 0.02$). This is caused both by the increase in the inflation rate of imported goods and by a change in the terms of the conflict over the domestic income distribution that had been previously established.

Indeed, by causing a strong shock to the real exchange rate, the shock to the foreign inflation rate leads to a reduction in the wage share desired by firms (see Equation 7), which increases the gap between the wage share desired by firms and that desired by workers. In the literature, this gap is known as the aspiration gap, and it is directly related to the level of the domestic inflation rate, as it leads to higher nominal wage and price adjustments as each class tries to come closer to its desired income share

[19] Such shock produces a similar result to a shock on the nominal exchange rate, which would also have implications for the domestic inflation. Since we are mostly concerned with the distributive effects of monetary policy when reacting to foreign shocks, that is, under the inflation targeting regime, we do not report a no-reaction scenario (which would only capture the distributive impact of the foreign shock). In such a scenario, the results for the main distributive variables (wage share and ratio between real wages) fall between the results for the ER and UT scenarios and do not present the permanent effects captured in the Baseline and UT scenarios. These results are available upon reasonable request.

[20] All parameters and initial values for the Baseline configuration are reported in Table A1 in the Appendix section. Note that, since the parameters of the two different channels refer to different variables that are measured in different ways, we chose their values to obtain different economic structures that achieve the same stationary levels for inflation and inequality before the shock. Therefore, the different magnitudes are not comparable and should not be regarded as reflecting any previously determined assumption.

[21] The shock is only applied after the steady state has been reached and all scenarios have reached the same values for the relevant variables. This allows us to be confident that their different trajectories after T_i are due to their different responses to the foreign shock.

Table 1. Parameter values.

Parameter	Description	Baseline	ER	UT
γ	sensitivity of capacity utilization to the real interest rate	5	0	5
ξ	sensitivity of the nominal exchange rate to changes in the interest rate differential	2	2	0

Note: ER: exchange rate channel, UT: capacity utilization channel.

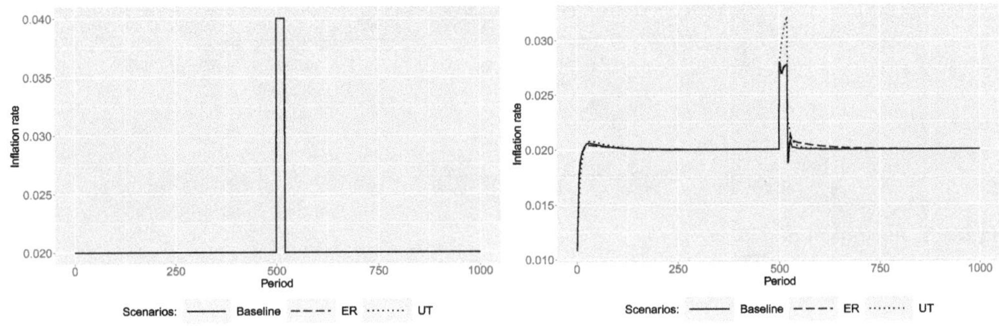

Figure 2. Inflation rates. (a) Foreign inflation rate and (b) Domestic inflation rate.

Note: ER: exchange rate channel, UT: capacity utilization channel. The Baseline scenario includes both channels.

(Lavoie 2022; Rowthorn 1977). As shown in Figure 3, at the beginning of the simulation period (before the shock), the aspiration gap slowly adjusted towards a stable value that was compatible with the targeted inflation rate. The shock to the foreign inflation rate increases the aspiration gap above this level, indicating that also the domestic prices are now growing at a higher rate and thus contributing to the increase in the inflation rate experienced by the domestic economy. After the shock, the dynamics of the aspiration gap is also explained by the response of the monetary authority, and it slowly decreases towards the level compatible with the inflation rate target.

The initial impact of the increase in the foreign inflation rate on the interest rate is to decrease its real level because of the pass-through effect on the domestic inflation rate (Figure 4). However, under the inflation targeting regime, the monetary authority responds by raising the nominal interest rate. Consequently, the real interest rate starts to grow when the increase in the nominal interest rate is large enough to compensate for the effect associated with the inflation rate. In all scenarios, the nominal and real interest rates are kept at a higher level after the shock to the foreign inflation rate finishes, characterizing a new steady state. This is because the response of the inflation targeting regime described in Equation 12 is such that the interest rate is adjusted only when there is a gap between the actual and targeted inflation rate.[22] When the foreign inflation rate returns to the Baseline value, it contributes to the decrease of the domestic inflation rate towards the targeted inflation rate, and the nominal interest rate is no longer adjusted when the target is reached. Yet, there are no factors causing a return of the nominal

[22]This specification captures policy decisions by the monetary authorities in many countries, wherein policymakers justify changes in the interest rate based on the extent to which the current inflation deviates from the target.

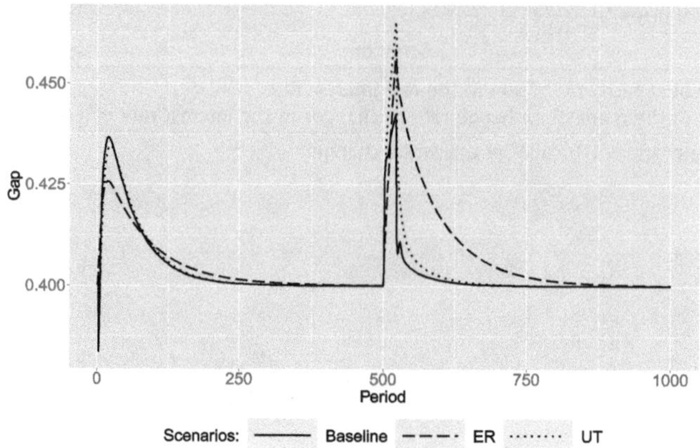

Figure 3. Aspiration gap.

Note: ER: exchange rate channel, UT: capacity utilization channel. The Baseline scenario includes both channels.

interest rate back to its initial values, which suggests a long-term effect of the temporary shock to the foreign inflation rate.

The increase in the interest rate is smaller in the Baseline scenario than in the other two, which is due to the combination of the two transmission mechanisms that contribute to lowering the domestic inflation rate. This, in turn, means that the inflation target is reached with a weaker response by the monetary authority than would be the case if only one transmission mechanism was in place. Note that after the foreign shock is over, there is a slight decrease in the real interest rate in the Baseline and ER scenarios before it stabilizes - this is associated with the adjustment after the foreign shock is over, in particular to the dynamics of the nominal exchange rate, which is important for the impact that the foreign inflation rate has on domestic inflation.

The dynamics of the model can be further discussed by analyzing the transmission mechanisms of monetary policy. As reported in Figure 5, when the exchange rate channel is active (Baseline and ER scenarios), the response of the monetary authority leads to a reduction in the nominal exchange rate. Such reduction is larger in the ER

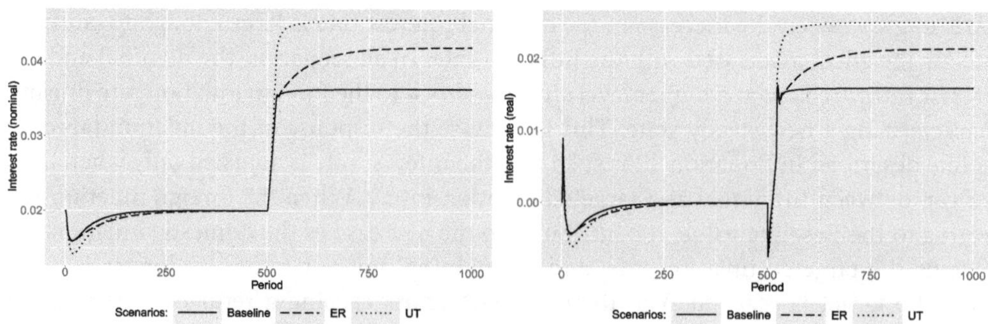

(a) (b)

Figure 4. Interest rates. (a) Nominal interest rate and (b) Real interest rate.

Note: ER: exchange rate channel, UT: capacity utilization channel. The Baseline scenario includes both channels.

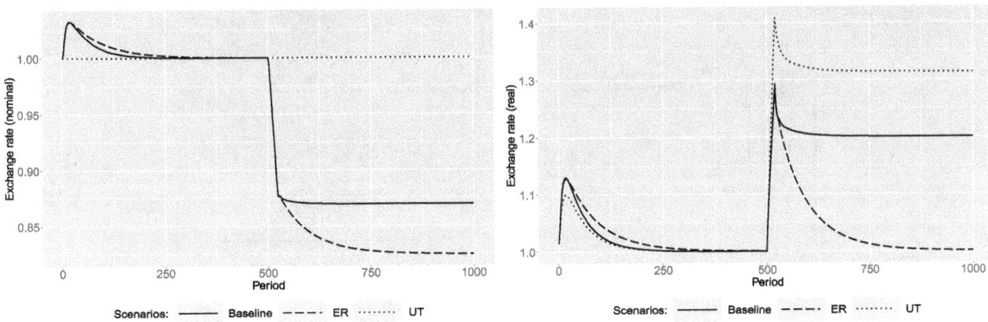

(a) (b)

Figure 5. Exchange rates. (a) Nominal exchange rate and (b) Real exchange rate.
Note: ER: exchange rate channel, UT: capacity utilization channel. The Baseline scenario includes both channels.

scenario than in the Baseline scenario due to the stronger increase in the nominal interest rate in the former, as discussed above. Thus, while all scenarios are characterized by a significant initial increase in the real exchange rate resulting from the large increase in the foreign price level with respect to the domestic price level (increase in the numerator of Equation 15 relative to its denominator), when a nominal currency appreciation takes place, the increase in the real exchange rate is much smaller than otherwise.[23]

This indicates that the nominal currency appreciation attenuates the effect of the shock on the foreign inflation rate by reducing the size of the real currency depreciation, with important implications for the dynamics of the domestic inflation rate. The nominal currency appreciation reduces the increase in the price of commodity goods when converted to the domestic currency, thus reducing the imported inflation component. While this contributes to the reduction of the domestic inflation rate, there is also an important effect of the smaller increase in the real exchange rate on the aspiration gap, since the extent to which firms reduce their desired wage share will be smaller. Consequently, the real currency appreciation also contributes to the reduction of the domestic inflation rate by reducing the aspiration gap through an adjustment that is mostly related to firms' behavior. Conversely, when the real exchange rate does not return to its initial value (Baseline and UT scenarios), it contributes to reducing the desired wage share by firms in a permanent manner, which has the potential of creating inflationary pressures - this potential does not become reality because there are compensatory factors associated with capacity utilization.

In comparison, when the economic activity channel is active (Baseline and UT scenarios), the response of the monetary authority leads to a reduction in the capacity utilization rate due to the increase in the real interest rate - this takes place after an initial increase in capacity utilization due to the fall in the real interest rate at the time of the shock, as observed in Figure 6. This reduction is larger in the UT scenario than in the Baseline scenario due to the larger increase in the real interest rate in the former. The

[23]For simplicity, we are assuming that the foreign sector's monetary policy does not change throughout the simulation. However, if this was not the case and the foreign interest rate increased as well, the domestic policy rate would have to rise further in order to increase the interest rate differential for the exchange rate channel to work. In this case, the domestic interest rate would be higher, affecting the magnitude but not the conclusion of our experiments.

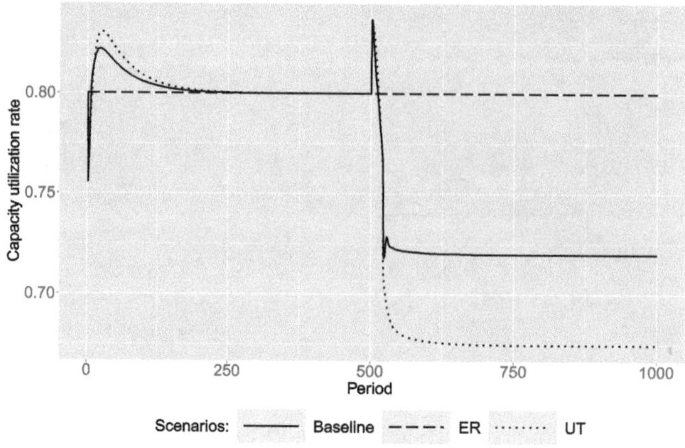

Figure 6. Capacity utilization rate.
Note: ER: exchange rate channel, UT: capacity utilization channel. The Baseline scenario includes both channels.

decrease in the capacity utilization rate is assumed to lead to an increase in the unemployment level, exerting a negative effect on workers' bargaining power. In the model, this is captured by a decrease in the wage share desired by workers (Equation 10). Consequently, this channel contributes to the reduction of the domestic inflation rate by reducing the aspiration gap through a reduction in the wage share desired by workers. As discussed further below, this mechanism concentrates the burden of the inflation control on workers.

Regardless of the transmission mechanisms, the results suggest a long-term effect on key variables such as the nominal exchange rate and the capacity utilization rate, which helps to understand the long-term effect on the interest rate that was discussed above and, in particular, why there are no factors causing a reduction of the interest rate back to its initial level.[24] The main explanation for these long-term effects is the fact that the temporary increase in the foreign inflation rate means a permanent effect on the foreign price level and, unless compensated by other mechanisms, a permanently higher real exchange rate. Since domestic prices adjustments are a positive function of the real exchange rate, a higher level of foreign prices (or nominal exchange rate) leads to inflationary pressures. This permanent (potential) inflationary pressure requires a permanently higher level of the interest rate.

This dynamics occurs differently in each of the scenarios analyzed. In the ER scenario, since the exchange rate channel is the only transmission mechanism of the monetary policy, the nominal interest rate increases until it fully compensates for the increase in the foreign price level and reaches the initial real exchange rate, which is the level compatible with the inflation rate target. When such a value is reached, no further increases in the nominal interest rate are required, and an appreciated domestic currency is maintained to compensate for the higher level of foreign prices. This adjustment is not present in the UT scenario, which is why the real exchange rate is kept at a much higher level (which has the potential of strengthening the distributive conflict). Since

[24]More precisely, one could expect that the higher level of the interest rate when the foreign shock is over would cause an inflation rate below the target, thus triggering a new adjustment of the interest rate back to its initial level.

this leads to higher inflationary pressures, the inflation target can only be achieved by keeping a lower capacity utilization rate, as economic activity is the sole transmission mechanism in this case.[25] In other words, in this case it is necessary to keep lower workers' bargaining power to induce lower nominal wage growth rates to compensate for the higher real exchange rate. Therefore, the inflationary pressures caused by the stronger strength of firms in the conflict over the domestic income distribution (expressed by a higher real exchange rate) is compensated by reducing workers' strength, meaning that inflationary control through the economic activity channel hampers workers in the long run. As the Baseline scenario is a combination of the dynamics described for both the ER and UT scenarios, these long-term effects are also observed therein, only with different magnitudes.

4.2. Income and Inflation Inequalities Dynamics

The previous section emphasized the different natures of the inflation control through monetary policy depending on its transmission mechanisms. We now analyze the implications of these dimensions to inequality captured by two different variables: the wage share and the difference in inflation rates for high- and low- wage workers. While the former captures the functional income inequality, the latter captures the dynamics of the inflation inequality. Combined, they offer a more comprehensive understanding of the effects of foreign inflationary shocks and the response of the monetary authority.

Figure 7 shows the dynamics of the wage share. In all scenarios, the increase in the foreign inflation rate is accompanied by a decrease in the wage share in the domestic economy in the short run. As previously discussed, this occurs because this shock leads to a strong increase in the real exchange rate, which tends to benefit firms and cause a change in the functional income distribution towards profits. More precisely, this is associated with a decrease in $\omega_{f,t}$ in Equation 7 that, *ceteris paribus*, leads to a lower wage share.

Nevertheless, the nature of the inflationary control is of primary importance to the long-run dynamics of the wage share. In the ER scenario, the inflation rate is controlled through a nominal currency appreciation, which brings the real exchange rate back to its initial level (Figure 5). Therefore, while the initial shock benefited firms (causing a decrease in $\omega_{f,t}$), the nominal currency appreciation controls the inflation rate through a reduction in the aspiration gap that is generated by increasing $\omega_{f,t}$ back to its initial level (and, thus, closer to the wage share desired by workers). Consequently, the wage share also returns back to its initial level.

The opposite process occurs in the UT scenario, in which the wage share stabilizes at a lower level. As discussed above, in this scenario the inflation rate is controlled by keeping the capacity utilization rate at a lower level (even in the long run). This means that the aspiration gap is reduced through a decrease in the wage share desired by workers ($\omega_{w,t}$ in Equation 10), bringing it closer to the wage share desired by firms, which had been

[25]This explains why a lower capacity utilization is not associated with a decrease in the inflation rate after the foreign inflationary shock is over. Consequently, there is no reason for a reduction of the nominal interest rate through the inflation targeting regime. This means that our results suggest that such shock is not neutral in the long run if it is the only shock upon the economy. In reality, we usually have multiple shocks that lead to a more complex dynamics of monetary policy.

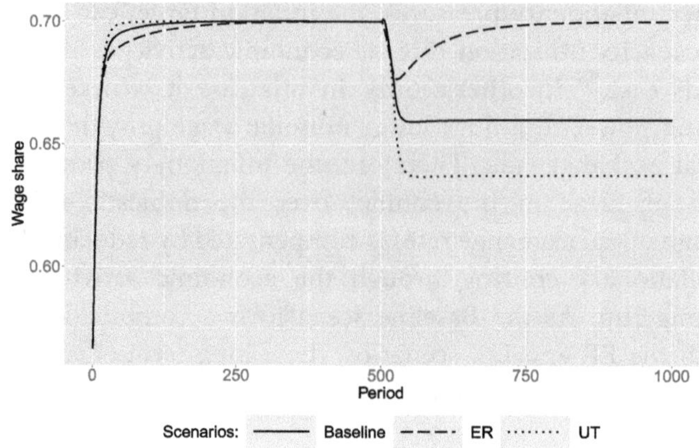

Figure 7. Wage share.
Note: ER: exchange rate channel, UT: capacity utilization channel. The Baseline scenario includes both channels.

(permanently) decreased by the shock in the foreign inflation rate. Therefore, the increase in interest rates when the economic activity is the sole transmission mechanism of the monetary authority leads to a further decrease in the wage share.

Since the Baseline scenario is an average of both effects, the decline in the wage share is not as large as in the UT scenario, but it is also characterized by a lower wage share in the long run, as capacity utilization is permanently kept at a lower level. This suggests that whenever controlling the inflation rate requires a reduction in capacity utilization (and higher unemployment rates), lasting effects on the functional income distribution may arise. These lasting effects are associated with the need of keeping a lower capacity utilization rate to compensate for the permanently higher real exchange rate, as already mentioned.

The combination of a lower wage share and higher prices of commodity goods, as well as higher prices of non-commodity goods, leads to a reduction in the real wage of both groups of workers (Figure 8). These real wages are calculated by considering the group-specific consumption baskets and, thus, a larger share of commodity goods for low-wage

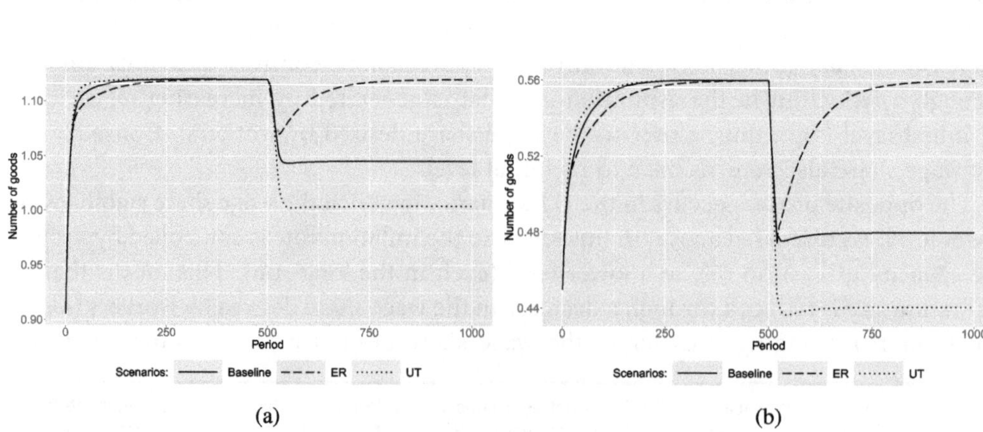

Figure 8. Real wages. (a) High-wage workers and (b) Low-wage workers.
Note: ER: exchange rate channel, UT: capacity utilization channel. The Baseline scenario includes both channels.

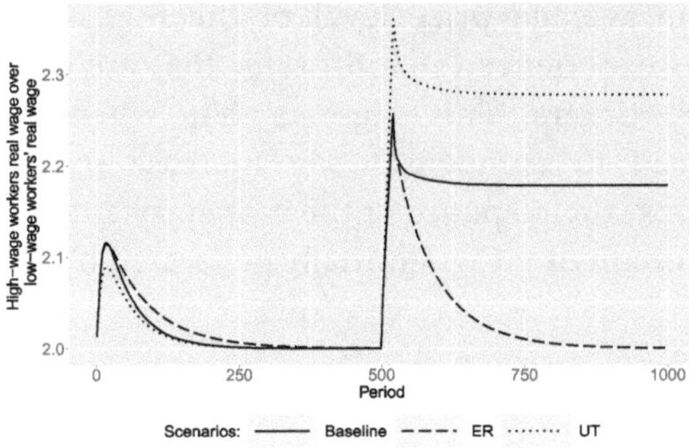

(a)

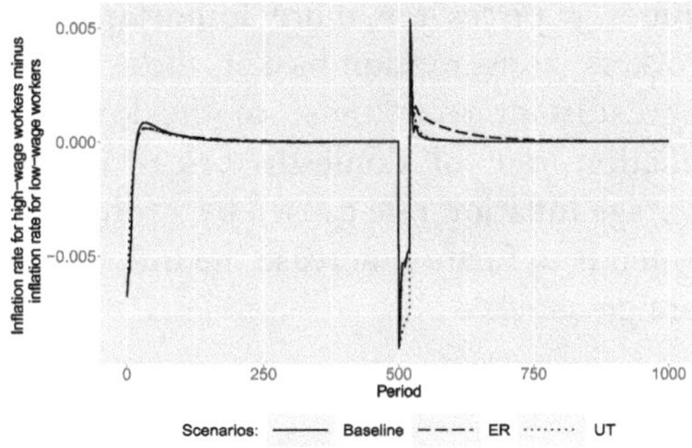

(b)

Figure 9. Inflation inequality indicators. (a) Real wage ratios and (b) Difference in group-specific inflation rates.

Note: ER: exchange rate channel, UT: capacity utilization channel. The Baseline scenario includes both channels.

workers. Consequently, the loss in purchasing power is much larger to the low-wage workers than the high-wage workers, as expressed by the larger decrease in the real wage of the former in comparison to the latter.

This indicates that these workers are experiencing different inflation rates.[26] Indeed, Figure 9 shows that the shock to the foreign inflation rate causes an increase of the real wage of high-wage worker relative to that of the low-wage workers and a lower inflation rate experienced by the high-wage workers relative to that experienced by the low-wage workers. Moreover, the ratio between the real wages increases more in the UT scenario than in the ER scenario, with the Baseline representing an intermediate case. This reflects the fact that in the UT scenario the gap between the group-specific inflation rates increases more than in the other scenarios.

The dynamics of inflation inequality described in Figure 9 is strongly linked with how inflation is controlled in each scenario or, in other words, the specific transmission mechanisms. In the ER scenario, the inflation rate is controlled by an exchange rate appreciation. While the exchange rate is appreciating ($\Delta e_t < 0$), the price in domestic currency of the commodity goods grows less than the price denominated in foreign currency. This attenuates the higher levels of the foreign inflation rate during the period of the shock. When the shock is over, the domestic currency continues to appreciate for a while (until the real exchange rate reaches its initial value). This continues to reduce the growth rate of the price of commodity goods in domestic currency, which leads to a lower growth rate of commodity goods prices relative to non-commodity goods prices. As a consequence, for some periods after the shock is over the high-wage workers are experiencing a higher inflation rate than the low-wage workers. Overall, in the ER scenario, since there is a lower growth rate of commodity goods prices in domestic currency relative to the other scenarios, the increase in inflation inequality caused by the foreign shock is attenuated.

In contrast, in the UT scenario the inflation rate is controlled through a reduction in the growth rate of nominal wages and, consequently, of domestic prices. Since the

[26]Recall that the ratio between their nominal wages is kept constant throughout the simulation periods.

domestic prices are more important to the average price level of the high-wage workers' consumption basket, these workers experience inflation rates that are even more distant from those of the low-wage workers. This suggests that, when the inflation rate of domestic prices is reduced to compensate an increase in the average inflation rate caused by a foreign shock, the response of the monetary authority tends to further increase the inflation inequality that was initially generated by the foreign shock.

5. Conclusion

The nature of foreign price shocks means that they are an external factor influencing the class conflict between domestic agents. Their direct effect on the prices of certain goods tends to lead to: i) a real depreciation of the domestic currency; ii) an increase in the inflation rate; iii) an increase in profits in some sectors (increasing the aggregate profit share), and; iv) an increase in inflation inequality, reducing the real wage of workers who are more exposed to these shocks (most likely low-wage workers). Moreover, as workers seek to protect themselves and firms try to benefit from the higher real exchange rate, there is a secondary inflationary pressure arising from the domestic economy dynamics. When monetary policy responds to these inflationary pressures, it can either worsen or attenuate these distributive effects depending on the strength of its transmission mechanisms.

This offers a very specific example of the interaction between the many layers that impact the distributive effects of monetary policy, as discussed by Rolim and Marins (2022). In the case of foreign price shocks, the reaction of the IT regime can amplify the distributive consequences by not acting directly on the source of the shock (and thus requiring lower bargaining power of workers to fight it), but it may also attenuate these consequences when it is possible to affect the real exchange rate. Therefore, there is no policy prescription that fits all countries when it comes to fighting inflationary pressures created by foreign price shocks. Moreover, it seems inappropriate to claim that fighting inflation is always a tool to protect the poor, in particular if lower economic activity is required, since workers will face higher unemployment and an even lower wage share, while low-wage workers will be in a worse position relative to high-wage workers.

While we consider these as very robust conclusions that should be taken into consideration when discussing the distributive effects of monetary policy, we highlight two main caveats. First, our model does not capture interest payments to creditors or the effect of interest rates on asset prices, so it represents better the changes in distribution among workers and firms. Secondly, we do not consider the possible effects of the wage share and real exchange rate, which would be related to the type of demand regime (wage- or profit-led), and the effects of real wage inequality on demand. Finally, we recognize that the international context is also relevant. For instance, the sensitivity of the exchange rate to the domestic interest rate can change according to external conditions. Moreover, the exchange rate channel is less effective when all countries are facing an inflationary shock and responding with higher interest rates. Considering these aspects is part of our future research agenda.

Acknowledgments

We thank Eckhard Hein, Ryan Woodgate, Marc Lavoie, and the participants of the Monetary Policy and Income Distribution Workshop held in Toronto (Canada) in 2022 and of the Demand-led Growth Workshop in Rio de Janeiro (Brazil) in 2023 for helpful comments and suggestions.

Disclosure statement

No potential conflict of interest was reported by the author(s).

Funding

LR greatfully acknowledges funding from the Sao Paulo Research Foundation (FAPESP, process number 2018/21762-0). This study was also financed in part by the Coordenação de Aperfeiçoamento de Pessoal de Nível Superior — Brasil (CAPES) — Finance Code 001.

ORCID

Lilian Rolim http://orcid.org/0000-0002-9880-2823
Nathalie Marins http://orcid.org/0000-0002-1374-2666

References

Andrade, R. P., and D. M. Prates. 2013. 'Exchange Rate Dynamics in a Peripheral Monetary Economy.' *Journal of Post Keynesian Economics* 35 (3): 399–416.

Ari, M. A., M. N. Arregui, M. S. Black, O. Celasun, M. D. M. Iakova, M. A. Mineshima, V. Mylonas, et al. 2022. 'Surging Energy Prices in Europe in the Aftermath of the War: How to Support the Vulnerable and Speed Up the Transition Away from Fossil Fuels.' International Monetary Fund Working Paper (2022/152).

Bastian, E. F., and M. Setterfield. 2020. 'Nominal Exchange Rate Shocks and Inflation in An Open Economy: Towards a Structuralist Inflation Targeting Agenda.' *Cambridge Journal of Economics* 44 (6): 1271–1299.

Beaudry, P.. 2023. 'No Two Ways About It: Why the Bank is Committed to Getting Back to 2%.' Bank of Canada - Remarks by Deputy Governor.

Berman, N., P. Martin, and T. Mayer. 2012. 'How Do Different Exporters React to Exchange Rate Changes?.' *The Quarterly Journal of Economics* 127 (1): 437–492.

Bhaduri, A., and S. Marglin. 1990. 'Unemployment and the Real Wage: The Economic Basis for Contesting Political Ideologies.' *Cambridge Journal of Economics* 14 (4): 375–393.

Blecker, R. A. 1989. 'International Competition, Income Distribution and Economic Growth.' *Cambridge Journal of Economics* 13 (3): 395–412.

Blecker, R. A. 2011. 'Open Economy Models of Distribution and Growth.' In *A Modern Guide to Keynesian Macroeconomics and Economic Policies*, edited by E. Hein and E. Stockhammer. Edward Elgar Cheltenham.

Conti, B. M., D. M. Prates, and D. Plihon. 2014. 'A Hierarquia Monetária E Suas Implicações Para As Taxas De Câmbio E De Juros E a Política Econômica Dos Países Periféricos.' *Economia e Sociedade* 23 (2): 341–372.

Dutt, A. K. 1984. 'Stagnation, Income Distribution and Monopoly Power.' *Cambridge Journal of Economics* 8 (1): 25–40.

Dutt, A. K. 1987. 'Alternative Closures Again: A Comment on "Growth, Distribution and Inflation".' *Cambridge Journal of Economics* 11 (1): 75–82.

Farhi, M. 2007. 'Análise Comparativa Do Regime De Metas De Inflação: Pass-Through, Formatos E Gestão Nas Economias Emergentes.' *Texto para Discussão, Instituto de Economia, UNICAMP* 127: 1–57.

Gouvêa, R. 2022. 'Large Devaluations and Inflation Inequality: Replicating Cravino and Levchenko (2017) with Evidence From Brazil.' *Journal of Applied Econometrics* 37 (3): 657–664.

Ha, J., M. A. Kose, F. Ohnsorge, and H. Yilmazkuday. 2019. 'Sources of Inflation: Global and Domestic Drivers.' In *Inflation in Emerging and Developing Economies: Evolution, Drivers, and Policies*, edited by J. Ha, M. A. Kose and F. Ohnsorge. World Bank Washington, DC: World Bank Publications.

Hein, E., and M. Mundt. 2012. 'Financialisation and the Requirements and Potentials for Wage-Led Recovery: A Review Focussing on the G20.' ILO Working Paper, Conditions of Work and Employment Series, No. 37.

Hein, E., and E. Stockhammer. 2010. 'Macroeconomic Policy Mix, Employment and Inflation in a Post-Keynesian Alternative to the New Consensus Model.' *Review of Political Economy* 22 (3): 317–354.

Hein, E., and L. Vogel. 2008. 'Distribution and Growth Reconsidered: Empirical Results for Six OECD Countries.' *Cambridge Journal of Economics* 32 (3): 479–511.

Hobijn, B., and D. Lagakos. 2005. 'Inflation Inequality in the United States.' *Review of Income and Wealth* 51 (4): 581–606.

IPEA. 2023. 'Inflação por Faixa de Renda.' *Carta de Conjuntura.*

Kalecki, M. 1971. 'Class Struggle and the Distribution of National Income.' *Kyklos* 24 (1): 1–9.

Kaltenbrunner, A. 2015. 'A Post Keynesian Framework of Exchange Rate Determination: A Minskyan Approach.' *Journal of Post Keynesian Economics* 38 (3): 426–448.

Lavoie, M. 2022. *Post-Keynesian Economics: New Foundations.* 2nd ed. Cheltenham, UK, Northampton, MA, USA: Edward Elgar.

Lima, G. T., and M. Setterfield. 2010. 'Pricing Behaviour and the Cost-Push Channel of Monetary Policy.' *Review of Political Economy* 22 (1): 19–40.

Morlin, G. S. 2023. 'Inflation and Conflicting Claims in the Open Economy.' *Review of Political Economy* 35 (3): 762–790.

Pivetti, M. 1991. *An Essay on Money and Distribution.* London, UK: Palgrave Macmillan.

Powell, J. H. 2022. 'Restoring Price Stability.' *Remarks at "Policy Options for Sustainable and Inclusive Growth" 38th Annual Economic Policy Conference National Association for Business Economics.*

Ramos, R. A. 2016. 'Financialization and Its Implications on the Determination of Exchange Rates of Emerging Market Economies.' PhD thesis, Université Sorbonne Paris Cité; Universidade Estadual de Campinas.

Ribeiro, R. S. M., J. S. L. McCombie, and G. T. Lima. 2017. 'Some Unpleasant Currency-Devaluation Arithmetic in a Post Keynesian Macromodel.' *Journal of Post Keynesian Economics* 40 (2): 145–167.

Ribeiro, R. S. M., J. S. McCombie, and G. T. Lima. 2020. 'Does Real Exchange Rate Undervaluation Really Promote Economic Growth?.' *Structural Change and Economic Dynamics* 52: 408–417.

Rochon, L.-P., and M. Setterfield. 2007. 'Interest Rates, Income Distribution, and Monetary Policy Dominance: Post Keynesians and the "Fair Rate" of Interest.' *Journal of Post Keynesian Economics* 30 (1): 13–42.

Rolim, L., G. T. Lima, and C. T. Baltar. 2022. 'The Impact of International Trade Shocks on Domestic Output, Income Distribution, and Inflation in An Agent-Based Model.' *Texto para Discussão, Instituto de Economia, UNICAMP* 441: 1–30.

Rolim, L., and N. Marins. 2022. 'Inflation Targeting Regime and Income Distribution in Emerging Market Economies.' In *The Future of Central Banking*, edited by S. Kappes, L.-P. Rochon and G. Vallet. Cheltenham, UK: Edward Elgar Publishing.

Rossi, D., and J. Galbraith. 2016. 'Exchange Rates and Industrial Wage Inequality in Open Economies.' *UTIP Working Paper* 71: 1–23.

Rowthorn, R. E. 1977. 'Conflict, Inflation and Money.' *Cambridge Journal of Economics* 1 (3): 215–239.

Sasaki, H., R. Sonoda, and S. Fujita. 2013. 'International Competition and Distributive Class Conflict in An Open Economy Kaleckian Model.' *Metroeconomica* 64 (4): 683–715.
Weber, I. M. 2022. 'Big Oil's Profits and Inflation: Winners and Losers.' *Challenge* 65 (5-6): 151–159.
Weber, I. M., and E. Wasner. 2023. 'Sellers' Inflation, Profits and Conflict: Why Can Large Firms Hike Prices in An Emergency?.' *Review of Keynesian Economics* 11 (2): 1–21.
Wildauer, R., K. Kohler, A. Aboobaker, and A. Guschanski. 2023. 'Energy Price Shocks, Conflict Inflation, and Income Distribution in a Three-sector Model.' *Energy Economics* 127: 106982.

Appendix. Parameters and Initial Values in Baseline Specification

Table A1. Parameters and initial conditions.

Parameter	Description	Value
$\alpha_{H,L}$	share of non-tradable goods in the consumption goods basket for group *H*, *L*	(0.95, 0.5)
γ	sensitivity of capacity utilization to the real interest rate	5
δ	ratio between high- and low-wage workers' nominal wages	2
λ	sensitivity of workers' desired wage share to the capacity utilization rate	0.5
μ	foreign price inflation shock	0.02
ρ	sensitivity of the nominal interest rate to the inflation gap	0.1
φ	sensitivity of price adjustments to the difference between the desired wage share by firms and realized wage share	0.1
ψ	sensitivity of firms' desired wage share to the real exchange rate	0.2
Ω	sensitivity of wage adjustments to the difference between the desired wage share by workers and realized wage share	0.1
$\omega_{\max}$	maximum wage share desired by firms	0.7
$\omega_{\min}$	minimum wage share desired by workers	0.5
ξ	sensitivity of the nominal exchange rate to changes in the interest differential	2
e_0	initial nominal exchange rate	1
i^f	nominal interest rate in the foreign sector	0.02
i_0	initial nominal interest rate	0.02
n_H	share of high-wage workers in total employment	0.25
p_0^d	initial price of non-tradables (in domestic currency)	100
$\hat{p}_{t-i}$	initial inflation rate for $i = 1, \ldots, T_i$	0.02
$\hat{p}^T$	inflation rate target	0.02
p_0^f	initial price of tradables (in foreign currency)	100
$\hat{p}_f^*$	foreign inflation rate (no shock)	0.02
T_i	initial period for shock on the foreign inflation rate	500
T_e	number of periods for exchange rate adjustment to changes in the interest rate differential	4
T_f	final period of shock on the foreign inflation rate	520
T_p	number of periods considered by the monetary policy rule	4
u_0	capacity utilization rate when the real interest rate is equal to zero	0.8
u_0	initial capacity utilization rate	0.8
$w_{L,0}$	initial nominal wage for low-wage workers	44

Dealing with Rising Inequality: Is the Fed Up for the Task, or Will Everyone Get Fed Up?

Steven Pressman

ABSTRACT
Recently, considerable research effort has been devoted to studying the impact of monetary policy on inequality. This paper summarizes the literature on the causes of rising inequality and looks at the empirical work on interest rates and inequality. It argues that growing empirical evidence concerning the impact of monetary policy on inequality is mixed and that the conflicting results concerning monetary policy and inequality involve, to a large extent, how one measures inequality. Overall, it seems that loose monetary policy increases incomes of those at the bottom of the distribution but reduces their income relative to those at the top of the distribution. The paper also examines some post-Keynesian monetary policy rules to deal with inequality and finds them wanting in many respects. Going further, the paper argues that monetary policy is too a blunt instrument for reducing inequality and that reducing inequality needs to be the job fiscal policy, which is better suited to dealing with this problem and which has the political authority to deal with distributional problems.

1. Introduction

Both income and wealth inequality have risen sharply in developed nations over the past 40 years (Piketty 2014, 2020; Saez and Zucman 2019; Wolff 2017). In what follows, we mainly focus on income inequality — partly because greater wealth inequality generates greater income inequality through some Piketty-like mechanism and partly because income distribution data is more reliable than wealth distribution data (see Pressman 2016).

Recognizing a problem naturally leads to a search for causes. The impact of monetary policy on inequality has received scant attention until very recently. Carstens (2021, Graph 2) finds a growing use of 'inequality' in central banker speeches — from 1 per cent between 2004 and 2010 to 10 per cent between 2016 and 2021. Kashkari (https://www.afr.com/policy/economy/neel-kashkari-pushes-federal-reserve-to-battle-us-income-inequality-20171219-h06w2g), President of the Minneapolis Fed, claims that monetary policy can play the same sort of redistributive role as fiscal policy and set up an Opportunity and Inclusive Growth Institute at the Minneapolis Fed to study this. Still, the direction of the impact remains in dispute — even among central bankers. Draghi (2016), former head of the ECB, argues that monetary easing reduces inequality because the unemployed can find jobs and low-income workers can find new jobs with higher wages. Conversely, former Fed Chair Bernanke (2015) notes that inequality rises when interest rates fall due to surging asset prices.

Economists outside central banks have also raised concerns about recent monetary policy *contributing to* rising inequality (Stiglitz 2015). Some have pushed for central banks to do more to address the problem. Muelibauer (2014) advocates a quantitative easing (QE) for the people, effectively a (temporary) basic income provided to individuals by central banks. Similarly, Buetzer (2022) of the IMF supports a policy of 'outright transfers' by central banks in times of crisis. Such proposals take monetary policy outside its traditional function of controlling interest rates.

This interest is welcomed, albeit strange, given numerous critiques over the years that central banks serve the interests of the financial community rather than the general public. Greider (1987) castigated the Volcker Fed for engineering a deep recession in the early 1980s. Smithin (1996) calls late 20th-century monetary policy 'the revenge of the rentiers' because it was so good to wealth holders. Many others (Rochon 2021; Seccareccia 2017; Dietsch et al. 2018) complain that central bank policy supports those with wealth over those without wealth. A more recent example of this phenomenon took place during the 2008 financial crisis when the Fed bailed out financial institutions but did nothing for underwater homeowners who were given mortgages they couldn't possibly repay (Blinder 2013).

This paper takes a different approach. It argues that empirical evidence concerning the impact of monetary policy on inequality is mixed and that a good deal of the dispute concerning monetary policy and inequality involves how one conceptualizes tight (and loose) monetary policy and how one defines inequality. Going further, the paper argues that monetary policy is a blunt instrument for reducing inequality, especially when there is a better alternative — fiscal policy.

Toward this end, Section Two summarizes the literature on the causes of rising inequality. Sections Three and Four, respectively, look at the theoretical and empirical literature on interest rates and inequality. Section Five examines some post-Keynesian interest rate rules to deal with inequality. Finally, Section Six pulls things together and argues that monetary policy shouldn't try to deal with rising inequality; rather, this problem should be left to fiscal policy, which is better suited to the task.

2. Why Inequality Is Rising

The literature on the causes of inequality is enormous. It is impossible to do it justice here. Several literature reviews discuss this issue in economics (Alfani 2021; Levy and Murnane 1992) and political science (Boix 2010; Schlozman et al. 2017). This section focuses on a few prominent explanations — marginal productivity theory, Piketty's $r > g$, a battle between education and technology, globalization, market power, and fiscal policy.

2.1. Marginal Productivity

According to standard neoclassical economic theory, workers get paid based on their marginal productivity, or how much additional revenue they bring to the firm that hires them.

The problems with this theory are well-known. Firms cannot know the marginal productivity of workers when they are hired. Moreover, worker productivity is not independent of what other workers do, or the pay distribution; so it is hard to identify the marginal productivity of each worker and then pay them accordingly. Considerable empirical research has found that when productivity depends upon team effort, unequal rewards actually harm productivity (Bloom 1999; Cowherd and Levine 1992; Bloom and Michel 2002). Also, income distribution is highly skewed; it does not follow a normal distribution. In contrast, attributes like intelligence follow a normal distribution; so we should expect worker productivity and incomes to do so as well. Finally, the Cambridge capital controversy undermines the foundation of the marginal productivity theory (Harcourt 1972).

2.2. Piketty

Piketty's (2014) explanation for rising inequality is that returns on assets (r) exceed overall economic growth (g), where g determines average income gains, and he adduces considerable evidence that this has been the case over a long stretch of history. Piketty tries hard to explain why $r > g$ from a neoclassical perspective, but his effort suffers due to the flaws with this perspective. Nonetheless, it should be pointed out that Piketty's results follow algebraically from a post-Keynesian model of distribution (Zorn and Pressman 2020) and his results can be explained based on compounding without resorting to any economic theory (Pressman 2016).

The big problem with Piketty's explanation for rising inequality is that it has difficulty explaining why inequality has fallen during some historical epochs without resorting to a great deal of adhockery. For Piketty, the two world wars destroyed capital or wealth, and so less income went to the very rich due to the high returns on wealth. But there is little in *Capital in the Twenty-First Century* that explains why inequality remained so low in the several decades following World War II. More recently, Piketty (2020) attributes this to ideology, pushing the question out of the realm of economics and raising issues regarding measuring ideologies.

2.3. Technology and Education

The technological change story goes back to Ricardo's (1819[1951]) concerns about the distributional impact of machinery. More recently, Bound and Johnson (1992) and Brynjolfsson and McAfee (2012, 2014) argue that technological improvements favor skilled workers, who are adept at using the new technology, and hurt unskilled workers, who are not. When machinery replaces human labor, those lacking other skills find it hard to get a good job. As automated assembly lines replace people doing routine jobs, a greater supply of low-skilled workers reduces wages for this group. At the same time, new technology requires educated laborers who can use, create and maintain it. This increases the demand for skilled workers, raising their pay. The result is greater inequality.

Tinbergen (1975) takes things a step further, viewing changing income inequality as the outcome of a race between education and technology. Expanding education reduces the supply of less-educated workers, pushing up the wages of the remaining low-skilled workers. If education improves more rapidly than technology, income inequality declines; if technology has the upper hand, income inequality becomes greater (also see Goldin and Katz 2010).

This story is hard to evaluate, in large part because there is no good measure of technology or technical change. Technological change is qualitative rather than quantitative. Taking von Böhm-Bawerk's (1889[2008]) famous example, people first get water from the nearby stream using buckets rather than their hands. Later, water gets piped into our homes. While we recognize such qualitative changes, it is impossible to say *how much* technology has grown in these particular cases or to figure out when one technological change is greater than another.

Moreover, several studies have questioned this explanation. Caselli (1999) and Atkinson (2008) point out that technical change is not always skill-biased and does not always lead to larger wage differentials and greater inequality. Sometimes technological change and inequality do *not* move together. For example, the computer revolution began in the 1980s, while a larger increase in inequality in the US took place between 1979 and 1982 — before the introduction of computers (Howell 1994).

2.4. Globalization

Another story about rising inequality concerns globalization (Wood 1994; Friedman 2005). This story operates along multiple channels. Its theme is that greater world trade, increased movement of capital around the world, and increased flows of labor (immigration) across national borders, all contribute to greater income inequality. When firms outsource production, US workers have to compete with foreign workers willing to accept lower pay; if they don't, firms will move production to low-wage countries. Likewise, the immigration of unskilled workers from other countries puts downward pressure on wages and incomes within the US, especially for unskilled US workers. As a result, more mobile capital (and labor) gains at the expense of less mobile capital (and labor).

The globalization story suffers from the same limitation as the technical change story — it is not clear how to measure globalization. The standard economic measure, exports plus imports as a fraction of GDP, has been rising consistently over time. Moreover, some studies found this factor to be insignificant (Moller et al. 2003), others found it to be a moderate force toward greater inequality (Richardson 1995), and yet others have found that international trade leads to a rise in inequality (Alderson and Nielsen 2002). Reviewing the extensive literature on this topic, Haskel et al. (2012, p. 136) conclude that 'there is little evidence that globalization through the classic channel of international trade in goods, intermediates and services has been raising inequality between more-skilled and less-skilled workers'.

Last, but not least, while standard (Heckscher–Ohlin) trade theory predicts rising inequality for developed countries due to trade — because the gains go to skilled capital and labor — modern trade theory predicts that gains will go to the largest and most productive *firms*. Globalization thus benefits the top and the bottom of the distribution, while the middle part of the distribution loses (Leamer 2007; Venables 2009).

2.5. Market Power

Two strands of thought emphasize the importance of market power in generating inequality.

Labor economists see unionization leading to collective bargaining and more equal wage outcomes (Freeman and Medoff 1984). Nonetheless, there is reason for skepticism about the union explanation. Reduced union membership might be the result of other forces that are also generating inequality (such as greater corporate power). And, of late, the link between unionization and inequality seems to have broken down (Baccaro 2011).

Post-Keynesians see greater industrial concentration or market power as leading to a greater markup by firms over their costs when setting prices (Lee 1998), thereby increasing the incomes of capitalists at the expense of workers. Similarly, Stiglitz (2015) contends that rising inequality stems from rising monopoly power and the failure of the government to control it. Lack of competition yields rents via imperfections in corporate governance and bargaining between workers and firms. It also leads to market manipulation, insider trading, predatory lending and abusive credit card practices. Wealthy shareholders and senior executives of large companies win; workers lose. Two examples of this are non-compete clauses and no-poach agreements among franchises like McDonald's and Planet Fitness. Such agreements are required by nearly 60 per cent of major US franchises, up from 36 per cent in 1996 (Starr et al. 2019). Starr et al. (2017) estimate that 20 per cent of workers with a high school education level or less are subject to some such clause as well as 12 per cent of workers making less than $40,000 a year such as hair stylists, health care aids, janitors and house cleaners.

Measured by concentration ratios, market power has risen at the same time that inequality has grown. And, in the USA, market power has enabled firms to require no-poaching and non-compete clauses from their employees. The market power explanation seems to have some explanatory power.

2.6. Financialization

According to Epstein (2001, p. 1), 'Financialization refers to the increasing importance of financial markets, financial motives, financial institutions, and financial elites in the operation of the economy, and its governing institutions'. It can be measured by the relative size of the financial sector in the economy and the rise in household and corporate debt levels, as well as greater public debt.

James Galbraith (2012) and Palley (2008) argue that the increasing role of the financial sector is responsible for rising inequality. Finance pressures corporate executives to maximize shareholder value, or risk being bought out by another firm that will improve the financial performance of the firm. On the one hand, this leads to stock buybacks to increase stock prices, financed by greater debt (Lazonick 2014). On the other hand, there is greater pressure to cut worker wages and benefits, leading to a rise in CEO pay relative to the pay of average workers, and a divergence between the growth of worker productivity and the growth of worker wages.

Like the globalization and technical change explanations, this explanation falls short because it is hard to measure financialization, and because financialization has increased steadily since the 1950s while inequality has not. Alexiou et al. (2022) examine the relationship between financialization and inequality and find that only two out of four measures of financialization significantly are associated with rising Gini coefficients, when using disposable income to calculate the Gini, and conclude that the relationship between financialization and inequality is 'not so straightforward'.

2.7. Fiscal Policy

Fiscal policy is like a double-edged sword when it comes to understanding inequality. According to standard economic theory, low taxes create incentives to make money by letting people keep more of what they earn. It also creates incentives for people to work hard and be productive employees. This is the heart of supply-side economics, which has dominated US policy since the early 1980s. Over more than four decades, the top marginal tax rate in the US for married couples fell from 70 to 37 per cent. There were similar cuts for single household heads and large corporations, as well as lower tax rates on dividends and capital gains, forms of income that go mainly to the very wealthy.

Further, a feedback loop runs from lower taxes to making political contributions, to even lower tax rates. Wealth provides access to elected representatives (Task Force on Inequality and American Democracy 2004), and elected members of Congress tend to represent the views of their high-income constituents more than the views of their average constituents (Bartels 2008; Gilens 2014).

On the other hand, tax cuts do stimulate the economy and create more jobs. This should make the distribution of income more equal. Which is the stronger of these two forces is unclear. The same thing is true regarding the impact of government spending on inequality The question is who gains most from government expenditures. For military spending, it is the owners of firms making the equipment and the ammunition. For interest on the government debt, nearly all the gain goes to the top 1 per cent (Piketty 2014). Likewise for so-called tax expenditures. Social expenditures, on the other hand, tend to benefit the poor and middle class.

Government rules and regulations also impact income distribution. One contentious issue concerns the minimum wage. Card and Krueger (1994) looked at contiguous counties in two different states that were similar in many respects. They then examined hiring at fast food restaurants before and after New Jersey increased its minimum wage but Pennsylvania did not. They found no difference in hiring in the two locations as a result of the increase in the minimum wage.

Fiscal policy can clearly impact income distribution through spending and tax policy, and through regulation. Before addressing this question in greater detail, we turn to a relatively new explanation for rising inequality — monetary policy.

3. Monetary Policy and Income Distribution

As inequality has increased over the past few decades, the literature on monetary policy and inequality has mushroomed. This work identifies ways monetary policy can impact income inequality or the transmission mechanisms of monetary policy.

The most common form of monetary policy involves central banks changing short-term interest rates. Today this is done by setting a floor on overnight bank loans by paying interest on bank reserves and a ceiling with the central bank lending rate to banks (the discount rate in the US). Such changes can impact employment and wages, essentially a *Keynesian Effect*, although Keynes (1936, p. 173) was skeptical that monetary policy could impact employment, noting the many slips between the cup and lip. Nonetheless, lower interest rates should increase borrowing, spending and demand. Business firms will hire more workers, creating jobs for the unemployed and more hours for those currently employed. As such, lower interest rates should promote wage equality. However, lower interest rates also impact the wages of people near the top of the income distribution because the demand for more managers and senior executives will also rise. They will have more opportunities for advancement, receive higher pay and larger bonuses, and have greater opportunities to move to another firm offering higher wages. Given that monetary policy should increase wages over the entire income distribution, whose wages will rise the most and how this will impact wage inequality is unclear based on theory.

Another monetary policy transmission mechanism is the wealth effect. Lower interest rates impact financial asset prices (Bernanke 2015). When firms pay less to borrow money, and spending rises due to lower interest rates, firm profits rise, as do stock prices. Also, low-interest rates lead firms to borrow money in order to buy outstanding shares of stock, pushing up stock prices (Lazonick 2009, Ch. 6, 2014). Stock ownership as a percentage of household wealth increases as household wealth rises. Higher equity prices provide capital gains for their owners, whether or not they are realized; and, on the Haig-Simons definition of income, changes in wealth get counted as part of income. Also, lower rates make it easier for households to afford a mortgage and so should increase home prices. Since home equity is a major source of household wealth for the middle class, lower interest rates should increase the wealth of the middle class, and thus their income according to the Haig-Simon definition. Low-income households (the bottom 50 per cent of the wealth distribution) own few or no assets; their wealth will be affected only minimally by interest rate changes. Overall, the asset price effect of lower interest rates should worsen inequality.

Besides wages and capital gains, many people own businesses and receive business income, which is typically more responsive to monetary policy than wage income (Gornemann et al. 2016). It is not clear whether this will increase or decrease inequality; the answer to this question depends on where individual entrepreneurs lie in the overall income distribution.

Finally, interest rate changes impact interest on savings. Lower rates reduce interest income and higher rates increase it. As such, interest rate cuts hurt older and middle-class households that typically keep a larger proportion of their assets in savings accounts. For wealthy households, the impact of lower interest rates on interest income is unclear. They may be more willing and able to take greater risks for higher returns, balancing out the loss of interest income from government bonds and savings accounts. Or, this might not happen, reducing their returns on savings accounts and bonds.

In brief, the impact of monetary policy on income distribution can't be determined by economic theory. It is an empirical question, to which we now turn.

4. Some Empirical Results

To examine the distributional consequences of monetary policy empirically requires dealing with numerous issues, some of which we encountered previously. Here are just a few. What interest rate are we talking about? How do we measure income and income inequality? Inequality of what? Over what time period does distribution change?

Central banks typically focus on very short-term interest rates, the rates they charge to banks and the overnight lending rate among banks. But they purchase other assets and target other rates, ranging from medium-term or long-term rates on securitized assets and government bonds to various rates on consumer borrowing and savings. This raises the question of whether QE has different distributional consequences than standard monetary policy.

Regarding income, do we look at taxable income, total income, or something more comprehensive such as the Haig-Simons definition? Also, issues arise surrounding our *unit of analysis*. Do we look at individuals or at households? If the latter, what equivalence scales do we use? Further, it should be remembered that government benefits are a form of income. Programs such as unemployment insurance compensate for the loss of income due to monetary policy; some benefits are in-kind (such as health insurance) that should be counted as part of income.

Next, there is the question raised by Sen (1982) — 'inequality of what?'. We can focus on income inequality, wealth inequality, educational inequality, health inequality, social and political inequality, equality before the law, equality of capabilities, etc. Following Pressman and Scott (2009), we can subtract debt repayments from income and look at consumption inequality. Most empirical work looks at income inequality, but the other inequality notions need to be kept in mind, especially the one that deals with household debt.

There are also different measures of inequality, each giving different weights to different parts of the distribution (Pressman and Scott 2022). The Gini coefficient gives excess weight to the middle of the income distribution. Relative and absolute poverty rates focus only on the bottom of the distribution. Piketty emphasizes the top of the distribution — the share of total income going to the richest 1 per cent. Decile ratios focus on just two points in the entire income distribution.

Most studies of monetary policy and inequality regress changes in interest rates and changes in inequality (however defined). However, they don't control for all the other forces that can impact inequality (noted in Section Two). Many fail to control fiscal policy and various government programs that might mitigate the distributional impact of monetary policy.

Another issue concerns timing. Monetary policy is known to have long and variable lags. The theory is silent about how long it takes for changes in interest rates to impact distribution or whether the impact will dissipate over time. Complicating matters, central banks may increase interest rates at any time during the year, and they usually change interest rates over several years when undertaking a cycle of raising or cutting rates. Yet, income data is typically collected annually, either via surveys or tax returns. Consequently, it is hard to line up interest rate and income data. Having quarterly or monthly income data would help; lacking such data it is harder to draw conclusions about how and when monetary policy impacts distribution.

A related problem concerns the nature of monetary policy. Studies typically examine how interest rate 'shocks' impact inequality, but provide no clear definition of this term. Usually, a shock is taken to be a change of a certain number of basis points (bp). Standard theory holds that only 'unexpected' interest rate changes will lead to economic and distributional changes. If an interest rate change is expected, the distributional changes should have been baked into the economy and the existing distribution of income *before* the central bank started raising rates. For example, at least a 200 bp change was expected in the US in early 2022, when it was necessary to end a regime of easy monetary policy due to the covid pandemic and deal with rising inflation. In contrast, a 25–50 bp hike in interest rates can be a true surprise. For example, in September 2022 everyone expected a 75 bp hike by the Fed; the only surprise would have been a smaller increase and a real surprise would have been no increase. What is needed is a way to identify an actual shock. One possibility, following Bernanke and Kuttner (2005), is to look at interest rate changes right before and right after monetary policy announcements. Following this suggestion, Hansen and Stein (2015) and Gürkaynak et al. (2005) examine changes in two-year bond yields on days that central banks announce changes in monetary policy. However, this doesn't solve the problem. It excludes times when no change is the shock — as in the September 2022 example above. Finally, if central banks follow (either explicitly or implicitly) a rule such as the Taylor Rule (Taylor 1993), then there should be no monetary policy shocks.

A related complication is that since the late 1990s central banks have provided forward guidance or hints about what they plan to do next. Called the 'signaling channel', this is now a key component of monetary policy (Bernanke 2020). Studies looking at only interest rate changes at one point in time ignore the forward guidance provided by central banks on a regular basis (Bundick and Smith 2022). When central banks do change rates, following the guidance they provided previously, this change should be expected rather than unexpected.

Given the theoretical problems and the data limitations, it is unsurprising that the empirical literature on interest rate changes and distributional changes is rather inconclusive. Nonetheless, Kappes (2023) comes to a different conclusion. Examining 14 papers on the topic, Kappes concludes that, for conventional monetary policy, interest rate cuts lead to greater equality and rate increases lead to greater inequality. He arrives at this conclusion, despite the fact that seven studies reached this conclusion and seven reached the alternative conclusion, by claiming that the seven papers finding that stimulative monetary policy reduces inequality are stronger. However, Kappes doesn't explain how he selected these 18 papers, or whether they are representative samples of the empirical work on this topic. Nor does he discuss their methodological flaws or how they go about solving some of the empirical problems noted above. In addition, he counts two different versions of the same paper (by Saiki and Frost) among his seven studies showing that conventional monetary expansion increases inequality.

Colciago et al. (2018) provide another literature survey. This work looks at 13 papers, 7 of which are covered by Kappes, and 2 different versions of one paper (by Mumtaz and Theophilopoulou). Of the remaining six papers, conventional monetary easing increases inequality according to four papers and reduces it according to two. Combined, we have 20 different papers covered in these 2 surveys. Nine say that expansionary monetary policy increases inequality and seven say it reduces inequality.

Searching further, I found five additional papers on the topic not included in either survey. Two (Villarreal 2014; von Wachter et al. 2009) find that tight monetary policy increases income inequality; and one that easy monetary policy increases inequality (Andersen et al. 2020). One paper finds no change in inequality (Meh et al. 2010), while Lenza and Slacalek (2021) come up with ambiguous results — greater inequality in the short run, a decline in the medium term, and no change in the long run. Overall, the empirical results seem evenly split. The impact of conventional monetary policy on inequality seems to be: 'it depends'. This result should not be surprising given the problems we noted above concerning measurement, control variables, and timing issues.

Results for unconventional monetary policy, or QE, are also mixed. Kappes finds that, in four different papers studying this question, two reduce income inequality, one increases income inequality, and one has negligible effects. Colciago et al. (2018) report the same outcome for four different papers. I found one study not covered in either of these two literature reviews. It concluded that QE leads to greater inequality (Bonifacio et al. 2021). Again, the results are mixed.

The results regarding wealth inequality are likewise inconclusive. Of three papers studying this topic, according to Kappes (2023), two find greater wealth inequality from lower rates and one finds insignificant changes. Colciago et al. (2018) report on nine additional studies of the impact of monetary policy on wealth inequality. Of these, two find less wealth inequality, four find greater wealth inequality, and three negligible or insignificant results. I found a few additional studies on this topic. Gabriel and Lutz (2017) find that loose monetary policy increases the value of real estate assets in the US. This implies that wealth inequality rises since households below the median for both income and wealth possess little wealth. Greenwald et al. (2021) find this result holds for all wealth in the US, and Amberg et al. (2021) find this holds for Sweden. On the other hand, Mäki-Fränti et al. (2022) find only small effects on wealth inequality in Finland due to lower interest rates. Domanski et al. (2016) estimate something similar for the US.

Finally, central banks might affect income distribution through the regulations they impose on financial institutions. Macroprudential regulation, such as higher capital requirements for banks and more stringent loan-to-value limits, seek to constrain bank lending and prevent a Minsky-like bubble of the sort leading to the Great Recession. By reducing lending, these regulations should reduce economic growth and increase inequality. This is what the empirical work on this issue indicates. Frost and van Stralen (2016) find that higher capital requirements increase inequality, while Carpantier et al. (2016) find that more stringent loan-to-value limits increase inequality. The real-world impact, or *economic significance*, however, is quite small in these cases.

I conclude this empirical survey with one important observation — inequality is difficult to measure with a single number, and different measures yield different results. Amberg et al. (2021) shed considerable light on this issue. It studies the impact of monetary policy using several different measures of inequality. Their results (reproduced as Table 1) make clear that the distributional impact of interest rate cuts depends on the measure of inequality adopted to a large extent. The share of income received by the top 1 per cent, Piketty's measure of inequality, changes most on a percentage basis. The Gini coefficient, which weights middle-income groups most heavily, changes the least because the big changes occur at the top and bottom of the income

Table 1. Two-year impact of 25 basis point shock.

Distribution measure	Per cent change
Gini	0.09
Top 1%	1.95
Top 10%	0.55
Std Dev. Log Inc	−0.43
90/10 Ratio	−0.43
90/50 Ratio	0.11
50/10 Ratio	−0.55

Source: Amberg et al., AER Insights, 2021, p. 299.

distribution and cancel each other out. Inequality falls when looking at 90–10 and 50–10 ratios. Dividing income gains into capital and labor income, the bottom 20 per cent gain the most in terms of labor income, the top 1 per cent gains the next most, and the middle-income group gains little. For capital income, gains go to the top decile and the largest gains go to the top 1 per cent. It should be noted here that these are dividends, interest income and realized capital gains. Adding unrealized capital gains (which the paper does not do) would show income inequality rising even more due to monetary policy easing.

My takeaway from this literature is that expansionary monetary policy involves a trade-off between making those at the bottom better off in absolute terms (with more jobs and hours), and relative to those in the middle of the distribution, but at the expense of doing relatively worse compared to the rich. A similar trade-off exists for tight monetary policy. By reducing asset prices it reduces inequality, but in absolute terms, it hurts those with low incomes the most. A further takeaway from the literature is that there is still a great deal of empirical work that needs to be done, including a meta-analysis of previous studies.

5. Post-Keynesian Rules

Post-Keynesians have been particularly interested in the impact of monetary policy on income distribution. Rochon and Seccareccia (2021, p. 13) contend that high-interest rates lead to slower wage growth, which increases inequality, and argue that inflation targeting in Canada (which resulted in higher interest rates) led to high unemployment and a falling wage share. However, as noted above, income consists of more than just wages, and wages are only one part of the story about the impact of monetary policy on inequality. As noted in the previous section, when you add appreciating assets, the empirics indicate that *higher interest rates reduce asset price inequality*. Further, aggregate US data over several decades fails to support their view. The Fed began lowering interest rates in the 1980s and kept them low through 2021. Over this time period wage growth has *not* kept up with productivity growth (https://www.epi.org/productivity-pay-gap/) and the income share received by the top 1 per cent has grown remarkably (Piketty 2014).

Nonetheless, many post-Keynesians have proposed using easy monetary policy to reduce inequality. They have developed several rules that put central banks on automatic pilot regarding interest rates, leaving fiscal policy to deal with stabilization issues (Lavoie 1992; Lavoie and Seccareccia 2019, p. 161). These rules provide precise instructions about what to do (usually each quarter) in response to changes taking place in the economy. This differs from allowing central banks to make discretionary interest rate changes —

m into considerable trouble. Total factor productivity is a dubious notion (Metcalfe 97), especially for economists who understand the problems with the notion of an gregate production function (see Harcourt 1972). Labor productivity would have n a much better choice for their monetary policy rule. Further, there are several ferent inflation measures (CPI, core CPI, PCE, etc.) as well as different interest es. Seccareccia (2019; Seccareccia and Lavoie 2016) wants central banks to control g-term bond rates, which he takes to be a classic form of income for rentiers. wever, this is not easy for central banks to do, and it would likely damage the ısing market, where mortgage rates depend on the rate of 10-year government nds, and thereby impact housing prices, where most middle-class households (as posed to the rich) have their wealth stored.

An even bigger problem is what Lavoie and Seccareccia (2019) would require from tral banks under certain circumstances. Labor productivity in the US *fell* by 7.3 per t in the first quarter of 2022 and by 4.6 per cent in the second quarter; inflation s around 2 per cent in each quarter. This would have required an interest rate of .3 per cent, for the first quarter and −2.6 per cent for the second quarter of 2022, ich would come up against the zero-lower-bound problem. In contrast, for 2021, or productivity grew 1.9 per cent and inflation was 7.1 per cent, The Pasinetti Rule uld have had the Fed set the interest rate at 9 per cent (on average) that year, something virtually everyone would regard as being too high, including post-Keynesians, who nplained as central banks raised interest rates above 5 per cent. Finally, it is worth considering a hypothetical case. If labor productivity rose from 2 to 4 per cent at a time of 0 cent inflation, the Pasinetti Rule would call for central banks to increase the rate of erest from 2 to 4 per cent. It is not clear why central banks should slow an economy eriencing 0 per cent inflation and rapid productivity growth, especially if a rising re of income went to labor.

Problems with the Kansas City rule are easier to identify. What happens when ation is high and rising in the US, and it is necessary to slow demand? The KC e says the Fed should do nothing and leave stabilizing the economy to fiscal policy. what if Republicans will accept only cuts in government spending to reduce ation, while Democrats will allow only tax hikes on the wealthy, which won't do ch to lower effective demand? And what if there are good political economy sons that politicians don't want to use fiscal policy to lower inflation? For example, ir constituents will want neither higher taxes nor cuts in government programs m which they benefit. Fiscal policy becomes impossible from a practical standpoint, ving only monetary policy to lower inflation. This is why politicians prefer letting tral banks take away the proverbial punch bowl. Monetary policy has its problems, it needs to be tried in the absence of viable alternatives. Without monetary policy, have few policy options other than letting 'the market' deal with inflation, which ans not dealing with the problem at all. This is not a good policy given that it ms inflation hurts poor families most <https://www.dallasfed.org/research/nomics/2023/0110>.

While the Kansas City Rule errs by having central banks do too little, the Smithin Rule by having central banks do too much. If there is deflation, the Smithin Rule calls for ative nominal rates, which raises the issue of the zero lower bound. Bigger problems e when inflation is high. Smithin, remember, wants a 0 per cent real rate, claiming it

based partly on economic variables, and partly on observations and i
what is going on in the economy. Post-Keynesians have developed
rules.

One, put forward by Pasinetti (1980–81, 1981, Ch 8), has been cal
interest'; it is supported by many post-Keynesians (Gnos and Roch
Stockhammer 2010; Kriesler and Lavoie 2007; Setterfield 2009; Roch
2008). According to Lavoie and Seccareccia (1999, p. 140), this is 't
that will leave unchanged the distribution of income between interes
income'. Rates greater than this lead to a larger share of income go
lower rates to a larger share of income going to labor. The Kansas
1998, 2007; Tymoigne 2009) calls for setting the nominal interest
and keeping it there, while the Smithin Rule (2007, 2018, 2020; also su
mourgos 2011) would set the real interest rate at 0 per cent via nomina
rate changes.

One test of a monetary policy rule is empirical. Would a partic
desired economic effect? The previous section found that changes i
don't seem to have a large impact, if any, on income distribution;
depends on the measure of inequality that you use. Moreover, to the ex
policy impacts inequality, there is a trade-off between greater equality
for those at the bottom of the distribution. Another test for any polic
accords with our intuitions about the right action at a particular
another test is whether the rule is logically consistent in its own ter
Keynesian Rules come up short on these last two tests.

Pasinetti's 'fair interest rate' is not the least bit fair. As its advocates
keep the wage share in the economy constant. It is really a stable rate a
this. If you start with a low-wage share, because it has fallen for sever
2015), the so-called 'fair rate' merely maintains the existing status quo
Lavoie and Seccareccia (2021, p. 26) go so far as to maintain that 'the
anism to get wages to catch up with long-term productivity'. More s
stable rate doesn't sit well with the philosophical literature on what is a
income. Two approaches to this question are well-known. Rawls (1971
imizing the gains for those at the bottom of the distribution, while N
that fairness is about just acquisitions (both originally and through inh
tributional implications of these two approaches are quite different. Fo
help those at the bottom of the distribution. For Nozick, we should r
any distribution of wealth or income reached in a just manner. I stru
why two post-Keynesians, concerned about rising income inequal
quences, would side with Nozick rather than Rawls here.

Another problem with Pasinetti's approach is that it is hard to fo
not clear and simple to follow. Lavoie and Seccareccia (1999) point
labor and profit shares require that wages grow in line with producti
ductivity grows faster than wages, because of greater markups, the
to lower interest rates regardless of the economic circumstances a
wages grow faster than productivity, central banks should raise
this, Lavoie and Seccareccia (2019) want central banks to set the
rate equal to the inflation rate plus the rate of overall productivity

will lead to constant purchasing power for rentiers or owners of finance capital. This will require much higher nominal rates in times of inflation.

During the first half of 2022, a 0 per cent real interest rate would have required a nominal rate of around 9 per cent in the US. Besides hurting low-income households, this would hurt households in debt, which are low-income and middle-class households. Those priced out of home ownership must still live somewhere, thus increasing apartment demand and rents. Moreover, attempting to reduce inflation that is mainly due to supply problems (which central banks cannot control), such tight monetary policy would have likely brought on a recession, which would worsen the economic condition of those at the bottom of the income distribution. The Smithin Rule might produce greater equality as asset prices tumbled, but we would also get an economy with less income from employment and more suffering by those at the bottom of the distribution — the opposite of what Smithin wants.

There are two additional practical problems with monetary policy rules. Data gets revised in the short term and also in the long term, as our economic knowledge, sampling, and statistical techniques improve. Sometimes these changes can be significant. For example, the Boskin Commission (1996) in the US, led to large changes in measured inflation. It is hard to follow rules when not just the goalposts, but the entire football field moves. A second issue is that monetary policy rules result in central banks moving much too slowly during times of crisis, such as the bankruptcy of Lehman Brothers in September 2008 or the onset of the coronavirus pandemic in March 2020. In these instances we need monetary policy to act quickly; this is its comparative advantage relative to fiscal policy. But economic data comes out with a lag — one month for inflation data and several months for GDP data (depending on whether central banks rely on preliminary data or the final data revision). So, in times of crisis, monetary policy is behind the curve with any monetary policy rule. It is in worst shape with the Kansas City Rule, which keeps interest rates permanently fixed and thereby keeps monetary policy from dealing with a crisis that fiscal policy does not move quickly to remedy.

Finally, the post-Keynesian monetary rules seem designed for a world that existed a long time ago, when Keynes (1936, p. 376) supported the 'euthanasia of the rentier'. Wray (2007, p. 136) and Smithin (1996, p. 84) seem to follow Keynes in this regard. However, rentiers are no longer the coupon clippers of the 19th and early 20th centuries. Today the rich own stocks, and benefit greatly from low interest rates that push up stock prices. There are ways to euthanize today's rich, but cutting interest rates won't do the trick. Instead, rate cuts will push up stock prices and increase inequality. Rather than relying on monetary policy to generate greater equality, we need fiscal policy — a progressive individual income tax system, high corporate income tax rates, and high taxes on inheritances.

6. The Case Against Central Banks Dealing with Inequality

We have seen that theoretical arguments and empirical studies regarding the impact of monetary policy on inequality are inconclusive and the post-Keynesian case for monetary policy rules is flawed. Central bank policy can increase incomes and wealth for some people, but these income changes do *not* follow a neat linear path where (as central banks lower rates) incomes rise but the rise diminishes with increasing income (or wealth) levels. To the extent that monetary policy can improve income distribution, it requires higher interest rates to reduce asset prices, which will lead to slower economic growth, higher unemployment, and worsening economic circumstances for those at the bottom of the distribution. The cure here may be worse than the disease. On the other hand, hoping that central banks can reduce inequality by keeping interest rates low, or following some monetary policy rule, is a false hope, given the empirical evidence summarized in the previous section.

We close with a few more arguments against having central banks try to deal with the problem of inequality, and the case for using fiscal policy to deal with inequality.

Central banks can do little to remedy inequality stemming from greater monopoly power or supply-side problems. Interest rate hikes won't reduce monopoly power. They also can't remedy supply-side problems by producing more grain (to make up for the losses due to the war in Ukraine); and, unlike Aladdin, central bankers can't rub some money and magically create more workers (to make up for the losses due to covid). They can't do anything about globalization, a slowdown in educational achievement, or regressive tax policy.

Second, there is Tinbergen's (1952) problem — two policy objectives require two tools. Central banks already have several objectives (controlling inflation and ensuring financial stability, and for some countries controlling unemployment) and two main tools (changing interest rates and changing bank regulations). Regulation can promote financial stability, leaving one tool to deal with other policy goals. Problems become greater if inequality gets added as a policy objective for central banks. In contrast, fiscal policy has many tools at its disposal to impact income distribution. While taxes are cut for the poor and middle class, tax rates on capital gains, interest, and dividends can be raised, and top marginal income tax rates can be increased on both individual and corporate income taxes (see Zorn and Pressman 2020). Also, estate taxes can be increased, limiting the transfer of large wealth to the next generation and giving children of the very wealthy great advantages over others. It is hard to see central banks doing anything similar to impact inequality.

One way around this problem would have central banks make direct payments to individuals, something like dropping 'helicopter money' on the economy (Bernanke 2016; Sims 2016). Buetzer (2022) argues that on distributional matters this is better than QE, which increases asset prices, and the wealth (and income) of the rich.

While correct, this solution runs into a third problem with using monetary policy to impact distribution — legal and political issues. Central banks were established to deal with inflation, and in some cases (like the US) unemployment also. Nowhere have they been given mandates to deal with inequality. Buetzer (2022, p. 44) himself notes that this approach has no 'clear and unambiguous legal foundation'. And it is unlikely to get one in the near future. Politicians want credit if people are happy. When unemployment rises, tax cuts and spending increases give politicians the credit rather than central bankers. On the other hand, politicians prefer to have central bankers take away the proverbial punch bowl when spending needs to be reduced and have them take the blame when unemployment rises. But taking the punch bowl away from everyone is different than directly taking drinks away from some people and giving them to others. This is a political decision for the legislative branch of government, including how much redistribution there should be and the acceptable levels of inequality and redistribution for the nation. These decisions should be made by elected representatives of the people. Any orchestrated change in income distribution is a political act and should be performed by politicians subject to recall by the voters.

The key takeaways from this paper are that monetary policy has an uncertain and small impact on income distribution, that its impact differs based on the measure of income distribution, and that dealing with distributional issues is not the job of central bankers. Nonetheless, the distributional impact of monetary policy needs to be understood better. This is research that central banks should undertake, and such an undertaking would be most welcomed. But this is very different from using monetary policy to change income distribution.

To end on a positive note, there are better alternatives. Rather than devising monetary policy rules, we can push for more diverse voices on the governing board of central banks — not only voices that represent labor and the indebted but also more liberal voices. The Fed has had a few such voices in the past. Some names that come to mind are Alan Blinder, Ed Gramlich and Janet Yellen. Gramlich, in particular, deserves kudos. In the mid-2000s he was writing to Fed Chair Greenspan about a housing bubble and the severe economic consequences if it were allowed to continue. He even wrote a book on his deathbed expressing his fears about this (Gramlich 2007). Had there been more Gramliches on the Fed at the time, we may not have had to go through the Great Recession and its negative distributional consequences. With more Gramliches on the Fed now, we might have better monetary policies and a more equal distribution of income.

Acknowledgements

This paper was presented at a conference on Central Banks and Inequality, held in Toronto in September 2022. The author thanks the conference participants for their questions and comments, and also the journal referees for their comments on an earlier version of this paper.

Disclosure Statement

No potential conflict of interest was reported by the author(s).

References

Alderson, A., and F. Nielsen. 2002. 'Globalization and the Great U-Turn: Income Inequality Trends in 16 OECD Countries.' *American Journal of Sociology* 107: 1244–1299.

Alexiou, A., E. Transchanas, and S. Vogiazas. 2022. 'Inequality and Financialization: A Not So Straightforward Relationship.' *Journal of Economic Studies* 49: 95–111.

Alfani, G. 2021. 'Economic Inequality in Preindustrial Times: Europe and Beyond.' *Journal of Economic Literature* 59: 3–44.

Amberg, N., T. Jansson, M. Klein, and A. Picco. 2021. 'Five Facts About the Distributional Income Effects of Monetary Policy.' Sveriges Riksbank Working Paper No. 403.

Andersen, A., N. Johannesen, M. Jørgensen, and J.-L. Peydró. 2020. 'Monetary Policy and Inequality.' CEPR Working Paper DP15599.

Aspromourgos, T. 2011. 'Can (and Should) Monetary Policy Pursue a Zero Real Interest Rate, Permanently?' *Metroeconomica* 64: 635–655.

Atkinson, A. 2008. *The Changing Distribution of Earnings in OECD Countries.* New York: Oxford University Press.

Baccaro, L. 2011. 'Labor, Globalization and Inequality: Are Trade Unions Still Redistributive?' *Research in the Sociology of Work* 22: 213–284.

Bartels, R. 2008. *Unequal Democracy: The Political Economy of the New Gilded Age.* Princeton, NJ: Princeton University Press.

Bernanke, B. 2015. 'Monetary Policy and Inequality.' https://www.brookings.edu/blog/ben-bernanke/2015/06/01/monetary-policy-and-inequality/.

Bernanke, B. 2016. 'What Tools Does the Fed Have Left? Part 3: Helicopter Money.' https://www.brookings.edu/articles/what-tools-does-the-fed-have-left-part-3-helicopter-money/.

Bernanke, B. 2020. 'The New Tools of Monetary Policy.' *American Economic Review* 110: 943–983.

Bernanke, B., and K. Kuttner. 2005. 'What Explains the Stock Market's Reaction to Federal Reserve Policy?' *Journal of Finance* 60: 1221–1257.

Blinder, A. 2013. *After the Music Stopped: The Financial Crisis, the Response, and the Work Ahead.* New York: Penguin.

Bloom, M. 1999. 'The Performance Effects of Pay Dispersion on Individuals and Organizations.' *Academy of Management Journal* 42: 25–40.

Bloom, M., and J. Michel. 2002. 'The Relationships Among Organizational Context, Pay Dispersion, and Managerial Turnover.' *Academy of Management Journal* 45: 33–42.

von Böhm-Bawerk, E. 1889[2008]. *Capital and Interest.* Vol. 2. Gloucestershire: Dodo Press.

Boix, C. 2010. 'Origins and Persistence of Economic Inequality.' *Annual Review of Political Science* 13: 489–516.

Bonifacio, V., L. Brandao-Marques, N. Budina, B. Csonto, C. Fratto, P. Engler, D. Furceri, D. Igan, R. Mano, M. Narita, M. Omoev, G. K. Pasricha, and H. Poirson. 2021. 'Distributional Effects of Monetary Policy.' IMF Working Paper WP/21/2021.

Boskin Commission. 1996. *Final Report of the Advisory Commission to Study the Consumer Price Index.* Washington, DC: Government Printing Office.

Bound, J., and G. Johnson. 1992. 'Changes in the Structure of Wages in the 1980s: An Evaluation of Alternative Explanations.' *American Economic Review* 82: 371–392.

Brynjolfsson, E., and A. McAfee. 2012. *Race against the Machine: How the Digital Revolution is Accelerating Innovation, Driving Productivity, and Irreversibly Transforming Employment and the Economy.* Aventura, FL: Digital Frontier Press.

Brynjolfsson, E., and A. McAfee. 2014. *The Second Machine Age: Work, Progress, and Prosperity in a Time of Brilliant Technologies.* New York: W.W. Norton.

Buetzer, S. 2022. 'Advancing the Monetary Policy Toolkit Through Outright Transfers.' IMF Working Paper WP/22/87.

Bundick, B., and A. Smith. 2022. 'Evaluating Quantitative Easing: The Importance of Accounting for Forward Guidance.' *Economic Review*, Federal Reserve Bank of Kansas City, 3rd Quarter: 5–20.

Card, D., and A. Krueger. 1994. 'Minimum Wages and Employment: A Case Study of the Fast-Food Industry in New Jersey and Pennsylvania.' *American Economic Review* 84: 772–793.

Carpantier, J.-F., J. Olivera, and P. van Kerm. 2016. 'Macroprudential Policy and Household Wealth Inequality.' Ku Leuven, Department of Economics, Discussion Paper DPS17.06.

Carstens, A. 2021. 'Central Banks and Inequality.' Bank for International Settlements. https://www.bis.org/speeches/sp210506.htm.

Caselli, F. 1999. 'Technological Revolutions.' *American Economic Review* 89: 78–102.

Colciago, A., A. Samarina, and J. de Haan. 2018. 'Central Bank Policies and Income and Wealth Inequality: A Survey.' De Nederlandsche Bank NV, Working Paper No. 594.

Cowherd, D., and D. Levine. 1992. 'Product Quality and Pay Equity Between Lower-Level Employees and Top Management: An Investigation of Distributive Justice Theory.' *Administrative Science Quarterly* 37: 302–320.

Dietsch, P., F. Claveau, and C. Fontan. 2018. *Do Central Banks Serve the People?* Cambridge, UK: Polity Press.

Domanski, D., M. Scatigna, and A. Zabai. 2016. 'Wealth Inequality and Monetary Policy.' *BS Quarterly Review* March: 45–64.

Draghi, M. 2016. 'Stability, Equity and Monetary Policy.' 2nd DIW Europe Lecture, Berlin, October 25.

Epstein, G. 2001. *Financialization, Rentier Interests, and Central Bank Policy*. Amherst, MA: Department of Economics, University of Massachusetts.

Freeman, R., and J. Medoff. 1984. *What Do Unions Do?* New York: Basic Books.

Friedman, T. 2005. *The World Is Flat*. New York: Farrar, Straus & Giroux.

Frost, J., and R. van Stralen. 2016. 'Macroprudential Policy and Income Inequality.' Unpublished Paper.

Gabriel, S., and C. Lutz. 2017. 'The Impact of Unconventional Monetary Policy on Real Estate Markets.' https://ssrn.com/abstract=2493873.

Galbraith, J. 2012. *Inequality and Instability: A Study of the World Economy Just Before the Great Crisis*. Oxford: Oxford University Press.

Gilens, M. 2014. *Affluence and Influence: Economic Inequality and Political Power in America*. Princeton, NJ: Princeton University Press.

Gnos, C., and L.-P. Rochon. 2007. 'The New Consensus and Post-Keynesian Interest Rate Policy.' *Review of Political Economy* 17: 369–386.

Goldin, C., and L. Katz. 2010. *The Race Between Education and Technology*. Cambridge, MA: Harvard University Press.

Gornemann, N., K. Kuester, and M. Nakajima. 2016. 'Doves for the Rich, Hawks for the Poor? Distributional Consequences of Monetary Policy.' International Finance Discussion Paper No. 1167.

Gramlich, E. 2007. *Subprime Mortgages: America's Latest Boom and Bust*. Washington, DC: Urban Institute Press.

Greenwald, D., M. Leombroni, H. Lustig, and S. van Nieuwerburg. 2021. 'Financial and Total Wealth Inequality with Declining Interest Rates.' NBER Working Paper No. 28613.

Greider, W. 1987. *Secrets of the Temple*. New York: Simon & Schuster.

Gürkaynak, R., B. Sack, and E. Swanson. 2005. 'Do Actions Speak Louder Than Words? The Response of Asset Prices to Monetary Policy Actions and Statements.' *International Journal of Central Banking* 1: 55–93.

Hansen, S. and J. Stein. 2015. 'Monetary Policy and Long-Term Real Rates.' *Journal of Financial Economics* 115: 429–448.

Harcourt, G. 1972. *Some Cambridge Controversies in the Theory of Capital*. Cambridge: Cambridge University Press.

Haskel, J., R. Lawrence, E. Leamer, and M. Slaughter. 2012. 'Globalization and U.S. Wages: Modifying Classic Theory to Explain Recent Facts.' *Journal of Economic Perspectives* 26: 119–140.

Hein, E., and E. Stockhammer. 2010. 'Macroeconomic Policy Mix, Employment and Inflation in a Post-Keynesian Alternative to the New Consensus Model.' *Review of Political Economy* 22: 317–354.

Howell, D. 1994. 'The Collapse of Low-Skill Male Earnings in the 1980s: Skill Mismatch of Shifting Wage Norms?' Levy Institute Working Paper 105.

Kappes, S. 2023. 'Monetary Policy and Personal Income Distribution: A Survey of the Empirical Literature.' *Review of Political Economy* 35: 211–230.

Keynes, J. M. 1936. *The General Theory of Employment, Interest and Money*. London: Macmillan.

Kriesler, P., and M. Lavoie. 2007. 'The New Consensus on Monetary Policy and Its Post-Keynesian Critique.' *Review of Political Economy* 19: 387–404.

Lavoie, M. 1992. *Foundations of Post Keynesian Economic Analysis*. Aldershot: Edward Elgar.

Lavoie, M., and M. Seccareccia. 1999. 'Fair Interest Rates.' In *Encyclopedia of Political Economy*, Vol. 1, edited by P. O'Hara. London: Routledge.

Lavoie, M., and M. Seccareccia. 2019. 'Macroeconomics and Natural Rates: Some Reflections on Pasinetti's Fair Rate of Interest.' *Bulletin of Political Economy* 13: 139–165.

Lavoie, M., and M. Seccareccia. 2021. 'Going Beyond the Targeting Mantra: A Dual Mandate.' Unpublished Paper, McGill University.

Lazonick, W. 2009. *Sustainable Prosperity in the New Economy?* Kalamazoo, MI: Upjohn Institute for Employment Research.

Lazonick, W. 2014. 'Profits Without Prosperity.' *Harvard Business Review* 92: 47–55.

Leamer, E. 2007. 'A Flat World, A Level Playing Field, A Small World After All, or None of the Above, A Review of Thomas L. Friedman's The World is Flat.' *Journal of Economic Literature* 45: 83–126.

Lee, F. 1998. *Post Keynesian Price Theory*. Cambridge: Cambridge University Press.

Lenza, M., and J. Slacalek. 2021. 'How Does Monetary Policy Affect Income and Wealth Inequality? Evidence from Quantitative Easing in the Euro Area.' Mimeo, European Central Bank.

Levy, F., and R. Murnane. 1992. 'US Earnings Levels and Earnings Inequality: A Review of Recent Trends and Proposed Explanations.' *Journal of Economic Literature* 30: 1333–1381.

Mäki-Fränti, P., A. Silvo, A. Guylan, and J. Kilponen. 2022. 'Monetary Policy and Inequality: The Finnish Case.' Bank of Finland Discussion Papers 3/2022.

Meh, C., J. Rios-Rull, and Y. Terajima. 2010. 'Aggregate and Welfare Effects of Redistribution of Wealth Under Inflation and Price-Level Targeting.' *Journal of Monetary Economics* 57: 637–652.

Metcalfe, J. S. 1997. 'The Evolutionary Explanation of Total Factor Productivity Growth: Macro Measurement and Micro Process.' *Revue d'Économie Industrielle* 80: 93–114.

Moller, S., D. Bradley, E. Huber, F. Nielson, and J. Stephens. 2003. 'Determinants of Relative Poverty in Advanced Capitalist Democracies.' *American Sociological Review* 68: 22–51.

Muelibauer, J. 2014. 'Combatting Eurozone Deflation: QE for the People.' VOX, CEPR. https://voxeu.org/article/combatting-eurozone-deflation-qe-people.

Nozick, R. 1974. *Anarchy, State and Utopia*. New York: Basic Books.

OECD. 2015. *The Labour Share in G20 Economies*. Unpublished Paper. Paris: OECD.

Palley, T. 2008. 'Financialization: What It Is and Why It Matters.' IMK Working Paper, No. 04/2008.

Pasinetti, L. 1980–81. 'The Rate of Interest and the Distribution of Income in a Pure Labor Economy.' *Journal of Post Keynesian Economics* 3: 170–182.

Pasinetti, L. 1981. *Structural Change and Economic Growth*. Cambridge: Cambridge University Press.

Piketty, T. 2014. *Capital in the Twenty-First Century*. Cambridge, MA: Harvard University Press.

Piketty, T. 2020. *Capital and Ideology*. Cambridge, MA: Harvard University Press.

Pressman, S. 2016. *Understanding Piketty's Capital in the Twenty-First Century*. London: Routledge.

Pressman, S., and R. Scott. 2009. 'Consumer Debt and the Measurement of Poverty and Inequality in the US.' *Review of Social Economy* 47: 127–146.

Pressman, S., and R. Scott. 2022. 'A Refundable Tax Credit for Children: Its Impact on Poverty, Inequality and Household Debt.' *Journal of Post Keynesian Economics* 45: 536–557.

Rawls, J. 1971. *A Theory of Justice*. Cambridge, MA: Harvard University Press.

Ricardo, D. 1819[1951]. *Principles of Political Economy and Taxation, The Works and Correspondence of David Ricardo*, Vol. 1, edited by P. Sraffa. Cambridge: Cambridge University Press.

Richardson, J. 1995. 'Income Inequality and Trade: How to Think, What to Conclude.' *Journal of Economic Perspectives* 9: 33–55.

Rochon, L.-P. 2021. 'The Inherent Biases of Monetary Policy.' In *Monetary and Budgetary Policy: Before and After the Global Crisis 2020*, edited by A. Giron. Mexico: Universidad Nacional Autónoma de México.

Rochon, L.-P., and M. Setterfield. 2008. 'The Political Economy of Interest-Rate Setting, Inflation, and Income Distribution.' *International Journal of Political Economy* 37: 5–25.

Rochon, L.-P., and M. Seccareccia. 2021. 'A Primer on Monetary Policy and Income Distribution: A Heterodox Approach.' *Ensayos Económicos* 1: 5–25.

Saez, E., and G. Zucman. 2019. *The Triumph of Injustice*. New York: W.W. Norton.

Schlozman, K., H. Brady, and S. Verba. 2017. 'Growing Economic Inequality and Its (Partially) Political Roots.' *Religions* 8: article 97.

Seccareccia, M. 2017. 'Which Vested Interests Do Central Banks Really Serve? Understanding Central Bank Policy Since the Global Financial Crisis.' *Journal of Economic Issues* 51: 341–350.

Seccareccia, M. 2019. 'From the Age of Rentier Tranquility to the New Age of Deep Uncertainty: The Metamorphosis of Central Bank Policy in Modern Financialized Economies.' *Journal of Economic Issues* 53: 478–487.
Seccareccia, M. and M. Lavoie. 2016. 'Income Distribution, Rentiers, and their Role in the Capitalist Economy.' *International Journal of Political Economy* 43: 200–223.
Sen, A. 1982. 'Inequality of What?' In *Choice, Measurement and Welfare.* Cambridge, MA: MIT Press.
Setterfield, M. 2009. 'Macroeconomics Without the LM Curve: An Alternative View.' *Cambridge Journal of Economics* 33: 273–293.
Sims, C. 2016. 'Fiscal Policy, Monetary Policy, and Central Bank Independence.' In *Designing Resilient Monetary Policy Frameworks for the Future,* 313–325. Kansas City: Federal Reserve Bank of Kansas City.
Smithin, J. 1996. *Macroeconomic Policy and the Future of Capitalism: The Revenge of the Rentiers.* Aldershot: Edward Elgar.
Smithin, J. 2007. 'A Real Interest Rate Rule for Monetary Policy?' *Journal of Post Keynesian Economics* 30: 101–118.
Smithin, J. 2018. *Rethinking the Theory of Money, Credit, and Macroeconomics: A New Statement for the 21st Century.* Latham, MD: Rowman & Littlefield.
Smithin, J. 2020. 'Interest Rates, Income Distribution and the Monetary Policy Transmission Mechanism under Endogenous Money: What Have We Learned 30 Years on from the Horizontalists and the Verticalists?' *European Journal of Economics and Economic Policies: Intervention* 17: 381–398.
Starr, E., J. Frake, and R. Agarwal. 2019. 'Mobility Constraint Externalities.' *Organization Science* 30: 961–980.
Starr, E., J. Prescott, and N. Bishara. 2017. 'Noncompetes in the U.S. Labor Force.' https://extranet.sioe.org/uploads/isnie2015/starr_prescott_bishara.pdf.
Stiglitz, J. 2015. 'New Theoretical Perspectives on the Distribution of Income and Wealth Among Individuals: Part I. The Wealth Residual.' NBER Working Paper 21189.
Task Force on Inequality and American Democracy. 2004. 'American Democracy in an Age of Rising Inequality.' *Perspectives on Politics* 2: 651–666.
Taylor, J. 1993. 'Discretion Versus Policy Rules in Practice.' *Carnegie-Rochester Conference Series on Public Policy* 39: 195–214.
Tinbergen, J. 1952. *On the Theory of Economic Policy.* Amsterdam: North Holland.
Tinbergen, J. 1975. *Income Distribution: Analysis and Policies.* Amsterdam: North Holland.
Tymoigne, E. 2009. *Central Banking, Asset Prices and Financial Fragility.* London: Routledge.
Venables, A. 2009. 'Rethinking Economic Growth in a Globalizing World: An Economic Geography.' *African Development Review* 12: 331–351.
Villarreal, F. 2014. 'Monetary Policy and Inequality in Mexico.' MPRA Paper No. 84588.
von Wachter, T., J. Song, and J. Manchester. 2009. 'Long-Term Earnings Losses due to Mass Layoffs During the 1982 Recession: An Analysis using US Administrative Data from 1974 to 2004.' Unpublished Paper, Columbia University.
Wolff, E. 2017. *A Century of Wealth in America.* Cambridge, MA: Harvard University Press.
Wood, A. 1994. *North-South Trade, Employment and Inequality: Changing Fortunes in a Skill Driven World.* Oxford: Clarendon Press.
Wray, L. R. 1998. *Understanding Modern Money.* Cheltenham: Edward Elgar.
Wray, L. R. 2007. 'A Post Keynesian View of Central Bank Independence, Policy Targets, and the Rules Versus Discretion Debate.' *Journal of Post Keynesian Economics* 30: 119–141.
Zorn, N., and S. Pressman. 2020. 'A Consensus on Taxing the Rich? Comparing Mainstream Economics, Piketty and Post-Keynesian Economics.' *International Journal of Political Economy* 49: 43–61.

Monetary Policy and the Gender and Racial Employment Dynamics in Brazil

Patricia Couto and Clara Brenck

ABSTRACT

Monetary policy has been historically concerned with controlling inflation, using the interest rate as its main tool. However, such policies are not gender- or race-neutral. This paper explores econometrically the effect of changes in the interest rate for female and black employment creation in Brazil. We conducted a fixed effects analysis for 13 states between 2012 and 2021 to estimate the effects of changes in interest rates on unemployment, separating it by gender and race. Our results show that the increase in the real interest rate has a positive effect on the relative unemployment of black men to white men, no effect on the relative unemployment of black women to white men, and a negative effect on the relative unemployment of white women to white men. These effects are intensified in regions where the black share of the population is lower. This paper contributes to understanding the challenges to closing gender and racial gaps, particularly in developing economies. We conclude that social stratification, if not considered, can lead to misleading policies that perpetuate unequal socioeconomic outcomes.

1. Introduction

In the current economic scenario, where inflation rates have been rising worldwide, monetary policy has become an object of research and intense debate. Many Central Banks apply an inflation-targeting regime, with the interest rate as the main policy instrument. The reasoning behind such a strategy starts from the assumption that inflation occurs due to demand pressures. In this way, changes in interest rates negatively affect demand, thus alleviating inflationary pressures. The adverse effect of this strategy is the increase in the unemployment rate, as theorized in a Phillips Curve approach.

In this context, empirical studies have shown that changes in the basic rate of interest have different impacts on different social groups (Zavodny and Zha 2000; Thorbecke 2001; Braunstein and Heintz 2008; Seguino and Heintz 2012). Depending on the productive structure, composition of the labor market, and income distribution, gender and race minorities are disproportionately affected by contractionary monetary policy. One of the main channels through which this occurs is the labor market: those social groups are concentrated in lower occupations and sectors that are more sensitive to changes in interest rates. In other words, since they are in vulnerable positions in the labor market, monetary policy may not be gender or racial-neutral.

Hence, within a framework that highlights distributive impacts, gender and race become indispensable in the debate for better strategies for economic policy. However, the monetary policy impact on social stratification is little explored. The majority of those who do it focus on developed economies (for the US, see Zavodny and Zha 2000; Thorbecke 2001; Seguino and Heintz 2012). The few works that focus on developing economies aggregate them in a panel data set, dismissing important dynamics of individual countries (Braunstein and Heintz 2008).

Brazil implemented inflation targeting in 1999 with the primary objective of containing price volatility and its adverse effects, considered the main challenge in the economic scenario of that period. Since then and in line with the practices of central banks in the world, the monetary policy in Brazil has inflation control as its primary objective and considers the basic rate of interest as its main tool (Barbosa-Filho 2015). In a country like Brazil, marked by its high inequality rates and where women represent 51 per cent and blacks 54 per cent of the population, including such variables when studying the impact of monetary policy is needed. The Brazilian context also includes important regional characteristics intrinsically connected to its racial and social inequality. Hence, a federal-level policy can exacerbate the already high level of inequality if regional differences are not considered.

In this paper, we investigate how the cost of interest rate hikes, the main policy instrument in combating inflation according to the Brazilian Central Bank, is distributed in the labor market among blacks and women relative to white men. It is important to clarify that it is not the purpose of this paper to argue whether the Central Bank's framework is appropriate — or to suggest alternative frameworks — but actually to evaluate the effects of that instrument on gender and racial unemployment.

To our knowledge, this is the first paper to do such an investigation for a peripheral country, so it also contributes to understanding the effects of interest rate changes in different social groups in the context of a developing economy. Comprehending these dynamics is essential for improving economic policy strategies. This paper is organized into five more sections in addition to this introductory one. The next section presents a brief review of the literature. In the third section, we present the empirical strategy and data used in the research. The fourth section presents the results, followed by the fifth section on robustness checks. In the last section, we discuss the implications of the results for monetary policy and inequality and conclude the paper.

2. Literature Review

The effects of monetary policy, especially interest rate policy, on inequality have received much attention recently. Kappes 2023 surveys the literature on monetary policy and income inequality and concludes that there is sufficient evidence that increases in interest rates have statistically significant effects on income distribution and that those effects are not temporary. The author also discusses the different transmission channels for such effects. Those include interest payments, labor incomes, financial wealth, housing wealth, and pension wealth. Changes in interest rates can directly affect the income of those who receive interest payments but also have indirect effects on income inequality through the labor market since an increase in interest rates tends to increase unemployment — and hence affect labor income. In addition to that, changes in the rate of interest mean changes in the value of assets, affecting wealth distribution.

As for gender and race inequality, however, the effect on employment has been the most studied in the literature. The disproportionate impact is caused by the unequal increase in unemployment — one of the main costs of controlling inflation via interest rate hikes. The lower rungs of the labor market ladder are more affected by contractionary monetary policies due to a greater labor supply elasticity for low-skilled workers (Blanchard 1995; Blanchard and Katz 1997).

Investigating the different impacts of monetary policy on unemployment rates in the United States, Abell 1991 concluded that the labor market is segregated in a way that favors white men during periods of contractionary monetary policies. Thorbecke 2001 found similar results, showing that African-American and Latino unemployment is 50 per cent to 90 per cent higher than white unemployment during periods of deflationary policies. Research later complemented by Carpenter and Rodgers 2004 highlighted that young black people with low education are the most affected by the increase in unemployment. Thorbecke 2001 also stresses that the explanation for the disproportionate impact in different social groups is due to the different sectoral impacts on the economy. The author estimates the impacts of contractionary monetary policies by sector and concludes that small business, construction industry, and durable goods sectors are more negatively affected. The coincident sectoral and racial segregation in the workforce then explains the results.

Seguino and Heintz 2012 estimate the impact of changes in interest rates on the unemployment of blacks and women relative to white men in the United States. The authors conclude that the effects vary according to the density of the black population in each US state and that the cost of policies to combat inflation is unevenly distributed among workers, negatively affecting more black women and black men, followed by white women and white men. In contrast to the results found for the US economy, the analysis conducted by Takhtamanova and Sierminska 2009 with nine OECD countries found no evidence of gender differences in unemployment rates associated with changes in interest rates.

To contribute to understanding the impact on the labor market by gender in developing countries, Braunstein and Heintz 2008 analyzed 17 low- and middle-income countries, including Brazil, and concluded that the rate of employment of women relative to men declines after episodes of contractionary monetary policy. During periods of expansionary monetary policies, there is no significant effect on women's employment compared to men. They also show that the negative effect could be reversed by maintaining a competitive exchange rate due to the greater employability of women in durable goods industries, which benefit from exchange rate devaluations.

In this connection, the literature shows that the sectoral composition is also an important channel in which the exchange rate affects gender and race inequality. Blecker and Seguino 2002, for example, develop a theoretical model where women are a source of cheap labor for the export sector in Semi-Industrialized Economies (SIE). Thus a devaluation would boost exports and increase female employment. Nonetheless, the exchange rate may also affect inflation (Ha, Stocker, and Yilmazkuday 2020), especially in countries that need to import capital goods, such as Brazil, possibly offsetting the effect found by the authors.

Given the importance of the exchange rate in affecting unemployment, especially in the export sector, Munyo and Rossi 2015 analyzed the dynamics of gender employment and domestic violence with changes in the exchange rate in Uruguay. The authors found a highly significant impact on domestic violence associated with an increased exchange rate, especially in regions where men are more allocated in tradable sectors. This is because an undervalued exchange rate affects employment in the tradable sector, affecting women's wages and bargaining power inside the home, then increasing domestic violence.

Erten and Metzger 2019 also contributed to this analysis by exploring the impact of changes in the exchange rate on women's labor force participation with a panel data set of 103 countries. The authors found no association in developed countries. Still, for developing countries at the early stages of development, an undervalued currency reduced the gender gap due to the expansion of female-dominated labor-intensive industries. Hence, they highlight the importance of the country's sectoral composition and stages of development where a currency undervaluation can reduce women's labor force participation by allocating resources to male-dominated technological-intensive industries — as in the East Asia region (Kucera and Tejani 2014; Tejani and Milberg 2016; Erten and Metzger 2019).

The exchange rate stands out as an important variable for developing economies, as it affects not only unemployment but also inflation itself. Changes in the interest rate influence the exchange rate by affecting capital flows, for example, which could have an additional effect on prices due to higher input costs. Hence, even though an inflation-targeting regime does not allow a fixed exchange rate, many monetary authorities in developing economies still intervene in the exchange rate market (Freddo 2019; Ribeiro, McCombie, and Lima 2017; Kaltenbrunner and Painceira 2017). Freddo 2019 shows that, in the case of Brazil, Chile and Colombia, most of the episodes where the target was not met happened at a time of strong currency volatility. Freddo 2019 therefore argues that the adoption of an inflation-targeting regime in the 1990s does not mean that the monetary authorities stopped intervening in the Foreign Exchange (FX) market — what became known as the 'dirty floating' regime. The author concludes that the exchange rate is an important measure for the conduction of monetary policy in Latin America.

3. Empirical Strategy

To address the effects of changes in the real interest rate on gender and racial unemployment, our empirical strategy was inspired by Seguino and Heintz 2012. We perform a fixed effects model with panel data for 13 Brazilian states. The fixed effects model considers regional differences between states that are constant over time and not observed in the data but can still affect outcomes, such as gender and racial norms. As we expect these unobserved variables to be correlated with some of the explanatory variables, the fixed effect model is our preferred specification. However, we also estimate random effects and pooled ordinary least squares (Pooled OLS) models.

We explore how the cost of increasing unemployment following a contractionary monetary policy, is distributed between different social groups. We conduct a regression model where we measure the effects of changes in the real rate of interest on our dependent variable: the relative unemployment rate of our group of interest (black women, black men, or white women) to white men. Gender and race estimates were carried out separately to assess better the impact of monetary policies on those different social groups.

Changes in the basic interest rate — the Selic rate in the Brazilian case– influence economic variables, mainly prices and output. According to the new consensus model, which is behind the inflation-targeting regime adopted in Brazil, the most common transmission mechanism is through aggregate demand effects, as consumption and investment decisions depend on the real rate of interest.[1] In this way, an increase in the real interest rate decreases aggregate demand, alleviating inflation but with the adverse effect of rising unemployment.

In the context of developing economies, the real rate of interest also affects exchange rates. As mentioned previously, an increase in interest rates tends to attract capital flows, appreciating the domestic currency and making imports cheaper — which also reduces price pressures if those imported goods are used as inputs for production. In addition to that, currency appreciation reduces exports and, consequently, aggregate demand. Hence, differently from Seguino and Heintz 2012, we use the exchange rate as a control variable in the model due to its importance in affecting inflation and the interest rate policy itself in the context of Brazil (Freddo 2019). In addition to the exchange rate, we include the labor force participation ratio between our group of interest (black men, black women, and white women) to white men, the state level growth rate and the black labor share of the economy as control variables.

We follow Seguino and Heintz 2012 and include the labor force participation rate as an explanatory variable to capture the possible bias of the unemployment rate as conventionally measured. This leads to a possible endogeneity problem, as the labor force is correlated with unemployment. However, as Seguino and Heintz 2012 argue, those variables are inversely correlated, which would lead to a lower-bound estimate of the effect on unemployment.

There's also a possibility of reverse causality between changes in the unemployment rate and the interest rate. Central Banks could respond to changes in real economic activity and not only to inflation, for example. However, since our estimations consist of the unemployment gap between black men, black women, and white women, relative to white men, we find it harder for the Central Bank of Brazil to respond to those unemployment measures. To confirm, we pursue a Granger-causality test with unemployment and the Selic Rate. We find that the real Selic Rate is not Granger-caused by any of our dependent variables. The test results are in the Appendix in Table A.

[1]There is, however, empirical evidence showing that this may not be the case. Cynamon, Fazzari, and Setterfield 2013 discusses the lack of sensitivity of consumption to changes in interest ratesFazzari, Ferri, and Greenberg 2010; Sharpe and Suarez 2015 and Sharpe and Suarez 2021 also show that this can be extended to the case of industries: it is also hard to find evidence of a great sensitivity of investment to changes in interest rates. The purpose of our paper is not, however, to confirm or deny any of those theories. We intend to show the effect of the main monetary policy tool, as argued by the Brazilian Central Bank, on gender and race inequality.

Since the beginning of the 2000s, the Brazilian economy experienced a trajectory of strong expansionary fiscal policy until 2014, with increasing social spending and public investments. That trajectory was interrupted in 2015, and austerity policies took place (see Dweck, Tonon, and Krepsky 2018 and Chernavsky, Dweck, and Teixeira 2020). As fiscal policy influences economic activity, Dweck, Tonon, and Krepsky 2018 shows that 'if in 2015 the government maintained the same the level of public investment in real terms as in 2014, there would be demand for 0.9 million more occupations'. To control for any change in unemployment that is due to economic activity — including due to decisions on fiscal policy — and not related to interest rate changes, we include the growth rate at the state level.[2]

Finally, Seguino and Heintz 2012 shows that the black labor share of the population is significant in explaining differences in unemployment by race and gender. Seguino and Heintz 2012 mention two opposing theories that can explain the relevance of the Black Labor Share for this analysis: the contact theory and the threat theory. Contact theory argues that higher contact with blacks and Hispanics would induce lower discrimination by whites. On the contrary, threat theory suggests that a greater share of blacks in the population could 'intensify racialist group identity in response to whites' perceived threat to their group position'. For the Brazilian context, we expect this variable also to be relevant to the dynamics of unemployment by race and gender: the higher the Black Labor Share of the state, the lower the propensity for discrimination. Hence, we decided to follow their strategy and include the Black Labor Share in our estimations. We estimate, then, the following equation:

$$U^j_{i,t} = \beta_1 Real\ Selic_t + \beta_2 LFP^j_{i,t} + \beta_3 gr_{i,t} + \beta_4 BLSH_{i,t} + \beta_5 ER_{i,t} + \eta_i + \epsilon_{i,t} \qquad (1)$$

where j represents the group of interest used to construct the dependent variables (white women, black women, or black men), i represents the state, t the time, U is the dependent variable (the ratio of unemployment between the group of interest j to white men), *real Selic* is the economy's interest rate minus inflation, *LFP* is the relative labor force participation (also calculated as a ratio between the labor force participation of the group of interest j to white men), *gr* is the rate of growth in output in each state, *BLSH* is the black labor share in each state, *ER* is the exchange rate (in log differences[3]), η is the fixed effect per state, and ε is the error term, assumed to be independent and identically distributed (iid).

After conducting the estimations with all available states, we separated them into two groups: (i) North and Northeast; and (ii) South, Southeast and Midwest, given the segregation of the Brazilian economic and racial structures. Figure 1 shows the share of the population by race and gender for each Brazilian state, separated by regions, in the 4th quarter of 2021. The contrast of racial composition in Brazil by regions becomes clear: black men and black women sum up to 70 per cent of the labor share in the

[2]Given the strong effect of public investment in employment found by Dweck, Tonon, and Krepsky 2018, we re-estimated the model including quarterly public investment (taken from historical series of treasury results by 'Tesouro Transparente') as a control variable, and the results did not change remarkably (signs and significance of coefficients continued the same). Because of that and to avoid high colinearity between public investment and the economic activity variable we prefer the model without the public investment variable.

[3]We reproduce these estimations with the exchange rate in level, but the results don't change significantly. We decided to keep it in log differences because the exchange rate series has a unit root, so we avoid bias.

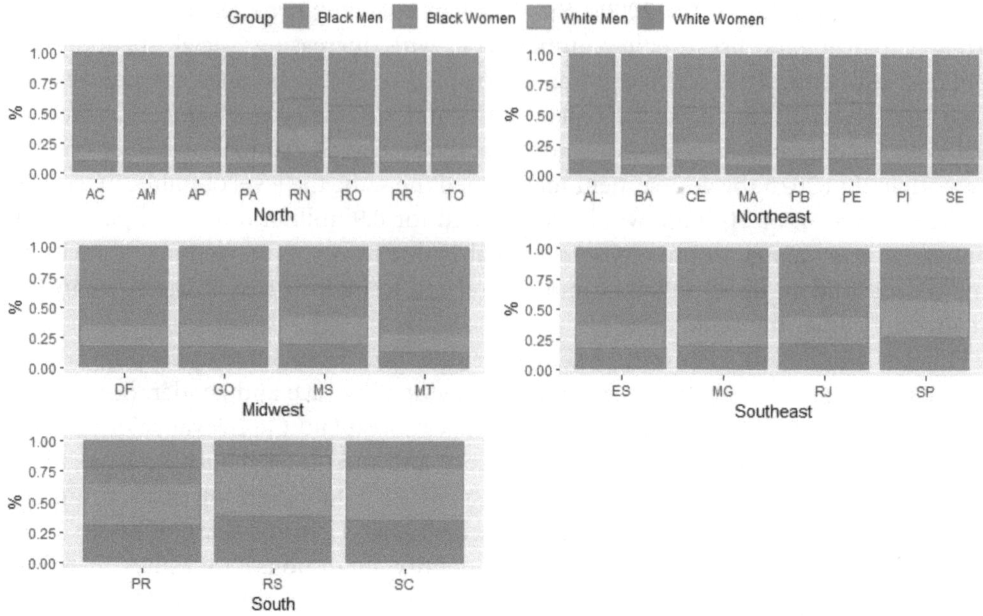

Figure 1. Brazilian states' Gender and Racial composition, separated by region, 4th quarter of 2021. Source: PNADc.

North and Northeast, while the South, Southeast and Midwest have a lower black labor share — an average of 43 per cent, for the states used in this estimation. In this way, the effect of monetary policy on gender and race may vary significantly among regions.

In terms of economic structure, the Brazilian regions also vary considerably. The North and Northeast regions had 21.2 per cent and 23.4 per cent, respectively, of total employment allocated to agriculture. In comparison, the Southeast and South regions had 7.4 per cent and 13.4 per cent, respectively, occupied in agriculture in 2015 (IPEA 2015).

Sectoral occupation also varies by race and gender. As can be seen in Figure 2, data from PNADc shows that, in 2019, 14.5 per cent of employed black men are in agriculture, 18 per cent in trade, and 17.8 per cent in construction. For white men, 27.8 per cent are allocated to transportation and commerce, 16.2 per cent to industry, and 9.8 per cent to construction. In the case of women, they are mostly allocated to education, health and domestic services. From total white women employed, 22 per cent are in education and health, 9 per cent in domestic services, and 32 per cent in other services.[4] On the other hand, 18.5 per cent of black women are allocated to education and health, 17.5 per cent are to domestic services and 29.4 per cent to other services.

In addition to that, there is still no consensus on the regional impacts of monetary policy in Brazil (Araújo 2004; Bertanha and Haddad 2008; Silva, Afonso, and Rodrıguez-Fuentes 2010; Guimarães and Monteiro 2014). The Selic rate is defined at a national level and can have different regional consequences. Regions concentrating more on

[4]Other services include Information, communication and financial, real estate, professional and administrative activities, Accommodation and food and Public administration, defense and social security

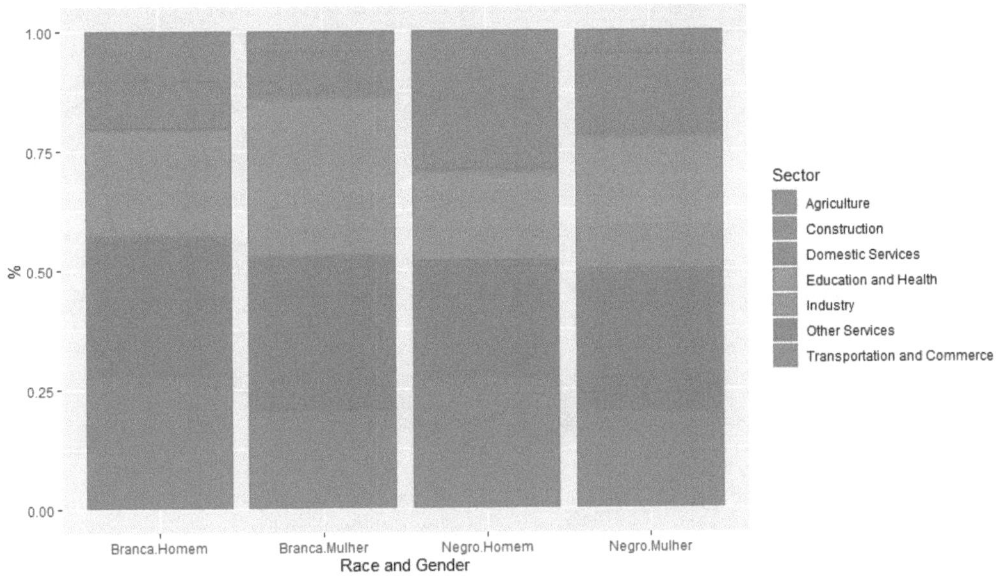

Figure 2. Sectoral Composition by Race and Gender in Brazil, first quarter of 2019. Source: PNADc.

interest-rate-sensitive industries, like construction and manufacturing, could be more affected by a contractionary monetary policy.

Hence, monetary policy effects by race can also reflect different regional effects. We hypothesize that blacks will be more negatively affected by contractionary monetary policy, but this effect will be lower in regions with a higher black population share. We also expect that white women will be the less affected group, compared to white men, since they are allocated to sectors that are not sensitive to the interest rate, like education and health.

3.1. Data

Our data consists of the period from the first quarter of 2012 to the last quarter of 2021 for 13 Brazilian states (Amazonas, Para, Pernambuco, Ceará, Bahia, Minas Gerais, São Paulo, Espirito Santo, Rio de Janeiro, Goiás, Paraná, Santa Catarina e Rio Grande do Sul). We used data from 13 of the 27 Brazilian states in our estimations due to the need for higher frequency data. Therefore, for economic activity data, we used the regional and national economic activity index (IBCR and IBC-Br) published by the Central Bank of Brazil but available only for those 13 states. We used the IBCR and IBC-Br rather than the GDP because the latter is only available annually at the state level, while the IBCR is available monthly. In addition, the IBCR provides an important distinction between regional and national economic dynamics. It is also the Brazilian government's main tool to develop the monetary policy strategy (BC 2018). These 13 states together corresponded to 85.5 per cent of the national GDP in 2019 and cover all five regions of Brazil.

To better access the impact of these variables at the state level, we follow Seguino and Heintz 2012 strategy and regress state IBCR growth on national IBC-Br growth data

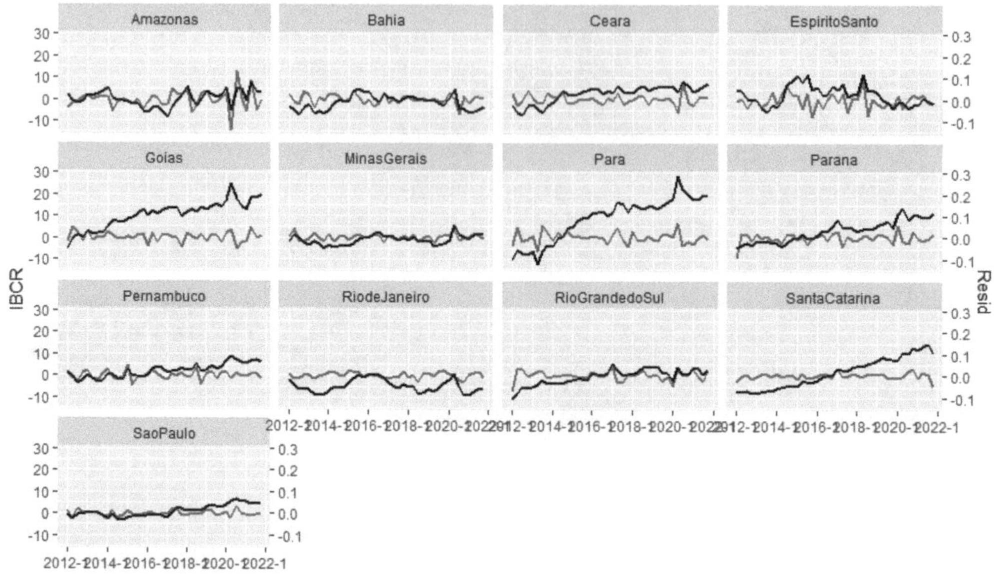

Figure 3. Quarterly IBCR state activity level (blue) and regression residuals (black) of state activity on national activity index, 2012–21. Source: Central Bank of Brazil and authors' estimations.

using a simple fixed-effect model. We use the residual of this regression as a regional activity or economic growth index. Figure 3 shows the original index and regression residuals after eliminating the national activity effect.

The time period was selected due to data availability. Unemployment and labor force participation rates disaggregated by gender and race were calculated directly from the main Brazilian household survey conducted by the Brazilian Institute of Geography and Statistics (IBGE): the National Continuous Household Sample Survey (PNADc), which started in 2012. The PNADc is a household survey conducted to produce quarterly indicators on the workforce and annual indicators on additional permanent topics (such as other forms of work, care economy and domestic work, and information and communication technology, among others). In this way, race and gender characteristics are self-reported. We used only two race categories (blacks[5] and whites) due to lack of sufficient observations from other racial categories, like indigenous. The survey asks the status of employment and, for those employed, a further question is asked on the condition of the occupation, with the alternatives being: employed in the private sector, domestic worker, employed in the public sector (including statutory and military servants), self-employed, and auxiliary family worker. In this way, informal workers are considered part of the employed population. The data used in our robustness checks on education and sectoral composition of employment were also taken from the PNADc.

Finally, the interest rate (Selic) and exchange rate data were downloaded directly from the Central Bank of Brazil website. The quarterly values of these monthly indices were obtained by the arithmetic mean of the three periods. We first collected data from the Broad Consumer Price Index (IPCA), taken from the Brazilian Institute of Geography

[5]We consider blacks the sum of those who reported being 'Pretos' (blacks) or 'Pardos' (browns).

and Statistics (IBGE) for inflation. As the Selic rate is reported in annual terms, we use annualized quarterly inflation to ensure consistency.[6]

4. Results

In this section, we present the estimation results. In each subsection, we present three tables: the first with the estimation considering all states, and the other two with the results for each subgroup of states. As previously mentioned, the racial dynamic in Brazil is related to regional characteristics, and hence separating the estimation into subgroups of states can provide a better understanding of how the monetary policy impacts gender and race.

There are three dependent variables for the estimations: the unemployment rate ratio between (i) black men to white men (BMWM); (ii) black women to white men (BWWM); and (iii) white women to white men (WWWM). The two first columns of each dependent variable group present the fixed effects estimation results. The second column includes the exchange rate as part of the explanatory variables (our preferred specification). Columns 3 (RE) and 4 (POLS) present the random effects and pooled OLS estimation results, respectively.

Table 1 provides the initial results with all 13 states. The coefficient associated with the real interest rate is positive and significant for the black men's and white men's relative unemployment rates. This means that an increase in the real interest rate is associated with an increase in the unemployment gap between black men and white men, as expected. The coefficient associated with black population share (BLSH) is significant only on the random effect and pooled OLS specification.

For the estimations for black women and white men's relative unemployment rate, only the coefficient associated with black population share (BLSH) is negative and significant. Hence, increases in the real interest rate seem to have no distinct effect on the unemployment of black women when compared to white men, and states with a higher share of blacks in their population would have a lower unemployment gap between black women and white men.

Finally, in the estimation of white women and white men's relative unemployment rate, the coefficient associated with the real interest rates is negative and significant. This result was surprising, as it means that a contractionary monetary policy would increase white men's unemployment more than white women's — i.e., reduce the gap. The coefficient associated with the black population share (BLSH) was also negative and significant, indicating that race characteristics can influence gender outcomes.

Tables 2 and 3 show the estimations separated by regions, with Table 2 showing the results for the North and Northeast regions, and Table 3 for the South, Southeast and Midwest.

The main results are maintained for the South, Southeast, and Midwest regions, with only the coefficient magnitudes changing. The coefficient associated with the real interest rates increases in magnitude for black men relative to white men and maintains its significance. This would suggest that the disproportional effect on black men, relative to

[6]To make the quarterly inflation rate in annual terms, we calculate the average price index (IPCA) for the quarter and then calculate the rate of change of this index to the same quarter of the previous year.

Table 1. Estimation for Black Men, Black Women and White Women relative to White Men — All 13 states.

	Black-men to White-men				Black-women to White-men				White-women to White-men			
	FE (1)	FE (2)	RE	POLS	FE (1)	FE (2)	RE	POLS	FE (1)	FE (2)	RE	POLS
(Intercept)			1.86***	1.31**			3.57***	2.00***			2.51***	1.68***
			(0.44)	(0.43)			(0.37)	(0.29)			(0.31)	(0.30)
Real Selic	0.93**	0.92**	0.89**	1.01**	−0.80	−0.85	−0.69	−0.27	−1.60***	−1.65***	−1.42***	−1.30**
	(0.30)	(0.30)	(0.30)	(0.38)	(0.47)	(0.46)	(0.47)	(0.57)	(0.35)	(0.34)	(0.35)	(0.39)
Growth	0.31	0.00	0.32	0.23	0.08	0.27	0.03	−0.12	−0.19	−0.13	−0.23	−0.35
	(0.49)	(0.50)	(0.49)	(0.62)	(0.78)	(0.80)	(0.78)	(0.97)	(0.58)	(0.59)	(0.59)	(0.67)
BLSH	−0.20	−0.65	−0.63**	−0.70***	−2.75***	−2.78**	−1.43***	−0.99***	−2.06***	−1.87**	−0.25	−0.00
	(0.46)	(0.49)	(0.19)	(0.05)	(0.82)	(0.87)	(0.28)	(0.09)	(0.57)	(0.59)	(0.16)	(0.06)
ER		−0.17				−0.18				−0.26		
		(0.13)				(0.21)				(0.16)		
LFP (BMWM)	−0.24	−0.28	−0.17	0.41								
	(0.43)	(0.43)	(0.42)	(0.42)								
LFP (BWWM)					−0.66	−0.58	−0.94*	0.90*				
					(0.54)	(0.54)	(0.45)	(0.36)				
LFP (WWWM)									−0.86*	−0.73	−1.21**	−0.26
									(0.41)	(0.41)	(0.38)	(0.38)
R2	0.60	0.61	0.04	0.33	0.58	0.58	0.06	0.33	0.28	0.30	0.05	0.02
Adj. R2	0.59	0.60	0.04	0.33	0.57	0.57	0.05	0.33	0.26	0.27	0.04	0.01
Num. obs.	520	507	520	520	520	507	520	520	520	507	520	520

***$p < 0.001$, **$p < 0.01$, *$p < 0.05$.

Table 2. Estimation for Black Men, Black Women and White Women relative to White Men — North and Northeast.

	Black-men to White-men				Black-women to White-men				White-women to White-men			
	FE (1)	FE (2)	RE	POLS	FE (1)	FE (2)	RE	POLS	FE (1)	FE (2)	RE	POLS
(Intercept)			1.26*	0.59			1.80**	0.51			1.92*	0.31
			(0.56)	(0.50)			(0.69)	(0.37)			(0.83)	(0.46)
Real Selic	0.31	0.32	0.36	0.46	−1.14	−1.17	−0.96	−0.83	−2.28***	−2.30***	−2.19**	−2.12**
	(0.43)	(0.43)	(0.44)	(0.46)	(0.71)	(0.71)	(0.73)	(0.76)	(0.68)	(0.67)	(0.69)	(0.74)
Growth	0.36	0.36	0.40	0.42	0.27	0.09	0.17	0.03	−0.14	−0.50	−0.21	−0.40
	(0.61)	(0.63)	(0.63)	(0.67)	(1.02)	(1.03)	(1.06)	(1.10)	(0.98)	(0.99)	(1.00)	(1.07)
BLSH	−0.23	−0.96	−0.54	−0.59**	−5.55**	−6.31**	0.57	1.75***	−3.14	−4.48*	0.67	2.54***
	(1.00)	(1.25)	(0.36)	(0.22)	(1.69)	(2.09)	(0.83)	(0.40)	(1.64)	(2.00)	(1.00)	(0.36)
ER		−0.02				−0.14				−0.24		
		(0.20)				(0.33)				(0.31)		
LFP (BMWM)	−0.10	−0.06	0.32	1.02*								
	(0.51)	(0.52)	(0.50)	(0.48)								
LFP (BWWM)					−0.74	−0.68	−0.70	−0.14				
					(0.75)	(0.77)	(0.71)	(0.53)				
LFP (WWWM)									−1.09	−0.96	−1.33*	−1.10
									(0.61)	(0.61)	(0.61)	(0.60)
R2	0.22	0.22	0.02	0.06	0.25	0.25	0.01	0.11	0.36	0.39	0.07	0.23
Adj. R2	0.19	0.18	−0.00	0.04	0.22	0.22	−0.01	0.09	0.33	0.36	0.05	0.21
Num. obs.	200	195	200	200	200	195	200	200	200	195	200	200

$***p < 0.001$, $**p < 0.01$, $*p < 0.05$.

Table 3. Estimation for Black Men, Black Women and White Women relative to White Men — South, Southeast and Mid-west.

	Black-men to White-men				Black-women to White-men				White-women to White-men			
	FE (1)	FE (2)	RE	POLS	FE (1)	FE (2)	RE	POLS	FE (1)	FE (2)	RE	POLS
(Intercept)			1.92**	3.26***			3.66***	4.13***			2.32***	2.16***
			(0.72)	(0.67)			(0.48)	(0.48)			(0.40)	(0.38)
Real Selic	1.33**	1.30**	1.29**	0.94	−0.53	−0.59	−0.47	−0.60	−1.11**	−1.14**	−0.91*	−0.88*
	(0.43)	(0.43)	(0.42)	(0.52)	(0.62)	(0.62)	(0.61)	(0.74)	(0.37)	(0.36)	(0.37)	(0.38)
Growth	0.31	−0.32	0.31	0.32	−0.12	0.53	−0.16	−0.22	−0.24	0.36	−0.23	−0.17
	(0.74)	(0.79)	(0.74)	(0.96)	(1.17)	(1.24)	(1.16)	(1.41)	(0.70)	(0.73)	(0.71)	(0.73)
BLSH	−0.07	−0.48	−0.28	−0.37***	−2.01*	−2.19*	−1.10*	−0.90***	−1.86***	−1.52**	−0.31**	−0.25***
	(0.54)	(0.55)	(0.33)	(0.08)	(1.02)	(1.04)	(0.48)	(0.11)	(0.54)	(0.54)	(0.11)	(0.07)
ER		−0.24				−0.21				−0.28		
		(0.18)				(0.28)				(0.16)		
LFP (BMWM)	−0.32	−0.41	−0.34	−1.60*								
	(0.71)	(0.72)	(0.70)	(0.66)								
LFP (BWWM)					−0.77	−0.58	−1.20	−1.95**				
					(0.76)	(0.76)	(0.64)	(0.62)				
LFP (WWWM)									−0.31	−0.10	−0.97	−0.79
									(0.59)	(0.58)	(0.52)	(0.49)
R2	0.49	0.50	0.05	0.13	0.45	0.42	0.04	0.17	0.14	0.14	0.04	0.05
Adj. R2	0.47	0.48	0.03	0.11	0.43	0.45	0.02	0.16	0.11	0.11	0.03	0.04
Num. obs.	320	312	320	320	320	312	320	320	320	312	320	320

***$p < 0.001$, **$p < 0.01$, *$p < 0.05$.

white men, is higher in the regions with a lower black population share, possibly pointing out a more pronounced racial bias in that region. There was no change in the results for the relative unemployment of black women to white men: the coefficient associated with the Selic rate continues to be insignificant. For the estimation of white women relative to white men, the coefficient associated with the Selic rate increased (became less negative), and maintained its significance.

However, for the North and Northeast regions, the effect of the real interest rate on the ratio between black men's and white men's unemployment rates becomes insignificant. This is an interesting result, as it points out the importance of differentiating regional dynamics. Again, the North and Northeast regions have a higher black population share, so racial discrimination in the labor market may be lower.

For the estimation of the relative unemployment between white women and white men in the North and Northeast regions, the coefficient associated with the real Selic rate decreases (becomes more negative), and maintains its significance. This means that the effect of reducing the unemployment gap between white men and white women, followed by an increase in interest rates, is more significant in the North and Northeast regions when compared to the South and Southeast. Table 5 summarizes the results, focusing on the coefficients associated with the real interest rate.

We also reproduced the estimations removing the data from the COVID-19 period. The COVID-19 pandemic was a unique period where companies had to shut down and only essential services were functioning, like health facilities, supermarkets and construction services. In addition, the real interest rate decreased sharply during that period. Hence, given the gender and racial composition of those sectors, the dynamics of this period could lead to some of the results found. The estimation results are in the Appendix in Table A2. The effect of the real interest rate changed only for blacks. The effect continues positive but becomes insignificant in all scenarios for the estimation of the relative unemployment between black men and white men. This can be due to lower observation points or less variability in the interest rate series. It can also point out different labor market dynamics that our model does not account for and thus needs further development in future research. For the ratio between black women and white men, the coefficient associated with the real interest rate becomes negative and significant for all 13 states and the South, Southeast, and Midwest regions. The lack of significance found previously for black women can also be associated with different directions taken by the unemployment gap before and during the pandemic. If the unemployment gap between black women and white men is negatively associated with real interest rates, it should have increased during the pandemic years, given that real interest rates were falling. However, that may not have been the case given that black women were concentrated in care services, viewed as essential during that period. The results are qualitatively similar for white women relative to white men, with the coefficient maintaining its negative sign and its significance for the estimation with all 13 states and the estimation for the South, Southeast, and Midwest regions but insignificant for North and Northeast regions.

Residual tests for cross-sectional dependence, contemporaneous correlation and serial correlation for our preferred estimation are presented in the Appendix B. Breusch–Godfrey test for serial correlation indicates that there's serial correlation when the estimate is conducted for the whole sample, but that correlation disappears when we exclude the pandemic period — possibly indicating that the COVID-19 pandemic was responsible for such correlation. Pesaran's cross-sectional dependence test results indicate that only for the estimation with white women in comparison to white men, there's a presence of cross-sectional dependence, that also disappears when we eliminate the pandemic period. The presence of nonorthogonal residuals does not interfere with the estimations but can alter the significance of t-test results.

The estimation results for the period before the COVID-19 pandemic shed light on possible different channels operating on the connection of the interest rate and labor market outcomes, especially when regional, gender, and racial differences are considered. To better understand our results, the next section conducts robustness checks on the estimations found, including sectoral and educational variables.

5. Robustness Checks

5.1. Including Educational, Work Condition and Sectoral Variables

In this section, we conduct a robustness check exercise. Following Seguino and Heintz 2012s model, we include sectoral occupation and education variables. Given the high level of informality in Brazil we decided to also include a variable on work condition as control. Those variables are the percentage of the labor force with some college education (complete and incomplete) and the employment composition in the industry, construction, domestic services, health and education sectors, and the percentage of workers employed in the private sector with a formal contract, all separated by gender and race. The data obtained for this exercise were also taken from PNADc.

The control variables for the robustness test are:

- College degree$_j$ = ratio between the percentage of group j with a college degree and the percentage of white men with a college degree.
- Work Condition$_j$ = ratio between the percentage of group j employed in the private sector with a formal contract and the percentage of white men employed in the private sector with a formal contract.
- Industry$_j$ = ratio between the percentage of group j employed in the industry and the percentage of white men employed in the industry.
- Construction$_j$ = ratio between the percentage of group j employed in the construction industry and the percentage of white men employed in the construction.
- Domestic Services$_j$ = ratio between the percentage of group j employed in the construction industry and the percentage of white men employed in domestic services.
- Education & Health$_j$ = ratio between the percentage of group j employed in the construction industry and the percentage of white men employed in the education and health services.

where, like before, j = black men, black women, white women are our groups of interest. Table 4 presents the results. We report, in this exercise, only the fixed effect estimation.

The effect of an increase in the real interest rate on black men's unemployment relative to white men maintains the positive and significant coefficient for the estimation with all states. It maintains the positive sign for the South, Southeast, and Midwest regions and

Table 4. Robustness checks: Fixed Effects Estimations for Black Men, Black Women and White Women, all relative to White Men.

	Black-men to White-men			Black-women to White-men			White-women to White-men		
	National	S, SE and MW	N and NE	National	S, SE and MW	N and NE	National	S, SE and MW	N and NE
Real Selic	1.23***	1.41**	0.75	−1.05*	−1.24	−0.68	−1.59***	−0.89*	−2.21**
	(0.33)	(0.45)	(0.50)	(0.53)	(0.68)	(0.85)	(0.35)	(0.39)	(0.71)
ER	−0.16	−0.23	0.00	−0.12	−0.22	−0.03	−0.27	−0.28	−0.24
	(0.13)	(0.18)	(0.20)	(0.21)	(0.29)	(0.33)	(0.16)	(0.16)	(0.31)
State Growth	−0.00	−0.49	0.35	0.30	0.51	0.13	−0.22	0.33	−0.26
	(0.50)	(0.79)	(0.63)	(0.80)	(1.27)	(1.01)	(0.59)	(0.75)	(0.99)
BLSH	−0.91	−0.68	−1.24	−2.16*	−1.57	−4.73*	−1.44*	−1.52**	−4.09*
	(0.51)	(0.61)	(1.28)	(0.90)	(1.10)	(2.13)	(0.60)	(0.58)	(1.99)
LFP	−0.34	−0.38	−0.15	−0.32	−0.56	−0.26	−0.84	−0.05	−1.11
	(0.44)	(0.73)	(0.53)	(0.56)	(0.80)	(0.78)	(0.45)	(0.67)	(0.68)
Construction	−0.04	−0.12	0.02	0.78	0.32	1.69*	0.37	1.02	0.17
	(0.05)	(0.07)	(0.06)	(0.52)	(0.71)	(0.77)	(0.26)	(0.52)	(0.36)
Industry	0.16*	0.14	0.16*	0.13	−0.20	0.39*	0.29**	−0.06	0.39**
	(0.07)	(0.15)	(0.07)	(0.13)	(0.23)	(0.16)	(0.10)	(0.18)	(0.14)
Education &	Health	0.05	−0.11	0.09	0.02	0.02	0.02	0.01	0.01
Health									
	(0.06)	(0.12)	(0.07)	(0.02)	(0.04)	(0.03)	(0.02)	(0.02)	(0.03)
Domestic Services	0.00	0.01	−0.00	0.00	0.00	0.00	0.00*	0.00	0.00*
	(0.01)	(0.01)	(0.01)	(0.00)	(0.00)	(0.00)	0.00*	0.00	0.00*
College Degree	0.22	0.28	0.12	−0.40**	−0.63*	−0.19	−0.04	−0.06	0.01
	(0.16)	(0.26)	(0.20)	(0.15)	(0.27)	(0.18)	(0.09)	(0.20)	(0.13)
Work Condition	0.02	0.10	−0.11	−0.08	−0.17	0.31	0.11	−0.00	0.18
	(0.06)	(0.09)	(0.10)	(0.13)	(0.16)	(0.25)	(0.11)	(0.14)	(0.18)
R2 (full model)	0.62	0.52	0.26	0.60	0.47	0.32	0.32	0.16	0.43
Adj. R2 (full model)	0.60	0.49	0.19	0.58	0.43	0.26	0.29	0.10	0.38
Num. obs.	507	312	195	507	312	195	507	312	195

***$p < 0.001$, **$p < 0.01$, *$p < 0.05$.

Table 5. Summary of Results for FE estimations, reported coefficients for the Real Selic Rate, with standard errors reported in parenthesis

		Agregated	South, SE, Midwest	North, NE
Full sample	Black Men	0.92	1.3	0.32
		(0.30)**	(0.43)**	−0.43
	Black Women	−0.85	−0.59	−1.17
		(0,46)	(0,62)	(0,71)
	White Women	−1.65	−1.14	−2.3
		(0.34)***	(0.36)**	(0.67)***
Without COVID-19	Black Men	0.76	0.93	0.49
		(0,52)	(0,69)	(0,79)
	Black Women	−2.45	−3.27	−1.13
		(0.78)**	(1.02)**	−1.22
	White Women	−2.03	−2.36	−1.49
		(0.57)***	(0.58)***	−1.15
Robustness	Black Men	1.23	1.41	0.71
		(0.33)***	(0.45)**	−0.49
	Black Women	−1.03	−1.18	−0.82
		(0,53)	(0,68)	(0,84)
	White Women	−1.46	−0.88	−1.96
		(0.35)***	(0.38)*	(0.68)**

* $p<0.05$ ** $p<0.01$ *** $p<0.001$.

increases its magnitude. This means that even controlling the sectoral composition, educational level and work conditions, the negative impact of a contractionary monetary policy is greater for black men when compared to white men. In other words, the unequal effect of contractionary monetary policy cannot be fully explained by different educational levels or work formality among these two groups, or for one group being employed in industries that are more sensitive to changes in the interest rate.

For black women, the coefficient remains negative but gains some significance for the estimation with all states. However, the results do not change qualitatively for the estimation separated by region: the interest rates continue not to impact the relative unemployment rate between black women and white men. Finally, for white women, the real interest rate maintained a negative and significant coefficient after the variables of education, sectoral composition and work conditions were included but slightly decreased in absolute values. This indicates that part of the previously found effect can be due to education, work conditions, or sectoral compositions. However, the employment behavior of this group needs to be further explored to fully understand this result.

We ran the regressions without the COVID-19 period data as in the previous estimations. The results in Table 4 changed significantly for black men's and black women's relative unemployment rates. As demonstrated in Table A3, in the Appendix, the real interest rates coefficient becomes insignificant for the estimation of the relative unemployment of black men to white men. The coefficient is negative and highly significant for black women's relative unemployment rates.

5.2. Estimation with Variables at the Level Form

To better understand the previous results, it is also important to look at the effects on each group individually. A ratio can increase because the numerator increases or the denominator decreases (or both). Hence, in this subsection, we conduct the estimations with the same variables, but instead of the unemployment rate ratios, we use the unemployment level for each gender-race group. Table 6 presents the fixed effect model estimation results.

As expected by the Phillips curve, real interest rates positively affect unemployment for almost every group and region. The most surprising result is for white women: an increase in the real interest rate has a negative relationship with unemployment for the estimation with the aggregated states, and for the North and Northeast regions. For the South, Southeast, and Midwest, the relationship is positive.

When looking at the magnitude of the coefficients associated with the real interest rate in the estimations, we can understand if the previous results were related to changes in the numerator or denominator. In the white men's estimation, an increase in the real interest rate positively affects white men's unemployment, but in a smaller magnitude when compared to black men and black women. Moreover, the Selic rate has no effect on white men's unemployment in the North and Northeast regions.

In this way, we can see that for the ratios between white women's and white men's unemployment, both the denominator and numerator are operating in the same direction: white women's unemployment is decreasing and white men's unemployment is increasing when interest rates rise. The coefficient for white women is positive for the South, Southeast, and Midwest regions, and the magnitude is smaller than for white

Table 6. Fixed effect estimations: variables in level.

	White Men			White Women			Black Men			Black Women		
	National	S,SE,MW	N,NE	National	S,SE,MW	N,NE	National	S,SE,MW	N,NE	National	S,SE,MW	N,NE
Real Selic	0.12***	0.25***	−0.06	−0.17***	0.12**	−0.55***	0.32***	0.43***	0.14*	0.21***	0.44***	−0.19*
	(0.03)	(0.03)	(0.06)	(0.04)	(0.04)	(0.08)	(0.04)	(0.04)	(0.06)	(0.05)	(0.06)	(0.09)
ER	−0.05***	−0.03*	−0.07**	−0.12***	−0.08***	−0.18***	−0.09***	−0.07***	−0.12***	−0.12***	−0.09***	−0.18***
	(0.01)	(0.01)	(0.02)	(0.02)	(0.01)	(0.03)	(0.01)	(0.02)	(0.02)	(0.02)	(0.02)	(0.03)
BLSH	0.03	−0.11**	0.24	0.02	−0.05	0.05	0.03	0.03	−0.09	−0.21**	−0.21**	−0.48*
	(0.05)	(0.04)	(0.15)	(0.07)	(0.05)	(0.22)	(0.05)	(0.05)	(0.15)	(0.08)	(0.08)	(0.19)
State Gr	0.03	0.06	0.04	−0.04	0.02	−0.06	0.02	−0.00	0.02	−0.04	−0.05	−0.04
	(0.04)	(0.04)	(0.07)	(0.06)	(0.06)	(0.11)	(0.05)	(0.07)	(0.07)	(0.06)	(0.08)	(0.09)
LFP	−0.17***	−0.06	−0.25***	0.05	0.26***	−0.09	−0.16**	−0.13	−0.20*	0.38***	0.32***	0.40***
	(0.04)	(0.06)	(0.07)	(0.05)	(0.05)	(0.08)	(0.05)	(0.07)	(0.09)	(0.06)	(0.06)	(0.10)
Construct	−0.37***	−0.37***	−0.45***	−1.04***	−1.02*	−1.08**	−0.38***	−0.28***	−0.57***	0.62	0.34	0.83
	(0.06)	(0.08)	(0.10)	(0.29)	(0.41)	(0.41)	(0.07)	(0.08)	(0.14)	(0.44)	(0.47)	(0.81)
Col Degree	0.16***	0.28***	−0.00	0.18***	0.29***	0.10*	0.48***	0.62***	0.27*	0.55***	0.79***	0.17*
	(0.03)	(0.03)	(0.06)	(0.03)	(0.03)	(0.05)	(0.06)	(0.07)	(0.11)	(0.05)	(0.05)	(0.08)
Industry	−0.26***	−0.50***	−0.09	0.00	−0.10	0.07	−0.43***	−0.39***	−0.32*	−0.14	−0.06	−0.12
	(0.06)	(0.06)	(0.10)	(0.10)	(0.10)	(0.16)	(0.07)	(0.08)	(0.15)	(0.08)	(0.08)	(0.17)
Dom Serv	0.39	0.64	0.32	0.08	0.00	0.28	0.70*	0.63	0.65	−0.07	0.01	0.08
	(0.31)	(0.39)	(0.47)	(0.11)	(0.11)	(0.17)	(0.34)	(0.37)	(0.71)	(0.10)	(0.11)	(0.18)
Educ & Halth	Heal	0.14	0.04	0.22	0.28***	0.12	0.35***	0.18	0.06	0.39	0.18*	−0.10
	(0.08)	(0.13)	(0.12)	(0.07)	(0.08)	(0.10)	(0.17)	(0.24)	(0.26)	(0.09)	(0.10)	(0.14)
Work Cond	0.25***	0.27***	0.18*	0.10	0.13	0.03	0.06	0.13	−0.16	−0.02	0.17	−0.33
	(0.05)	(0.06)	(0.09)	(0.09)	(0.10)	(0.14)	(0.06)	(0.07)	(0.11)	(0.10)	(0.12)	(0.17)
R2	0.57	0.75	0.49	0.48	0.72	0.47	0.66	0.71	0.63	0.66	0.75	0.67
Adj. R2	0.55	0.74	0.45	0.46	0.70	0.43	0.64	0.69	0.60	0.65	0.73	0.64
Num. obs.	507	312	195	507	312	195	507	312	195	507	312	195

* $p<0.05$ ** $p<0.01$ *** $p<0.001$.

men. This means that even when white women's unemployment increases in this region, it increases in a lower proportion compared to white men.

The opposite happens for black men and black women: the coefficient associated with the real interest rate is larger in magnitude when compared to white men. This means that an increase in the interest rate disproportionately affects the unemployment of black men in comparison to white men, explaining the positive coefficient found in the estimations for this group. For black women, the coefficient is smaller in terms of magnitude, which can explain the absence of significance found in the previous estimations.

For the estimation without the COVID-19 period data (Table A4, in Appendix), for all groups and in all regions, the relationship between unemployment and interest rates is positive. In this way, we understand that the negative results found in Table 6 for white women are due to the increase in the demand for healthcare workers during the COVID-19 pandemic, which is a female-dominated sector.

6. Concluding Remarks

Understanding the consequences of monetary policy for race and gender inequality is a fundamental step toward a more inclusive economic policy tool. Even though economic policy is not limited to monetary policy, there are few studies looking at monetary policy and gender and race inequality in Brazil. Hence, our main goal with this study is to contribute to the recent literature that explores the disproportionate impact of the current monetary policies on different social groups, especially in a country like Brazil, marked by the diversity of its population and high inequality rates.

We investigated the impact of real interest rates, as the primary monetary policy tool according to the Brazilian Central Bank, on unemployment by gender and race relative to white men. As mentioned previously, due to the lack of data, we could only conduct the estimations with quarterly periods from 2012 to 2021. We provided empirical evidence that social groups are disproportionately impacted when there is an increase in the interest rate, especially for black men relative to white men. This happens mainly in the regions with the lowest percentage of black share population: the South, Southeast, and Midwest regions. This result can be explained by the different positions of these two groups in the labor market or possible racial discrimination.

The effect for white women, however, is the opposite than expected: the unemployment of white women relative to white men reduces with increases in interest rates. We speculate that this can represent the need for white women to enter the labor market during periods of economic crisis. In addition to that, white women are mostly allocated to education and healthcare sectors, which are less affected by economic cycles. They are also the group with higher education but still receive lower wages compared to white men so that they could represent a source of cheap labor in crisis periods. However, a better investigation of the dynamics of this group in the labor market and how that relates to interest rates is needed.

Finally, for black women, the interest rate seems not to impact their employment relative to white men. For the estimation with all states, the effect is also negative, but smaller in magnitude when compared to white women. Their position in the labor market can explain this: most black women in Brazil are allocated to sectors that are not sensitive to changes in the interest rate, such as caretaking positions.

Aligned with previous studies, we conclude that the impact of contractionary monetary policies is not gender or racial-neutral. More importantly, the adverse effects vary according to different social groups, highlighting the importance of the intersection between race and gender when analyzing the impact of policy decisions. We can not stress enough that social stratification, if not considered, can lead to misleading conclusions that can perpetuate unequal socioeconomic outcomes.

It is also important to emphasize that the dynamics of monetary policies have different instruments and channels that can impact social groups differently. For the scope of this study, our strategy was to focus on employment and only one of these instruments — the interest rate. That can contribute to a more comprehensive understanding of how monetary policy impacts different social groups, especially in Brazil and other developing economies. Further studies are required to analyze income effects, other channels, and different intersections. In addition to that, there are other macroeconomic policies that impact employment and inequality. In the case of Brazil, fiscal policy — public investment, more specifically — played a significant role in affecting total employment (Dweck, Tonon, and Krepsky 2018). A complete framework should consider all effects to possibly design a better policy tool that fosters a sustainable and inclusive development path.

Finally, we also bring attention to the importance of understanding the impact of monetary policy in developing countries, even with data availability issues. As shown in the literature review, most of the studies conducted so far are concentrated in developed economies. The few that look to developing economies do so in an aggregated multi-country panel, dismissing important regional characteristics and leading to conclusions and recommendations that can, most of the time, perpetuate historical and structural issues that hamper the countries' development process itself.

Acknowledgements

We thank professors Stephanie Seguino, James Heintz, Jamee Moudud, Gilberto Tadeu Lima and Pedro Romero Marques for their comments and help on various draft versions of the paper. We would also like to acknowledge and thank the reviewers who carefully reviewed this article and aided in its publication.

Disclosure Statement

No potential conflict of interest was reported by the author(s).

ORCID

Clara Brenck http://orcid.org/0000-0002-0110-8668

References

Abell, J. D. 1991. 'Distributional Effects of Monetary and Fiscal Policy: Impacts on Unemployment Rates Disaggregated by Race and Gender.' *American Journal of Economics and Sociology* 50 (3): 269–284.

Araújo, E. 2004. 'Medindo o impacto regional da política monetária brasileira: uma comparação entre as regiões Nordeste e Sul.' *Revista Econômica do Nordeste* 35 (3): 356–393.

Barbosa-Filho, N. H. 2015. 'Monetary Policy with a Volatile Exchange Rate: The Case of Brazil Since 1999.' *Comparative Economic Studies* 57 (3): 401–425.

BC. 2018. 'Aspectos metodológicos e comparacões dos comportamentos do IBC-Br e do PIB, Estudo Especial n° 3/2018.' *Tech.* rep. Banco Central do Brasil.

Bertanha, M., and E. A. Haddad. 2008. 'Efeitos regionais da política monetária no Brasil: impactos e transbordamentos espaciais.' *Revista Brasileira de Economia* 62: 3–29.

Blanchard, O. J. 1995. 'Macroeconomic Implications of Shifts in the Relative Demand for Skills.' *Economic Policy Review* 1 (1): 48–53.

Blanchard, O., and L. Katz. 1997. 'The Natural Rate of Unemployment.' *Journal of Economic Perspectives* 11: 51–72.

Blecker, R. A., and S. Seguino. 2002. 'Macroeconomic Effects of Reducing gen- der Wage Inequality in an Export-Oriented, Semi-Industrialized Economy.' *Review of Development Economics* 6.1: 103–119.

Braunstein, E., and J. Heintz. 2008. 'Gender Bias and Central Bank Policy: Employment and Inflation Reduction.' *International Review of Applied Economics* 22 (2): 173–186.

Carpenter, S. B. e W. M. Rodgers. 2004. 'The Disparate Labor Market Impacts of Monetary Policy.' *Em: Journal of Policy Analysis and Management* 23 (4): 813–830.

Chernavsky, E., E. Dweck, and R. A. Teixeira. 2020. 'Descontrole ou inflexão? A polıtica fiscal do governo Dilma e a crise econômica.' *Economia e Sociedade* 29: 811–834.

Cynamon, B., S. Fazzari, and M. Setterfield. 2013. *After the Great Recession*. Tech. rep. New York: Cambridge University Press.

De Hoyos, R. E., and V. Sarafidis. 2006. 'Testing for Cross-Sectional Dependence in Panel-Data Models.' *The Stata Journal* 6 (4): 482–496.

Dweck, E., M. Tonon, and C. Krepsky. 2018. 'Assessing the Impact of Fiscal Consolidations on Unemployment and Growth in the Brazilian Economy.' Tech. rep. mimeo.

Elson, D. 1995. 'Gender Awareness in Modeling Structural Adjustment.' *World Development* 23 (11): 1851–1868.

Erten, B., and M. Metzger. 2019. 'The Real Exchange Rate, Structural Change, and Female Labor Force Participation.' *World Development* 117: 296–312.

Fazzari, S. M., P. Ferri, and E. Greenberg. 2010. 'Investment and the Taylor Rule in a Dynamic Keynesian Model.' *Journal of Economic Dynamics and Control* 34 (10).

Freddo, L. A. M. 2019. 'Inflation Targeting in Latin America: The Role of the Exchange Rate.' Masters diss., Universidade de São Paulo.

Guimarães, R. R. da S., and S. M. M. Monteiro. 2014. 'Monetary Policy and Regional Output in Brazil.' *Revista Brasileira de Economia* 68: 73–101.

Ha, J., M. M. Stocker, and H. Yilmazkuday. 2020. 'Inflation and Exchange Rate Pass-Through.' *Journal of International Money and Finance* 105: 102187.

IPEA. 2015. 'Retrato das desigualdades de genero e raca - 1995 a 2014.' Tech. rep. Instituto de pesquisa economica aplicada.

Kaltenbrunner, A., and J. P. Painceira. 2017. 'The Impossible Trinity: Inflation Targeting, Exchange Rate Management and Open Capital Accounts in Emerging Economies.' *Development and Change* 48 (3): 452–480.

Kappes, S. A. 2023. 'Monetary Policy and Personal Income Distribution: A Survey of the Empirical Literature.' *Review of Political Economy* 35 (1): 211–230. doi:10.1080/09538259.2021.1943159

Kucera, D., and S. Tejani. 2014. 'Feminization, Defeminization, and Structural Change in Manufacturing.' *World Development* 64: 569–582.

Munyo, I., and M. A. Rossi. 2015. 'The Effects of Real Exchange Rate Fluctuations on the Gender Wage Gap and Domestic Violence in Uruguay.' No. IDB-WP-618. IDB Working Paper Series.

Ribeiro, R. S. M., J. S. McCombie, and G. T. Lima. 2017. 'Some Unpleasant Currency-Devaluation Arithmetic in a Post Keynesian Macromodel.' *Journal of Post Keynesian Economics* 40 (2): 145–167.

Seguino, S., and J. Heintz. 2012. 'Monetary Tightening and the Dynamics of US Race and Gender Stratification.' *American Journal of Economics and Sociology* 71 (3): 603–638.

Sharpe, S. A., and G. Suarez. 2015. 'Why isn't investment more sensitive to interest rates: evidence from surveys'. In: Available at SSRN 2667352.
Sharpe, S. A., and G. A. Suarez. 2021. 'Why Isn't Business Investment More Sensitive to Interest Rates? Evidence from Surveys.' *Management Science* 67 (2): 720–741.
Silva, F. F., M. A. C. Afonso, and C. J. Rodrıguez-Fuentes. 2010. 'Limitacões teóricas da literatura convencional sobre impactos regionais de política monetária.' *Silva* 332: S586 l.
Takhtamanova, Y., and E. Sierminska. 2009. 'Gender, Monetary Policy, and Employment: The Case of Nine OECD Countries.' *Feminist Economics* 15 (3): 323–353.
Tejani, S., and W. Milberg. 2016. 'Global Defeminization? Industrial Upgrading and Manufacturing Employment in Developing Countries.' *Feminist Economics* 22 (2): 24–54.
Thorbecke, W. 2001. 'Estimating the Effects of Disinflationary Monetary Policy on Minorities.' *Journal of Policy Modeling* 23 (1): 51–66.
Wooldridge, J. M. 2010. *Econometric Analysis of Cross Section and Panel Data.* London: MIT press.
Zavodny, M., and T. Zha. 2000. 'Monetary Policy and Racial Unemployment Rates.' *Economic Review-Federal Reserve Bank of Atlanta* 85 (4): 1.

Appendix

A. Granger Causality Test

To guarantee that the real federal funds rate is not caused by changes in unemployment, we conducted a Granger causality test for our three dependent variables, using 4 lags. The null hypothesis of the test is that lagged x-values do not explain the variation in y. Table A shows the results. We conclude that we cannot reject the hypothesis that the real federal funds rate is not Granger-caused by changes in the relative unemployment of black and white men, black women and white men and white women and white men.

	F	P(>F)
UBMWM	0.317	0.867
UBWWM	0.645	0.631
UWWWM	1.746	0.139

B. Residuals Diagnosis Test

As residuals test diagnosis we pursue the Breusch-Godfrey serial correlation (or autocorrelation) test and the Pesaran Cross-Dependence (CD) test.

The Breusch-Godfrey test is an LM test applied to the residuals of the regression, where the null hypothesis is that there is no serial correlation in the errors (Wooldridge 2010).

The Pesaran CD test for cross-sectional dependence in panel data is best suited for panels with a finite T. The null hypothesis of the test is of no cross-sectional dependence (De Hoyos and Sarafidis 2006).

Table A1. *P*-values for Pesaran Cross-Dependence (CD) and Breusch-Godfrey/Wooldridge Serial Correlation Residuals Tests for Fixed-Effects Estimations (all states).

	Full sample		Without COVID-19	
	Pesaran CD	Breusch-Godfrey	Pesaran CD	Breusch-Godfrey
UBMWM	0.1878	0.0008168	0.2055	0.304
UBWWM	0.1867	0.001171	0.573	0.09982
UWWWM	0.02665	0.001041	0.246	0.5028

C. *Main Estimations Without the Covid Pandemic Period*

Table A2. Fixed Effects Estimation for Black Men, Black Women and White Women relative to White Men, excluding the COVID Pandemic period

	Black-men to White-men			Black-women to White-men			White-women to White-men		
	National	S, SE and MW	N and NE	National	S, SE and MW	N and NE	National	S, SE and MW	N and NE
Real Selic	0.76	0.93	0.49	−2.45**	−3.27**	−1.13	−2.03***	−2.36***	−1.49
	(0.52)	(0.69)	(0.79)	(0.78)	(1.02)	(1.22)	(0.57)	(0.58)	(1.15)
Growth	−0.02	−0.84	1.05	0.81	0.34	1.59	0.69	0.63	0.92
	(0.65)	(0.89)	(0.93)	(0.98)	(1.33)	(1.43)	(0.70)	(0.75)	(1.34)
ER	−0.20	−0.31	−0.02	−0.08	−0.32	0.29	0.05	−0.22	0.48
	(0.15)	(0.20)	(0.23)	(0.23)	(0.30)	(0.36)	(0.16)	(0.17)	(0.33)
BLSH	−0.35	−0.40	0.04	−1.69	−2.00	−1.71	−1.56**	−1.84**	−1.08
	(0.53)	(0.60)	(1.47)	(0.93)	(1.12)	(2.32)	(0.60)	(0.55)	(2.09)
LFP (BMWM)	−0.73	−0.87	−0.64						
	(0.55)	(0.93)	(0.66)						
LFP (BWWM)				−1.19*	−0.97	−1.39			
				(0.58)	(0.82)	(0.83)			
LFP (WWWM)							−0.83	−0.50	−0.91
							(0.43)	(0.65)	(0.64)
R2	0.02	0.03	0.02	0.06	0.08	0.05	0.06	0.11	0.05
Adj. R2	−0.02	−0.02	−0.04	0.02	0.03	−0.01	0.02	0.07	−0.01
Num. obs.	416	256	160	416	256	160	416	256	160

* $p<0.05$ ** $p<0.01$ *** $p<0.001$.

Table A3. Robustness checks: Fixed Effects Estimations for Black Men, Black Women and White Women, all relative to White Men

	Black-men to White-men			Black-women to White-men			White-women to White-men		
	National	S, SE and MW	N and NE	National	S, SE and MW	N and NE	National	S, SE and MW	N and NE
Real Selic	0.74	0.82	0.03	−2.80***	−4.06***	−1.46	−1.98**	−2.18**	−1.90
	(0.53)	(0.70)	(0.85)	(0.83)	(1.10)	(1.28)	(0.60)	(0.66)	(1.21)
ER	−0.22	−0.32	−0.07	−0.08	−0.38	0.30	0.03	−0.22	0.40
	(0.15)	(0.20)	(0.23)	(0.23)	(0.31)	(0.36)	(0.17)	(0.17)	(0.34)
State Growth	0.05	−0.69	1.19	0.92	0.21	1.67	0.80	0.73	1.54
	(0.65)	(0.92)	(0.94)	(0.98)	(1.40)	(1.46)	(0.70)	(0.79)	(1.35)
BLSH	−0.62	−0.54	0.26	−1.78	−2.17	−1.27	−1.28*	−1.94**	−0.84
	(0.58)	(0.71)	(1.53)	(0.98)	(1.21)	(2.36)	(0.61)	(0.60)	(2.10)
LFP	−0.76	−0.94	−0.56	−1.23	−1.09	−1.61	−0.81	−0.93	−0.95
	(0.56)	(0.96)	(0.67)	(0.87)	(0.95)	(0.48)	(0.75)	(0.71)	
Construction	−0.01	−0.01	−0.02	−0.00	−0.22	0.67	0.34	0.27	0.39
	(0.06)	(0.10)	(0.07)	(0.83)	(1.03)	(0.34)	(0.59)	(0.48)	
College Degree	0.26	0.25	0.24	−0.14	−0.34	−0.05	0.08	−0.28	0.17
	(0.20)	(0.32)	(0.25)	(0.18)	(0.31)	(0.21)	(0.10)	(0.19)	(0.14)
Industry	0.12	0.05	0.16	0.05	−0.43	0.35	0.26*	0.02	0.33*
	(0.10)	(0.18)	(0.12)	(0.17)	(0.27)	(0.22)	(0.12)	(0.20)	(0.16)
	Health	−0.10	−0.15	−0.08	−0.03	0.00	−0.06	−0.01	−0.01

(*Continued*)

Table A3. Continued.

	Black-men to White-men			Black-women to White-men			White-women to White-men		
	National	S, SE and MW	N and NE	National	S, SE and MW	N and NE	National	S, SE and MW	N and NE
Education & Health									
	(0.09)	(0.13)	(0.11)	(0.03)	(0.05)	(0.05)	(0.02)	(0.03)	(0.03)
Domestic Services	0.00	−0.00	0.01	0.00	0.00	0.00	0.00	−0.00	0.00
	(0.01)	(0.01)	(0.01)	(0.00)	(0.00)	(0.00)	(0.00)	(0.00)	(0.00)
Work Condition	−0.00	0.12	−0.26*	−0.27	−0.20	−0.35	−0.07	0.06	−0.17
	(0.08)	(0.10)	(0.12)	(0.15)	(0.18)	(0.30)	(0.12)	(0.16)	(0.20)
Num. obs.	416	256	160	416	256	160	416	256	160
R2 (full model)	0.62	0.50	0.28	0.64	0.52	0.38	0.38	0.24	0.48
Adj. R2 (full model)	0.60	0.47	0.20	0.62	0.48	0.31	0.35	0.18	0.43

* $p<0.05$ ** $p<0.01$ *** $p<0.001$.

Table A4. Robustness test: Fixed Effects Estimation for Unemployment Rates by Demographic Group.

	White Men			White Women			Black Men			Black Women		
	National	S,SE,MW	N,NE	National	S,SE,MW	N,NE	National	S,SE,MW	N,NE	National	S,SE,MW	N,NE
Real Selic	0.26***	0.30***	0.15	0.21***	0.31***	0.14	0.52***	0.54***	0.48***	0.34***	0.42***	0.17
	(0.04)	(0.04)	(0.08)	(0.05)	(0.05)	(0.10)	(0.05)	(0.06)	(0.09)	(0.07)	(0.08)	(0.11)
LFP	−0.03	0.08	−0.13	0.31***	0.49***	0.14	0.02	0.26**	−0.27*	0.52***	0.53***	0.39**
	(0.05)	(0.07)	(0.09)	(0.05)	(0.06)	(0.09)	(0.07)	(0.09)	(0.12)	(0.07)	(0.08)	(0.13)
State Gr	−0.01	0.06	−0.08	0.02	0.06	−0.01	0.00	−0.01	0.03	0.06	−0.00	0.19
	(0.05)	(0.05)	(0.09)	(0.06)	(0.06)	(0.11)	(0.06)	(0.07)	(0.10)	(0.07)	(0.09)	(0.11)
ER	−0.05***	−0.02*	−0.07**	−0.08***	−0.06***	−0.11***	−0.07***	−0.06***	−0.08**	−0.11***	−0.10***	−0.12***
	(0.01)	(0.01)	(0.02)	(0.01)	(0.01)	(0.03)	(0.01)	(0.02)	(0.03)	(0.02)	(0.02)	(0.03)
BLSH	0.04	−0.10*	0.14	−0.06	−0.12*	−0.15	0.08	0.10	−0.17	−0.13	−0.23**	−0.29
	(0.05)	(0.04)	(0.16)	(0.06)	(0.05)	(0.19)	(0.06)	(0.06)	(0.16)	(0.07)	(0.08)	(0.19)
Construct	−0.30***	−0.22**	−0.42***	0.03	−0.14	0.10	−0.44***	−0.33***	−0.62***	0.58	0.25	0.77
	(0.07)	(0.08)	(0.10)	(0.29)	(0.43)	(0.42)	(0.08)	(0.09)	(0.16)	(0.45)	(0.49)	(0.85)
Col Degree	0.19***	0.28***	0.09	0.21***	0.29***	0.15***	0.41***	0.41***	0.35**	0.48***	0.69***	0.23**
	(0.03)	(0.04)	(0.06)	(0.03)	(0.03)	(0.05)	(0.07)	(0.08)	(0.13)	(0.05)	(0.06)	(0.08)
Industry	−0.32***	−0.55***	−0.13	−0.05	−0.12	−0.04	−0.44***	−0.42***	−0.37	−0.19*	−0.11	−0.40*
	(0.06)	(0.06)	(0.10)	(0.08)	(0.12)	(0.13)	(0.09)	(0.10)	(0.19)	(0.08)	(0.09)	(0.19)
Educ\	Heal	0.18	0.06	0.29*	0.40***	0.12	0.50***	0.19	0.35	−0.01	0.29***	−0.04
	(0.09)	(0.16)	(0.14)	(0.06)	(0.09)	(0.09)	(0.19)	(0.27)	(0.30)	(0.08)	(0.11)	(0.14)
Dome Serv	0.56	0.85*	0.35	0.27**	0.29**	0.21	1.32**	1.09*	2.24**	0.28**	0.23*	0.47*
	(0.33)	(0.40)	(0.53)	(0.09)	(0.11)	(0.14)	(0.40)	(0.46)	(0.81)	(0.09)	(0.11)	(0.19)
Work Cond	0.24***	0.34***	0.14	0.10	0.33**	−0.11	0.13	0.14	−0.13	0.05	0.14	−0.14
	(0.05)	(0.07)	(0.09)	(0.08)	(0.11)	(0.12)	(0.07)	(0.07)	(0.14)	(0.11)	(0.13)	(0.19)
R2	0.60	0.76	0.52	0.58	0.72	0.51	0.69	0.74	0.66	0.70	0.76	0.69
Adj. R2	0.58	0.74	0.47	0.55	0.70	0.45	0.67	0.73	0.62	0.69	0.74	0.65
Num. obs.	416	256	160	416	256	160	416	256	160	416	256	160

* $p<0.05$ ** $p<0.01$ *** $p<0.001$.

OPEN ACCESS

Monetary Policy and Income Distribution in a Multisectoral AB-SFC Model

Matheus Trotta Vianna

ABSTRACT

Restrictive monetary policy can not only fail to achieve the conventional macroeconomic goal of controlling inflation but also be seen as responsible for the increasing income inequality that has occurred in recent decades. This result is not clear, however, if one remains bounded to the traditional monetary policy transmission mechanisms and conventional models. In this article, we create an agent-based, stock-flow consistent, heterodox disequilibrium model to analyse and evaluate the effects of different basic interest rate levels, especially its distributive effects. Using computer simulations, we show that the basic interest rate plays a key role when firms compete in oligopolistic markets and face financial constraints and costs. In such circumstances, increases in the interest rate can be responsible for price increases, creating the price puzzle problem. In addition, it forces redistribution of income in favour of the financial system and pressures the profit rate of industrial firms, which will raise prices and lower the wage share. The final distributive effect of an interest rate policy will ultimately depend on the power of these agents: the bargaining power of the workers to claim higher wages and the market power of the firms to raise prices.

1. Introduction

Income distribution has changed significantly in several countries during the previous five decades. The Gini index has increased in developing countries such as South Africa and China but also in developed countries such as the United States and the United Kingdom when compared with data from the 1960s. The Gini index is, however, inconclusive for many countries as a result of its limitations, including its low sensitivity to distribution extremes (Cobham, Schlögl, and Sumner 2016; Palma 2014). If we then observe the share of income earned by the top 1 or 10 per cent of the population, the evidence for a strong income concentration is stark (Piketty and Saez 2006; Piketty 2014). These authors also point out that the recent increase in

This is an Open Access article distributed under the terms of the Creative Commons Attribution-NonCommercial-NoDerivatives License (http://creativecommons.org/licenses/by-nc-nd/4.0/), which permits non-commercial re-use, distribution, and reproduction in any medium, provided the original work is properly cited, and is not altered, transformed, or built upon in any way. The terms on which this article has been published allow the posting of the Accepted Manuscript in a repository by the author(s) or with their consent.

income concentration is driven by, among other factors, structural changes in labour and capital income.

When we observe the functional income distribution in OECD countries, for instance, the labour share of income has declined significantly in most countries since the 1980s (Dunhaupt 2013; Stockhammer 2009). The explanations for such a phenomenon, however, vary according to theoretical framework. These authors, for instance, highlight that, within a neoclassical framework, the declining labour share could be explained by technological and productivity changes that affect factor prices; however, from a Keynesian/Kaleckian theoretical perspective, pricing behaviour, profit rates, and aggregate demand can also play important roles. In addition, the macroeconomic consequences of this increased inequality are more pronounced when analysed according to non-orthodox theories (Stockhammer, Onaran, and Ederer 2009).

If aggregate demand can contribute to changes in functional income distribution, macroeconomic policies that affect aggregate demand can also have distributive impacts. In particular, interest rates affect profit rates and price decisions, showing that monetary policy is not neutral in the distributive sense. It is not a coincidence that, during the last five decades in which labour shares decreased in several countries, a significant policy shift in those countries was also observed; that is, restrictive monetary policy in the 1970s and 1980s resulted in shocks and was followed by global adoption of inflation targeting (IT). Samarina and Nguyen (2019) find evidence that expansionary monetary policy reduced income inequality in the eurozone between 1999 and 2014. Liosi and Spyrou (2022) reach the same conclusion, highlighting extra layers of consequences such as gender inequality.

The urge to tame inflation as the main policy goal is usually met with high interest rate levels, which slows down the economy and increases inequality. Moreover, under certain circumstances, increases in the basic interest rate can lead to higher rather than lower inflation — a self-defeating policy — which is in line with common critiques of IT and its overall inefficacy (Rochon 2022). This result is not clear, however, if one remains bound to traditional monetary policy theory, transmission mechanisms, and dynamic stochastic general equilibrium models.

Mainstream consensus on macroeconomics identifies the existence of several monetary policy transmission channels, which can contribute to greater or lesser efficacy of monetary policy in normal circunstances (not considering, for instance, the well-known issue of the zero-lower bound). However, all transmission channels in traditional theory generally point in the same direction: they all indicate a negative correlation between interest rates and inflation. In contrast, heterodox theories not only argue that some of the conventional channels might not be consistent with their world view but also argue for the existence of other transmission channels, not discussed in conventional models, which can have contradictory effects on monetary policy, for example the distributive channel. If heterodox transmission channels of monetary policy are in play, the efficacy of the IT regime is questioned and its impact on the distribution of income becomes more evident.

In this article, we discuss some heterodox transmission channels of monetary policy and the distributive role of the interest rate in terms of creating an agent-based, stock-flow consistent, heterodox disequilibrium model to analyse and evaluate the effects of different basic interest rate levels using computer simulations. The model presented here is an extension of an already existing model, from the Multisectoral Micro–Macro (MMM) family of models developed at the Federal University of Rio de Janeiro (Dweck 2006; Dweck, Vianna, and da Cruz Barbosa 2020; Possas and Dweck 2004; Possas, Dweck, and Visconti 2004; Trotta Vianna 2021). Our main goal is to analyse the distributive effects of different basic interest rate levels in a theoretical general economy.

To achieve our goal, this article is structured as follows: Section Two discusses alternative monetary policy transmission mechanisms and the theory behind them to show that, in contrast to the New Consensus whereby all transmission channels follow the same direction, the result of monetary policy is unknown and depends on the characteristics of each economy. Section Three describes the model, including its main characteristics and structure, and includes some equations regarding price formation, interest structure, and income generation and distribution. Section Four briefly presents the setting used for our experiments, noting the calibration of the model and focusing on the values of parameters and initial values we used. Section Five presents the results of our simulations. We first run a baseline configuration and show the main results of the model in general. Then, we test different basic interest rate levels and analyse the results. Last, but not least, we replicate the basic interest rate experiment in different economic conditions to try to understand when monetary policy is more or less effective and when it most affects the distribution of income. In Section Six, some final remarks conclude our article.

2. Monetary policy transmission mechanisms

2.1. Heterodox Transmission Channels

Arestis and Sawyer (2002) argue that the New Consensus view can be synthesized by a world described using three equations: an IS curve, a Phillips curve, and a monetary policy rule or central bank reaction function. In this reaction function, the basic nominal interest rate is the core policy instrument, defined by the monetary authority. The policy rules used by most monetary authorities follow some form or adaptation of Taylor's famous 1993 proposition. Interest rates affect aggregate demand and inflation via several channels.

Mishkin (1995, 1996) describes the main channels according the New Consensus view: the interest rate channel, asset price channel, exchange rate channel, expectations channel, credit channel (which is usually divided into two sub-channels), bank lending channel, and balance-sheet channel.[1] The literature concerning transmission mechanisms usually investigates which is the strongest or main channel, theoretically or empirically, and, while an individual channel may be criticised or obscured by another, the effectiveness of monetary policy is not questioned.

Monetary policy effectiveness is never checked because all channels produce the same final effect on demand, in terms of direction. The intensity might be weaker or stronger, depending on circumstances and which channel is operating, or the timing of monetary policy might be affected by several intermediate variables through which the channels pass, but the resulting effect, the negative correlation between the basic interest rate and demand, is always the same. If, via all channels, an increase in the basic interest

[1]This article has insufficient time and space to describe these already well-known transmission mechanisms. See Mishkin (1995, 1996) for detailed explanations.

rate reduces aggregate demand, the effectiveness of monetary policy in terms of taming inflation is also guaranteed, as an implicit hypothesis exists: inflation is always a phenomenon of demand. According to Gordon (1997), 'in the long run inflation is always and everywhere an excess nominal GDP phenomenon'.

Using a heterodox approach, this result is not guaranteed. One fundamental difference between the mainstream view and most of the heterodox economic approaches is how prices are defined and formed. Note that the idea that prices depend on level of demand, while supply is determined by real natural forces, is implicit according to the orthodox view and using the conventional transmission mechanisms. A perfect competition model is in play. In contrast, some heterodox approaches, for example the post-Keynesian and Kaleckian views, assume that firms have some market power in general, so they usually create prices by adding a mark-up to some measurement of unit cost within a more oligopolistic scenario. When market power is considered, the final link between demand and prices in all five channels might be compromised.

Moreover, inflation can have multiple sources, not merely demand. The post-Keynesian theory of inflation usually points to several cost factors, such as wages, markups, diminishing returns, imported costs, supply shocks, taxes, and even demand (Davidson 2011; Sicsú 2003). At the same time, outside the consensus view, many authors have pointed out other transmission mechanisms via which the interest rate can affect demand and inflation.

2.2. Exchange Rate Cost Channel

While the traditional exchange rate channel highlights only the indirect effect of the exchange rate on prices, via aggregate demand, even the central bank of Brazil (BCB 1999) recognises that the exchange rate directly affects prices and not demand. Usually, two sub-channels explain the direct effects of the exchange rate on prices.

First, an appreciation of the exchange rate decreases the cost of foreign products in domestic currency, and so, if consumers have access to the international market and domestic products compete with foreign products, this might force domestic firms to reduce prices in an attempt to retain demand.[2] Second, an appreciation of the exchange rate decreases the cost of both imported inputs and domestic production. If the unit cost of production is determined by price, it will lead to changes in price.

This channel has the same final effect on prices as traditional channels, even if not via aggregate demand: an increase in the basic interest rate will lead to a decrease in inflation. Summa and Serrano (2018) and Modenesi and de Araújo (2013), for example, argue that this is the main channel through which the inflation targeting regime was able to keep inflation under control during past decades in Brazil.

2.3. Inverse Bank Lending Channel

For theories that accept endogenous money, a horizontalist approach to money, which is common ground for most post-Keynesian economists, bank reserves have no causal

[2]Clearly this sub-channel depends on sectoral characteristics, the price elasticity of exports, and the degree of internationalisation of the domestic economy. For instance, Padrón et al. (2015) investigate why the price elasticity of Brazilian exports is low and affects this sub-channel.

relationship with the ability of banks to provide credit (Rochon and Setterfield 2008). Therefore, the traditional bank lending channel makes no sense. Another variable should be related to the banks' ability to lend, for instance, profitability.

Several recent empirical studies show some evidence of a possible inverse credit channel, but the effect of interest rates on bank profits was first investigated by Samuelson (1945). He argues that an increase in the interest rate, which increases the whole interest structure, improves the state of an individual bank and the banking system as a whole. The results of Borio, Gambacorta, and Hofmann's (2017) statistical study reveal a positive correlation between interest rates and bank profitability. Altavilla, Boucinha, and Peydró (2018) find similar results for banks in the eurozone, whereby accommodative monetary policy has a negative effect on bank profits; they argue, however, that this effect is counterbalanced by improvements in macroeconomic conditions via other channels. Kumar, Acharya, and Ho (2020) identify the same positive correlation for banks in New Zealand.

Using this channel, increases in the interest rate would lead to higher bank profitability and higher lending capacity. If investment has been financially constrained, it is possible that this channel generates higher investment and demand. In this case, with higher interest rates, higher investment can increase financial costs, indebtedness, and even financial instability.[3] However, better lending conditions do not necessarily mean that firms will increase investment, as reasons why they invest vary, such as expected demand, and credit is only a constraint to investment not a motivation for it.

2.4. Interest Rate Cost Channel

The interest rate also has direct effects on costs, and therefore on prices. Different to the exchange rate cost channel, the interest rate cost channel has an adverse impact on monetary policy effectiveness, as it explains the well-documented positive correlation between interest and prices. This correlation, as presented by Lima and Setterfield (2010), has several names: Gibson's paradox (Keynes 1930), price puzzle (Eichenbaum 1992), or Cavallo effect (Taylor 2009).

Hannsgen (2004) and Hannsgen (2007) study this effect in detail. It is very clear and direct: if interest rates are a cost of production and prices are based on costs, then increases in the interest rate will increase prices. In addition, recent studies conducted by Sicsú, Modenesi, and Pimentel (2020) and Passos and de Melo Modenesi (2021) identify that this interest cost channel influencing prices and inflation is even more pronounced in highly indebted economies. If, in general, firms can accumulate their own resources and not be hugely dependent on external finance to produce their products, the interest rate on loans will have almost no impact on the cost structure, and therefore on prices.

This is one of the most relevant channels for this investigation. First, it can only occur in oligopolistic markets, in situations where firms set prices based on their costs, in contrast to the traditional theory. Even so, the precise price formation rule is the topic of a long-running debate, even within heterodox economists.[4] Finally, this channel plays an

[3]The effect of monetary policy on financial instability is a topic for another article and is not investigated thoroughly here.
[4]See Lavoie (2014) for a useful taxonomy of different price-setting rules in heterodox economics.

important role in the distribution of income: higher interest rates will cause firms' profit margins to deteriorate if they do not compensate for this higher indirect cost with higher prices; however, their ability to adjust their prices is ultimately connected to their market power.

2.5. Distributive Channel

An important additional effect of interest rates, which is usually not considered by the conventional view, is the distributive effect. The interest rate is also a distributive variable that affects income flows and, consequently, also the income distribution of the economy. If someone pays interest, another person is getting paid on the other side. This implies that the interest rate affects the economic agents' income and expenditure flows. Surplus agents generally make resources available, and receive interest in return, whereas deficit agents generally depend on debt, and therefore pay interest. It becomes obvious that the interest rate has distributional effects, as it determines the cash flows of both deficit and surplus agents.

High interest rate policies generate income redistribution in favour of surplus agents. Households and firms in already consolidated positions generally have surplus resources, and are the ones that benefit from high interest rates. Banks and financial institutions also benefit from the distributional effects of high interest rates, as these rates directly determine profits from banking and financial activities. Households and firms in less comfortable positions, however, in general depend on loans and are borrowers of credit. These are the agents that pay the interest and do not benefit from high interest policies (Erber 2011, 2012). After all, as Smithin (2004) states, the product of labour must be divided into three parts: the profit share of capitalist activity, the wage share of workers, and the interest payment. Smithin levels strong criticism at the New Consensus policy recommendations and the theory that supports them, especially its apparent technocrat approach and ideas, such as the non-accelerating inflation rate of unemployment (NAIRU), natural interest rate, and so on, which mask the distributional effects of such policies.

Not only do interest rate policies affect income distribution but their distribution also has consequences for the rest of the economy. Surplus agents, those who usually receive interest payments — rentiers or financial capitalists — tend to have lower propensities to consume than industrial capitalists and workers, so a policy shift towards a higher interest rate that favours rentiers tends to decrease the average propensity to consume. As pointed out by Rochon and Setterfield (2008), for those who understand that economic growth is related to demand, both in the short and long run, income distribution has an impact on economic activity.

Argitis and Pitelis (2001) argue that restrictive monetary policy raised interest rates in the 1970s and 1980s in both the United Kingdom and the United States, leading to a redistribution of income in favour of financial income. Using a simple but still powerful post-Keynesian and Kaleckian theoretical framework and empirical evidence, they show that changes in interest rates might affect what they call *intracapitalist* distribution, which means between non-financial or industrial capital and financial capital, in line with a Marxian point of view. However, traditional functional income distribution between profits and wages, if interest is considered a cost by firms, and under the condition of oligopolistic competition, means that firms try to increase prices to compensate for the cost increase and thus consider the interest cost channel. Moreover, Argitis and Pitelis argue that the shift in income distribution, when reducing the profit share of firms, might disincentivise industrial production, thus reducing economic activity. Arestis and Howells (1994) go beyond simple redistribution from savers to debtors and describe the distributive effects of interest rates in terms of the increasing complexity of the financial system and thus financial relations.

2.6. Summary

In sum, the simple recognition that firms do not operate under perfect competition, not even in the long run, but instead operate within oligopolistic markets, setting prices as a mark-up on some measurement of the cost structure, changes completely the implications for monetary policy as the last link between demand and prices is not necessarily true. To go further, once it is recognised that several factors can affect cost structure, an eclectic range of explanations for inflation is suggested, including a rise in interest rates. The phenomenon of Gibson's paradox, or the price puzzle, can more easily be understood if the cost structure is taken into account. The basic interest rate can affect prices directly, not necessarily via demand but via the interest cost channel, for example, which is relevant for highly indebted economies, and the exchange rate cost channel, which is even more important in small, open economies.

By simply considering these two opposing direct cost channels, the final result on prices will depend on the circumstances and conditions of each specific economy and cannot be known *a priori*. With ambiguous effects on both prices and demand, as shown in Figure 1, monetary policy might not be effective in terms of providing price or output stability. In fact, the result can be in complete contrast to that expected, that is, increasing instability. As Hannsgen (2007) states, monetary policy is an extremely imprecise gun, which it might be best not to fire at all.

Considering the complexity of the topic, possible alternative channels, the existence of a price puzzle, individual critiques of each traditional transmission mechanism, distributive aspects, the relevance of financial conditions to the effectiveness of monetary policy, and, finally, a general methodological and theoretical critique, we seek an alternative framework, as Martins et al. (2017) propose. Rather than an aggregate DGSE model based on representative agents, we need a heterodox model that integrates micro and macro aspects and accounts for firm- and sectoral-level heterogeneities to gain some insights into the stabilising role of monetary policy and the effectiveness of a Taylor rule applied to a complex, financial, and evolving economy.

3. Existing Monetary Policy and Income Distribution Models

As previously discussed, the nexus between monetary policy and income distribution cannot be assessed in models that assume perfect competition and rely on representative agents, which renders redundant the vast majority of models in the economic literature. There are, however, some recent models that tackle such topics assuming other theoretical roots and/or methodology. For instance, there are some contributions in the new-Keynesian literature that assume oligopolistic competition and introduce heterogeneous

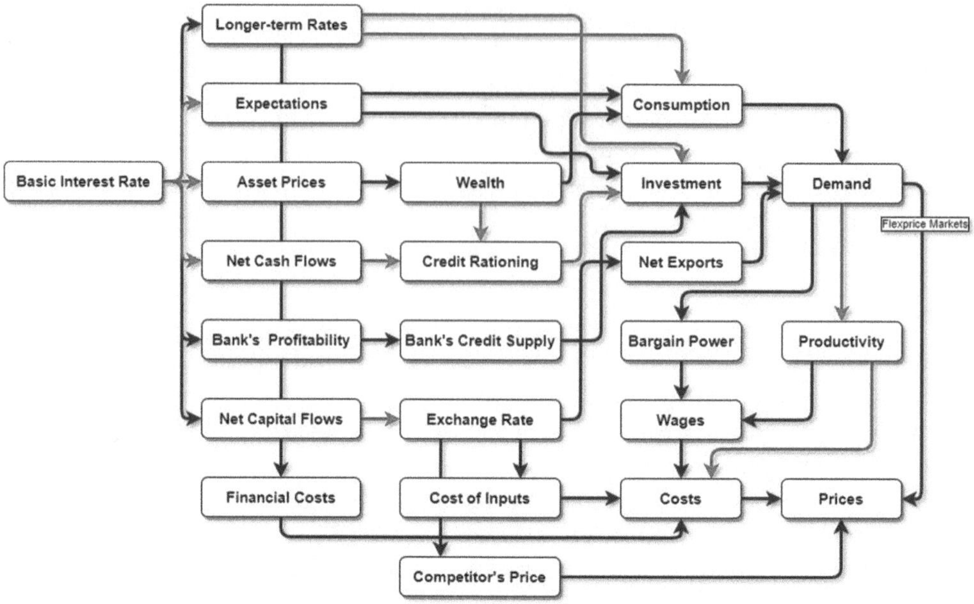

Figure 1. Traditional and Alternative Transmission Mechanisms of Monetary Policy. Source: Author's Elaboration. Green arrows represent a positive correlation from one variable to another; red arrows represent negative correlations.

agents. Simultaneously, there are also contributions in the agent-based modelling approach with post-Keynesian theoretical foundations. The present section reviews these models.

Auclert (2019) offers a comprehensive analysis of how monetary policy impacts consumption across heterogeneous households with varying marginal propensities to consume, classifying them among the winners and losers of policy changes. The study identifies three primary monetary policy redistribution channels: the earnings heterogeneity channel between wages and profits, the expected inflation channel between debt and credit, and the interest rate effect on maturity exposure. The model is a general equilibrium model but with more oligopolistic competition because firms set prices based on a markup over marginal costs. By identifying these three distributive channels within such a framework, in conjunction with the normal channels in general equilibrium models (aggregate income effect and intertemporal substitution effect), Auclert finds that monetary policy effectiveness is not very clear, as it depends on the heterogeneity of consumption behaviours among individuals. He suggests that the design of monetary policy should consider its redistributive impacts to achieve both macroeconomic stability and equitable income distribution.

Cairó and Sim (2018) employ similar methodology, that is, a general equilibrium model with heterogeneous agents (shareholders and workers), to analyse the effectiveness of monetary policy rules in unequal economies, which can even potentially lead to financial crises. Although they do not discuss distributive effects of monetary policy itself, they recognise that high levels of inequality can make conventional monetary policy rules suboptimal. Therefore, they argue that an optimal monetary policy rule should incorporate policy goals to offset existing inequality (although they also argue that monetary policy cannot affect and completely mitigate existing inequality). Despite being a general equilibrium model, Cairó and Sim's model incorporates some Kaleckian foundations, such as the pricing behaviour of firms and the role of demand in economies operating below full capacity.

Kaplan, Moll, and Violante (2018) propose a heterogeneous agent new-Keynesian (HANK) model to discuss monetary policy transmission channels. They argue that empirical evidence points out consumption's low sensitivity to interest rates so there must be another channel that explains the effects of monetary policy. They show that this channel depends on the distribution not of income but of assets, such as liquid short-term assets and illiquid long-term assets. The effectiveness of monetary policy depends on this distribution, which in turn arises from heterogeneity in propensity to consume, as savers tend to allocate their portfolio to illiquid assets. Despite this heterogeneity, the model assumes traditional new-Keynesian features, such as the Phillips curve and nominal price rigidities.

Although these models represent a departure from the representative agent assumption and perfect competition hypothesis, two necessary conditions when discussing income distribution and monetary policy effectiveness, they still rely on the general equilibrium approach, which imposes restrictive market clearing conditions and limits the possibility of more complex interactions and dynamics. Moreover, heterogeneity is characterised by two types of representative agent, and, rather than being a result of a model, it is instead imposed. Models that follow the agent-based approach allow for several heterogeneities and they can result from the complex interaction of agents, especially in conditions of equilibrium.

Dosi et al. (2013) can be considered pioneers in terms of contributing to this topic using macroeconomic agent-based modelling. The authors extend the established Keynes meeting Schumpeter (K+S) model (Dosi, Fagiolo, and Roventini 2010) to explore how income distribution interacts with monetary and fiscal policies to influence macroeconomic variables such as GDP growth, unemployment, and the occurrence of financial crises. The model encompasses heterogeneous consumption and capital firms following Kaleckian price behaviours, among other Keynesian and Schumpeterian behaviours. The main transmission channel present in this model is the impact of monetary policy on banks' credit supply, which can constrain consumption and investment while the aggregate demand effect can impact income distribution. They conclude that more unequal economies experience greater business cycle fluctuations, higher unemployment rates, and a higher probability of financial crises. Moreover, the agent-based approach, in contrast with the general equilibrium method, allows them to capture a non-linearity effect of monetary policy, which seems to result in reduced effectiveness until a certain threshold level and then, beyond that point, higher interest rates can lead to worse macroeconomic outcomes. Dosi et al. (2015) extend this analysis by combining monetary and fiscal policy. Not only do they find that monetary policy alone is not enough to achieve desired macroeconomic goals and needs to be combined with fiscal policy, but they also reinforce the idea that fiscal and monetary policies can have differential impacts depending on the distribution of income within the economy.

Schasfoort et al. (2017) present an agent-based model to study the complex interactions between several different monetary policy transmission channels: the expectations channel, bank lending channel, investment channel, asset price channel, consumption channel, cost channel, and exchange rate channel. Although most of these are conventional channels, Schasfoort et al. include the cost channel, since firms set price based on markup over costs, and interest can affect firms' funding costs. Their model does not discuss a distributive monetary policy channel or the impact of inequality on its effectiveness; rather, it presents a valuable contribution to studying several channels interacting at the same time. They conclude that the effectiveness of monetary policy obviously depends on the strength and interaction of each channel.

Rolim, Baltar, and Lima (2023), in turn, use an agent-based model with Keynesian features (in fact, there are many similarities between this model and the K+S family of models) to provide a comprehensive and detailed study of income distribution. The research delves into the mechanisms of productivity growth, wage bargaining and mark-up adjustments, exploring their implications for both functional and personal income distribution. Innovatively, the model assumes three classes of agents, capitalists, direct workers and managers, which allows them to draw conclusions on functional and personal income distribution. Although they do not discuss the direct impacts of monetary policy on income distribution, they find that policies that support workers' bargaining power, combined with measures to stimulate technological innovation and productivity, could mitigate the adverse effects of productivity growth on income equality.

The agent-based models reviewed above are complementary. Whereas that of Rolim, Baltar, and Lima (2023) emphasises determinants of distribution, Schasfoort et al.'s (2017) model focuses on several monetary policy transmission channels simultaneously, but without a direct distributive channel. Finally, Dosi et al. (2013, 2015) study the complex interaction between income distribution and monetary policy effectiveness but with limited transmission channels. The model developed in the next section aims to study this complex nexus wheni several transmission channels are in play, including direct and indirect monetary policy distributive channels.

4. The Model

This multisectoral micro–macro (MMM) dynamic simulation model combines theoretical foundations of post-Keynesian, Kaleckian and neo-Schumpeterian approaches as a useful tool to investigate general dynamic properties of capitalist economies. The present version of the MMM model describes a general theoretical economy composed of three productive sectors: one consumption goods sector populated with η^c firms, one intermediate goods sector populated with η^i firms, and one capital goods sector populated with η^k firms. The household sector is divided into H income classes, the financial sector is populated with B banks, and the government and the external sector complete the model. Figure 2 is a stylised representation of the model's structure and flows.

All firms make decisions to produce, set prices, invest, and conduct technological searches. To produce, all firms need capital and intermediate goods, and they produce based on expected demand, restricted to current productive capacity and current availability of inputs. All firms also employ labour, based on productivity and current level of production. Labour productivity is embodied in each vintage capital, which comprises

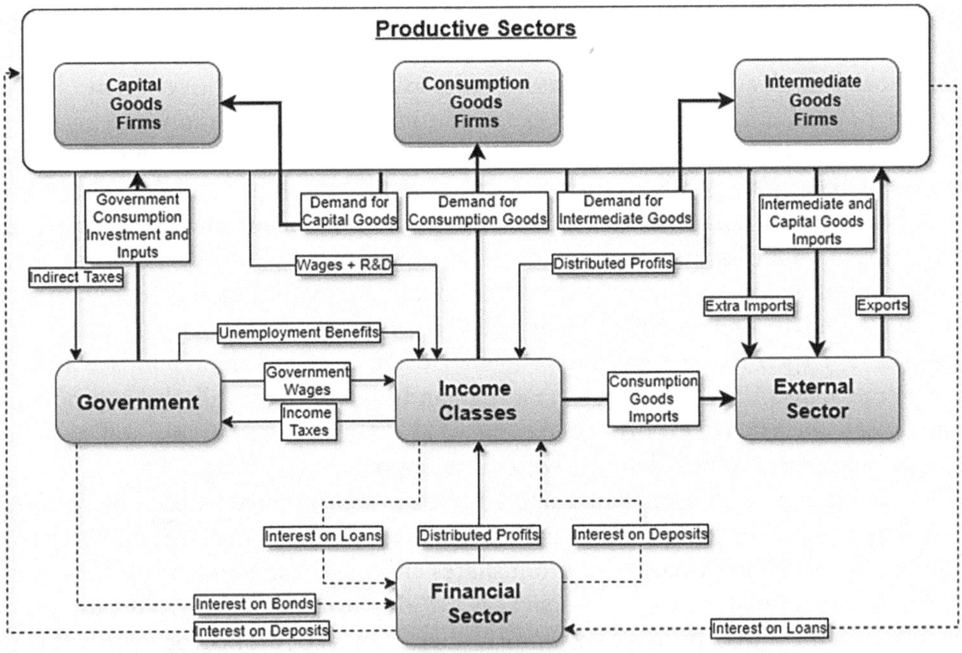

Figure 2. MMM Model Flows. Source: Author's Elaboration. Continuous arrows represent real flows; dashed arrows represent financial flows.

the total productive capacity of each firm, and the most productive sources of capital are used first. The aggregate level of production generates endogenous sectoral demand for intermediate goods, based on technical input coefficients.

Firms set prices based on their degree of monopoly under imperfect competition, as proposed by Kalecki (1954), as a weighted average between their desired price and the market average price, a reference price. Firms' desired price is determined by applying a long-term desired mark-up over variable unit cost. Their price, in addition to their delivery delay and product quality, affects their competitiveness, and subsequently their market share.

Firms also perform a technological search. The resources available depend on a fixed proportion of revenue, and are divided into innovation and imitation R&D. By conducting innovation R&D, firms are open to exogenous stochastic sectoral technological opportunities, and they search for new levels of both labour productivity (process innovation) and product quality and differentiation (product innovation). Imitation, in its turn, also involves a search for higher levels of productivity and quality but by examining other firms in the sector. Ensuring new product quality requires only labour; however, boosting labour productivity requires new capital goods thus affecting investment decisions.

Finally, firms undertake investment decisions, which can be subdivided into three main components: (i) physical depreciation, (ii) productive capacity expansion, and (iii) technological obsolescence and modernisation. Firms demand capital goods in order to have enough productive capacity to meet long-term expected demand, already bearing in mind physical depreciation. The third component is determined by a simple payback rule for each capital good, depending on the R&D success of the current period. Investment decisions can be financially constrained, and firms can use retained profits, loans, and available liquid assets (deposits) to finance investment. If total funds are not enough, firms prioritise expansion investment in relation to replacement investment. An aggregate level of investment decisions generates endogenous sectoral demand for the capital goods sector.

The banks in the financial sector collect deposits from firms and households, and provide loans to firms and households. The government can levy taxes on firms' revenue and/or household' income spend on public-sector wages and unemployment benefits, limited to one or more fiscal rules, such as a primary surplus target or a debt-to-GDP target. If the government has a deficit, it creates new bonds which are held by the banks. The external sector demands goods from all three productive sectors based on a fixed exports coefficient, real external income and real exchange rate, and it can meet unmet demand with extra imports.

The income generated by all banks and all firms is appropriated by each income class by a matrix of income appropriation coefficients: in general, this matrix is a 2×H matrix, composed by two H-sized vectors of profit shares and wage shares, where all elements of each vector should equal 1. In this version, we distinguish industrial profits, the profits generated by the three productive sectors, then financial profits, generated by the banks. We assume three income classes ($H = 3$), so we have a 3×3 matrix of income appropriation. To make it easy to identify the role of each source of income, we assume an identity matrix, so one class receives all financial profits, one class receives all industrial profits, and the final class receives all wages. Notice that the matrix of appropriation does not have to be an identity matrix and can be generalised to gain more realistic results. Besides the appropriation of functional income, the main difference between the classes is their propensity to consume.

Income classes demand consumption goods based on a fixed marginal propensity to consume over past average income, in which a share is demanded domestically and another share externally. However, autonomous consumption does not depend on income but evolves based on average quality of the consumption good sector. Income classes are also subject to balance sheet positions, as they can take on new loans to finance consumption decisions or accumulate deposits from unspent current income. Aggregate consumption decisions of all income classes generate endogenous sectoral demand for the consumption goods sector.

Appendix A provides a useful timeline of the events that happen in each time period of the model. Relevant equations can be found in Online Appendix B. A complete description of all equations used in the model can be found in Trotta Vianna (2021).

4.1. Simulation Settings

In order to evaluate the impact of the interest rate on income distribution, we perform simulations in a two-step process. First, we establish our baseline scenario and perform empirical validation of the standard case. Second, we conduct *policy experiments*, whereby we change the interest rate rule and generate the results. We then compare the variables for each case. We run 50 independent simulations for each case, each involving at least 600 periods, with one period representing a quarter. The first

200 periods are discarded to reduce the effects of the initial selected values of the stated variables, so that we can compute average values for the last 400 periods (100 years).

The model is written in LSD code, version 8.0.[5] LSD (Laboratory for Simulation Development) is both a language and a platform for writing simulation models. It is a simple to use, stand-alone program, which even non-experts can use to run and test results from simulation models. LSD is copyrighted by Marco Valente and Marcelo C. Pereira (version 7, plus additions). The version presented here can be found at https://github.com/thttnn/MMM_v.3.

4.2. Model Calibration

As we would like our model to replicate general dynamic properties and regularities, we do not want it to begin in a specific condition. So, the first hypothesis we made is the homogeneity assumption that all firms start in the same way, with the same market share, same productivity, same price, same costs. Firms' differentiation, competition, and selection will be generated endogenously during the simulation runs. Because of that we can simplify the calibration to sectoral level. This reduces the number of parameters to the number of sectors in the current specification, rather than having one parameter for each firm. The endogenous calculations are also simplified, as we are computing a more aggregate level of the model.[6]

As we would like the trends and trajectories, desirably endogenous growth and fluctuations, to be generated by the simulation process and not by the initial values, we stipulate no past growth. So, the initial configuration is a non-growth steady state, but it will not last even one time step, as the mechanisms which generate dynamics in the model will start to trigger from the first time step and so on. This could in fact generate some strong values at the very beginning, as the economy will rapidly change from the non-growth steady state to endogenous growth trajectories, but we will discard the first-time steps in our analysis to account for that problem, which is common good practice in the AB literature.

We assume that both the government and the external sector start in balance and we use stock and flow norms to calculate the initial values of many variables given some initial exogenous parameters. We will not discuss in detail the calibration method used here; however, its main advantage is that it reduces the parametric space and the degree of freedom of the modeller by imposing stock and flow restrictions. Appendix C presents a table of parameter values and baseline configurations.

5. Results

All results presented here are MonteCarlo averages of 50 independent simulation runs, discarding the first 200 of 600 time-steps, leaving us with 400 time periods, or 100 years in chronological time. We also present the MonteCarlo confidence interval, showing that the MonteCarlo average is statistically significant.

[5]The software can be downloaded in https://github.com/marcov64/Lsd.

[6]See Trotta Vianna (2021) for a complete exposition of the calibration procedure.

5.1. Baseline Results

The model is able to generate endogenous growth. Consumption is the largest and most stable component of GDP, while investment is the most volatile. The model can also generate endogenous business cycles. The cyclicality of the model can also be seen when looking at the average capacity utilisation rate, which fluctuates but is stable around the level desired by the firms. The model also generates endogenous positive inflation, with variations and a slight increasing trend, although stabilising at around 2 per cent a year.

Table 1 provides statistics for some relevant variables across simulation runs. For instance, it shows that the average GDP growth rate was, on average across simulations, 0.97 per cent, with a 0.0015 standard deviation across simulations, with the maximum being one simulation with an average GDP growth of 1.37 per cent and the minimum being one simulation with an average GDP growth of 0.34 per cent. This shows how the same set of initial conditions and parameters can generate different trajectories; however, for most variables the MonteCarlo average, the average across simulations, is representative. That is why we also present the MonteCarlo confidence intervals in the plots.

In Table 1 we can also see some of the distributive variables of the model, such as the profit and wage shares, calculated as shares of gross income, with profits accounting for both industrial and financial profits. We can also see the income share of the income classes, after distribution, income taxes, and non-taxable income transfers such as unemployment benefits. Class A appropriates all of the financial profits, class B the industrial profits, and class C the wages. On average, workers hold 39.5 per cent of disposable income, capitalists around 53 per cent, and rentiers, those who appropriate financial profits, 7.5 per cent. We might also be interested in seeing how this distribution changes during the simulation run, as these values are the averages of 100 years in each simulation.

Distribution changes during this 100-year period favour industrial profits reducing the wage share, which is a feature of recent capitalism as pointed out by several studies, such a (e.g., OECD 2015). This effect mainly occurs because the pass-through from productivity to wages is not full, smaller than one, meaning that wages grow

Table 1. Baseline results—Monte Carlo statistics.

Variable	Avg	SD	Min	Max
GDP growth	0.0098	0.0015	0.0034	0.0137
Volatility of GDP growth	0.0467	0.0120	0.0356	0.1040
Capacity utilisation	0.8992	0.0061	0.8729	0.9070
Volatility of capacity utilisation	0.0420	0.0087	0.0309	0.0778
Likelihood of recession	0.1034	0.0085	0.0850	0.1250
CPI inflation	0.0168	0.0002	0.0160	0.0173
Government debt/GDP	0.6736	0.0461	0.5829	0.8300
Profit rate	0.1903	0.0023	0.1814	0.1941
Profit share	0.6504	0.0025	0.6458	0.6578
Wage share	0.3496	0.0025	0.3422	0.3542
Class A Income Share	0.0741	0.0025	0.0693	0.0808
Class B income share	0.5299	0.0033	0.5226	0.5380
Class C income share	0.3960	0.0025	0.3883	0.4001
Basic interest rate	0.0034	0.0001	0.0033	0.0037
Firms' average debt rate	0.3743	0.0150	0.3357	0.4076
Classes' average debt rate	0.2813	0.0026	0.2692	0.2897
Financial sector default rate	0.0126	0.0023	0.0085	0.0213

slower than productivity and firms appropriate this difference in the form of profits, which explains increasing effective markups and profit rates.

The income share of class A, the rentiers, also grows, although slightly, mainly because of the increasing basic interest rate. This is one of the main features of the model due to its true heterodox theoretical foundations: as the traditional channels of monetary policy are not present, specifically, the last link from demand to prices, the central bank fails to tame inflation by adopting a single mandate Taylor rule. In fact, inflation exceeds the central bank's target, forcing it to increase the basic interest rate, and adjust the entire interest rate structure. However, as the average debt rate of the firms is not extremely high and the financial cost pass-through is also considerable, increases in the interest rate do not reduce completely the industrial profit rate. In the next sections we will perform some experiments with these key parameters.

5.2. Different Basic Interest Rate Levels

Given the baseline results described above, our first experiment involves changing the basic interest rate of the central bank. We tested four different levels: 0.003 (which is the same as the baseline scenario), 0.005, 0.007, and 0.009. Notice that this is the quarterly nominal interest rate. Table 2 presents a comparison of the alternative cases. The variables are presented as ratios in relation to the baseline, and we also perform a t-test against the null-hypothesis where no difference exists between the cases, so the ratio would be 1, thus presenting the statistical significance of the ratio.

We can already notice some relevant features: the interest rate level has no effect on the average growth rate but it increases volatility, mainly because the changes in the Taylor rule are proportional to the level. It increases inflation, characterising a price puzzle, and the exchange rate. Even with higher capital flows, as the domestic rate is higher than the external interest rate, the fall in the trade balance is higher than the increase in capital flows and so we get a more depreciated exchange rate. This increases input costs and prices. Also, as we know from the interest cost channel, increases in the basic rate leads to a higher rate on loans and, if firms adjust prices on the basis of financial

Table 2. Comparison between different basic interest rates.

Variable	0.003	0.005	0.007	0.009
GDP growth	0.0098	1.0153	1.0141	1.0145
Volatility of GDP growth	0.0467	1.0211	1.0704**	1.1055***
CPI inflation	0.0168	1.0200***	1.0404***	1.0623***
Exchange rate	0.8906	1.0112***	1.0217***	1.0328***
Primary surplus/GDP	0.0056	1.2186***	1.4515***	1.4815***
Profit rate	0.1903	0.9982	0.9961	0.9988
Profit share	0.6504	1.0010	1.0024**	1.0031***
Wage share	0.3496	0.9981	0.9955**	0.9942***
Class A income share	0.0741	1.0534***	1.1122***	1.1672***
Class B income share	0.5299	0.9946***	0.9889***	0.9826***
Class C income share	0.3960	0.9972	0.9938***	0.9919***
Firms' average debt rate	0.3743	0.9910	0.9886	0.9862*
Classes' average debt rate	0.2813	1.0005	1.0057**	1.0527***
Gini index	0.3202	1.0070***	1.0157***	1.0215***

Note: All results were subjected to a t-student test for signifficance. If a p-value is less than 0.05, it is flagged with one star (*). If a p-value is less than 0.01, it is flagged with 2 stars (**). If a p-value is less than 0.001, it is flagged with three stars (***).

costs, prices will go up. The positive effect of the interest rate on inflation corroborates the ineffectiveness of the Taylor rule, so persisting with such a monetary policy can be self-defeating.

Regarding distribution, there is only a slight change in profits and wage shares because they are mainly determined by the wage setting. However, intra-capitalist distribution is affected, as we see a significant increase in class A's income share and a fall in class B's. As the firms do not entirely pass financial costs to prices, increasing the interest rate level will eventually lead to a redistribution in favour of the rentier class. Another more direct mechanism corroborated this redistribution: with the same level of public debt, increases in the interest rate will lead to higher interest payments on public bonds. Banks hold these bonds, increasing their revenue and profits. Banks' profits are appropriated by the rentier class in our model.

Interestingly, as firms compensate for higher financial costs with higher prices, the profit rate and the average debt rate of the firms are practically unchanged. However, households, especially those from classes B and C which lost relative income, cannot generate more income to compensate for higher interest on their loans, and that is why we see an increase in the average debt rate of the income classes. We can assess the overall inequality of the economy by calculating a simple Gini index on income for the three classes, assuming their fixed shares in the population.[7] The average calculated Gini is 0.3202 and it increases significantly when the basic interest rate increases.

5.3. Experiment: Changing the Financial Cost Pass-Through

As we discovered that the financial cost pass-through might be mainly responsible for the price puzzle and the intra-capitalist distribution, we perform the same experiment, testing basic interest rate levels, but in different parameter configurations, first, with no financial cost pass-through and, second, with high financial cost pass-through. To be clear, we first set our parameter ξ_j^{fc} to zero and then to 1, recalling that in all experiments so far it assumed the value 0.5.

Table 3 shows the same variables when the test involves different interest rate levels with no financial cost pass-through.

First, and again, the interest rate has no effect on the growth trend. However, the positive effect on GDP volatility disappears. The price puzzle effect still persists, as increases in the basic interest rate lead to higher CPI inflation. However, the effect is lower than in the baseline case when financial costs are partially passed to prices. In the current scenario, the price puzzle effect occurs because of the exchange rate effect, as we see similar positive effect in the exchange rate and weaker effect on overall inflation when compared to the baseline experiment.

In line with our expectations, in the baseline case, the firms' profit rate is basically unaffected, as they maintain their profit margin by increasing prices. When they do not increase prices when facing higher financial costs, their profit rate on capital is reduce, a visible effect in this experiment. There was no significant effect on the firms'

[7]We assume 1, 29, and 70%, respectively, for classes A, B, and C. These values can be easily adjusted to approximate our theoretical economy from a specific country, but it is not the intention here.

Table 3. Comparison between different basic interest rates with no financial cost pass-through.

Variable	0.003	0.005	0.007	0.009
GDP growth	0.0094	1.0171	0.9944	1.0198
Volatility of GDP growth	0.0349	1.0232	1.0340	1.0341
CPI inflation	0.0172	1.0195***	1.0374***	1.0556***
Exchange rate	0.8874	1.0115***	1.0209***	1.0344***
Profit rate	0.1754	0.9932**	0.9865***	0.9767***
Profit share	0.6454	0.9992	0.9997	0.9979**
Wage share	0.3546	1.0015	1.0005	1.0039**
Class A income share	0.0926	1.0553***	1.1166***	1.1829***
Class B income share	0.5045	0.9897***	0.9800***	0.9662***
Class C income share	0.4029	1.0002	0.9983	1.0003
Firms' average debt rate	0.4669	0.9972	1.0043	1.0074
Classes' average debt rate	0.2862	1.0026	1.0031*	1.0352***
Gini index	0.2862	1.0026	1.0031*	1.0352***

Note: All results were subjected to a t-student test for signifficance. If a *p*-value is less than 0.05, it is flagged with one star (*). If a *p*-value is less than 0.01, it is flagged with 2 stars (**). If a *p*-value is less than 0.001, it is flagged with three stars (***).

average debt rate[8] as a result of changing the interest rate, but there is a relevant difference when we compare the two experiments, as the baseline average debt rate was 37 per cent in the first experiment and 47 per cent in the second. The effect on the household debt rate is stronger mainly because of inflation and distribution.

When we compare the two baselines, there no significant changes in functional distribution. However, we notice an interesting effect when we change the basic interest rate: the overall profit share falls and the wage share increases. The profit share falls because the fall in industrial profits is higher than the gain in financial profits, leading to an overall reduction of profit share and, as a result of complementarity, an increase in wage share. We can also visualise this effect by comparing the change in income share of classes A and B: class A has a higher gain when basic rates increase and firms do not compensate with higher prices, whereas class B has a greater drop in participation in the same circumstances.

When we look at the Gini index, the baseline with no financial cost pass-through generates a lower average index. In addition, there seems to be no significant difference when interest rates increase, except for when they are at really high levels. Intra-capitalist redistribution is not strong enough to have significant impacts on the Gini index, which is known to be a measure of inequality that is not very sensitive to extremes.

Alternatively, we test changing the basic interest rate in a scenario where firms pass financial costs to prices entirely, so we change our parameter ξ_j^{fc} to 1 first. Table 4 shows the results.

This exercise reinforces the general effects of the first experiments: a price puzzle and increased GDP volatility. The profit rate remains unchanged as does the average debt rate of the firms. When we compare the three baseline cases, with the same interest rate, the functional distribution between overall profits and wages is practically the same, but the effect on functional distribution is higher in this third cases: a higher basic interest rate increases bank profits and the income of the rentier class A, and it increases the financial costs of the industrial firms but they adjust prices accordingly, without losing profit

[8]The average debt rate might not be the best indicator as it masks most heterogeneity between firms. A better micro-level analysis would be required but it will not be carried out in this article.

Table 4. Comparison of different basic interest rates with high financial cost pass-through.

Variable	0.003	0.005	0.007	0.009
GDP growth	0.0105	0.9788	1.0054	0.9982
Volatility of GDP growth	0.0511	1.0301	1.0743*	1.1190***
CPI inflation	0.0165	1.0225***	1.0432***	1.0643***
Exchange rate	0.8893	1.0123***	1.0235***	1.0317***
Profit rate	0.1989	0.9998	1.0008	1.0048
Profit share	0.6536	1.0019***	1.0037***	1.0074***
Wage share	0.3464	0.9965***	0.9930***	0.9860***
Class A income share	0.0680	1.0519***	1.1079***	1.1726***
Class B income share	0.5399	0.9967***	0.9926***	0.9902***
Class C income share	0.3921	0.9955***	0.9915***	0.9836***
Firms' average debt rate	0.3440	0.9876*	0.9824**	0.9905
Classes' average debt rate	0.2782	1.0017	1.0105***	1.0849***
Gini index	0.3222	1.0096***	1.0178***	1.0312***

Note: All results were subjected to a t-student test for significance. If a p-value is less than 0.05, it is flagged with one star (*). If a p-value is less than 0.01, it is flagged with 2 stars (**). If a p-value is less than 0.001, it is flagged with three stars (***).

margins. Overall profits increase and squeeze the wage share because now workers face higher prices and higher indebtedness. The Gini index dynamic is very similar to that of the baseline scenario.

5.4. Experiment: Changing Workers' Bargaining Power

As another experiment, we can see how monetary policy affects distribution in a scenario whereby workers have higher bargaining power. In our model, this is represented by the two pass-through parameters in the wage equation, ξ_j^p and ξ_j^ϕ. Higher values of these parameters indicate that workers obtain higher wage adjustments when inflation and/or productivity rises. Higher wage adjustments also indicate more pressure on industrial firms, even when they incorporate financial costs in their price formation.

When we compare the scenario shown in Table 5 with the baseline, higher average inflation exists because the price–wage spiral is stronger, the average profit rate on capital is lower because of the cost pressures on industrial firms and lower appropriation of

Table 5. Different basic interest rates with high worker bargaining power.

Variable	0.003	0.005	0.007	0.009
GDP growth	0.0097	1.0044	0.9878	1.0093
Volatility of GDP growth	0.0433	1.0116	1.0295	1.0739**
CPI inflation	0.0173	1.0186***	1.0320***	1.0477***
Volatility of CPI inflation	0.0053	1.2040***	1.3698***	1.6217***
Exchange rate	0.9285	1.0092***	1.0193***	1.0282***
Profit rate	0.1597	0.9982	0.9981	0.9986
Profit share	0.5233	1.0042***	1.0098***	1.0163***
Wage share	0.4767	0.9954***	0.9893***	0.9821***
Class A income share	0.0709	1.0773***	1.1544***	1.2491***
Class B income share	0.4096	0.9935***	0.9888***	0.9824***
Class C income share	0.5194	0.9945***	0.9877***	0.9799***
Firms' average debt rate	0.3915	0.9993	0.9986	0.9943
Classes' average debt rate	0.3670	1.0066***	1.0259***	1.2565***
Gini index	0.1970	1.0226***	1.0487***	1.0794***

Note: All results were subjected to a t-student test for significance. If a p-value is less than 0.05, it is flagged with one star (*). If a p-value is less than 0.01, it is flagged with 2 stars (**). If a p-value is less than 0.001, it is flagged with three stars (***).

Table 6. Different basic interest rates with high worker bargaining power and no financial cost pass-through.

Variable	0.003	0.005	0.007	0.009
GDP growth	0.0092	1.0249	1.0171	1.0030
Volatility of GDP growth	0.0331	0.9898	0.9946	0.9764
CPI inflation	0.0179	1.0147***	1.0297***	1.0464***
Volatility of CPI inflation	0.0059	1.2993***	1.5108***	1.9777***
Exchange rate	0.9258	1.0100***	1.0190***	1.0286***
Profit rate	0.1427	0.9867***	0.9788***	0.9624***
Profit share	0.5170	0.9995	1.0015	0.9998
Wage share	0.4830	1.0006	0.9984	1.0002
Class A income share	0.0888	1.0802***	1.1568***	1.2731***
Class B income share	0.3830	0.9832***	0.9693***	0.9429***
Class C income share	0.5281	0.9987	0.9959***	0.9954***
Firms' average debt rate	0.4807	1.0066	1.0077	1.0154***
Classes' average debt rate	0.3711	1.0122***	1.0327***	1.6071***
Gini index	0.1938	1.0145***	1.0326***	1.0498***

Note: All results were subjected to a t-student test for signifficance. If a *p*-value is less than 0.05, it is flagged with one star (*). If a *p*-value is less than 0.01, it is flagged with 2 stars (**). If a *p*-value is less than 0.001, it is flagged with three stars (***).

productivity gains, and, perhaps the most significant difference, the average wage share is much higher (48 per cent compared to 35 per cent) and the average overall profit share is much lower (52 per cent compared to 65 per cent). When we look at the distribution between classes, it is clear that this difference exists in the industrial sphere, as the income share of class A, the financial capitalists, is practically unchanged. The bargaining power of workers is one of the main determinants of the distribution between wages and industrial profits. With smaller margins, firms face higher indebtedness and households, even if they increase their income, also face higher debt rates because of the inflationary effect. Despite the higher inflation and indebtedness levels for households, overall inequality measured by the Gini index falls considerably and has no adverse effect on GDP growth and volatility.

In such a scenario, higher interest rates have greater effects on functional distribution, increasing overall profit share. The income gains of class A are much higher because the dispute between industrial capitalists and workers is more fierce without affecting the rentiers. In addition, as both firms and households face higher indebtedness, the interest payments to banks and consequent redistribution of financial profits to rentiers are higher. Overall inequality is much more sensitive to changes in the interest rate in such a scenario because the Gini index increases significantly.

When firms do not adjust prices to higher financial costs, higher interest rates have no effect on functional distribution. Again, all income gains of the financial capitalist are a reduction of industrial capitalists' profits. Their profit rate declines and their indebtedness increases in comparison to the previous scenario. Even if the interest rate effect on the income of the rentiers is higher, the fall in overall inequality measured by the Gini index is not that sharp. Table 6 summarises this experiment. In contrast, when firms fully adjust prices to financial costs, their profit rate and indebtedness are almost unchanged as a result of the income share of the industrial capitalist. All income gains of the rentiers are passed to workers by firms and the decline in the wage share in the face of higher interest rates is greater. In this case, summarised by Table 7, the interest rate effect on overall inequality is much stronger.

Table 7. Different basic interest rates with high worker bargaining power and high financial cost pass-through.

Variable	0.003	0.005	0.007	0.009
GDP growth	0.0101	1.0093	0.9472*	0.9890
Volatility of GDP growth	0.0473	0.9911	1.1014***	1.0993***
CPI inflation	0.0166	1.0191***	1.0365***	1.0573***
Volatility of CPI inflation	0.0062	1.0791***	1.1985***	1.2824***
Exchange rate	0.9303	1.0103***	1.0214***	1.0334***
Profit rate	0.1709	1.0088***	1.0084***	1.0085***
Profit share	0.5287	1.0088***	1.0147***	1.0198***
Wage share	0.4713	0.9901***	0.9835***	0.9778***
Class A income share	0.0635	1.0821***	1.1623***	1.2482***
Class B income share	0.4235	0.9994	0.9968***	0.9918***
Class C income share	0.5129	0.9903***	0.9826***	0.9760***
Firms' average debt rate	0.3546	1.0062	0.9996	0.9910
Classes' average debt rate	0.3626	1.0028	1.0320***	1.2030***
Gini index	0.2013	1.0322***	1.0593***	1.0840***

Note: All results were subjected to a t-student test for signifficance. If a *p*-value is less than 0.05, it is flagged with one star (*). If a *p*-value is less than 0.01, it is flagged with 2 stars (**). If a *p*-value is less than 0.001, it is flagged with three stars (***).

6. Conclusions

The model presented in this article produced interesting results relating to the conduction of monetary policy in an economy when firms compete in oligopolistic markets and face financial constraints and costs. Even when introducing non-conventional channels of monetary policy and applying post-Keynesian and Kaleckian theories to production and pricing, monetary policy failed to tame inflation. In addition, the model also created the well-known Gibson's paradox, or price puzzle, whereby increases in the interest rate led to higher prices and inflation in contrast to the expectations of conventional theory. Higher interest rate levels also caused greater GDP volatility.

The main effect we captured, however, is the distributional effect of interest rates: regardless of circumstances, a higher basic interest rate increases interest payments on government bonds, thus increasing the income of bond holders, usually banks, financial institutions, and wealthy individuals. Higher interest rates affect the entire interest rate structure, increasing interest on loans for both firms and households. The difference is that firms have the power to increase their income and households do not. Households have no control over how much income they will receive, while industrial firms can adjust their prices to cope with higher financial costs.

The ability of firms to pass financial costs to prices is determinant on whether they can capture the effect of higher interest rates on so-called intra-capitalist distribution. Given the initial increase of financial profits, if firms adjust prices, they tend to maintain the same profit margin and the overall profit (industrial and financial) share increases, squeezing the wage share. If industrial firms do not adjust prices, the overall profit share might remain the same, relatively, although there is a shift in favour of financial capitalists.

When workers have more bargaining power with which to claim higher wages, there is another source of pressure on the profit rate of industrial firms. The wage spiral increases the indebtedness of workers and, consequently, the income of rentiers. Not only is the interest on loans higher but the amount of debt also increases, accelerating the redistribution of income in favour of rentiers. Although workers' higher bargaining power generates less unequal income distribution, it makes the effect of interest rates on distribution stronger.

The final effect of interest rate policies on overall functional distribution and intra-capitalist distribution will depend fundamentally on the power of banks, firms, and households. We found that the effect of interest rates on income distribution will depend on the ability of firms to increase prices when facing financial costs and the ability of household to claim higher wages. In this article, we treated the parameters that represent those abilities as fixed, changing them exogenously, but the next step of this research is to identify and examine how these abilities change or are related to current economic conditions, making them endogenous in the model. Still, we now know that, under any circumstances, a restrictive monetary policy will not benefit the majority of the population, the workers and wage earners.

Acknowledgements

The author is grateful for the comments provided by the participants in the Monetary Policy and Income Distribution Workshop (September 2022, Toronto, Canada) and the Agent-Based Models for Policy Workshop (November 2022, Pisa, Italy). No specific funding was used in this research. The usual disclaimers apply.

Disclosure Statement

No potential conflict of interest was reported by the author.

References

Altavilla, C., M. Boucinha, and J.-L. Peydró. 2018. 'Monetary Policy and Bank Profitability in a Low Interest Rate Environment.' *Economic Policy* 33 (96): 531–586.

Arestis, P., and P. Howells. 1994. 'Monetary Policy and Income Distribution in the UK.' *Review of Radical Political Economics* 26 (3): 56–65.

Arestis, P., and M. C. Sawyer. 2002. 'New Consensus' New Keynesianism, and the Economics of the'Third Way.'

Argitis, G., and C. Pitelis. 2001. 'Monetary Policy and the Distribution of Income: Evidence for the United States and the United Kingdom.' *Journal of Post Keynesian Economics* 23 (4): 617–635. doi:10.1080/01603477.2001.11490302.

Auclert, A. 2019. 'Monetary Policy and the Redistribution Channel.' *American Economic Review* 109 (6): 2333–2367.

BCB. 1999. *Relatório de Inflação*. Brasilia: Banco Central do Brasil.

Borio, C., L. Gambacorta, and B. Hofmann. 2017. 'The Influence of Monetary Policy on Bank Profitability.' *International Finance* 20 (1): 48–63.

Cairó, I., and J. Sim. 2018. 'Income Inequality, Financial Crises, and Monetary Policy.'

Cobham, A., L. Schlögl, and A. Sumner. 2016. 'Inequality and the Tails: The Palma Proposition and Ratio.' *Global Policy* 7 (1): 25–36.

Davidson, P. 2011. *Post Keynesian Macroeconomic Theory*. Edward Elgar Publishing.

Dosi, G., G. Fagiolo, and A. Roventini. 2010. 'Schumpeter Meeting Keynes: A Policy-Friendly Model of Endogenous Growth and Business Cycles.' *Journal of Economic Dynamics and Control* 34 (9): 1748–1767.

Dosi, G., et al. 2013. 'Income Distribution, Credit and Fiscal Policies in an Agent-Based Keynesian Model.' *Journal of Economic Dynamics and Control* 37 (8): 1598–1625.

Dosi, G., et al. 2015. 'Fiscal and Monetary Policies in Complex Evolving Economies.' *Journal of Economic Dynamics and Control* 52: 166–189.

Dunhaupt, P. 2013. 'Determinants of Functional Income Distribution: Theory and Empirical Evidence.'

Dweck, E. 2006. 'Uma análise da interação micro-macro com base em um modelo dinâmico multissetorial de simulação.' PhD diss., Universidade Federal do Rio de Janeiro.

Dweck, E., M. T. Vianna, and A. da Cruz Barbosa. 2020. 'Discussing the Role of Fiscal Policy in a Demand-led Agent-Based Growth Model.' *Economia* 21 (2): 185–208.

Eichenbaum, M. 1992. 'Interpreting the Macroeconomic Time Series Facts: The Effects of Monetary Policy.' *European Economic Review* 36 (5): 1001–1011.

Erber, F. S. 2011. 'As convenções de desenvolvimento no governo Lula: um ensaio de economia política.' *Brazilian Journal of Political Economy* 31 (1): 31–55.

Erber, F. S. 2012. 'The Evolution of Development Conventions.' *Revista de Economia Contemporânea* 16 (1): 1–22.

Gordon, R. J. 1997. 'The Time-Varying NAIRU and Its Implications for Economic Policy.' *Journal of Economic Perspectives* 11 (1): 11–32.

Hannsgen, G. 2004. 'Gibson's Paradox, Monetary Policy, and the Emergence of Cycles.'

Hannsgen, G. 2007. '13 The Transmission Mechanism of Monetary Policy: A Critical Review.' In *A Handbook of Alternative Monetary Economics*, edited by P. Arestis and M. Sawyer. *A Handbook of Alternative Monetary Economics.* Cheltenham: Edward Elgar Publishing.

Kalecki, M. 1954. *Theory of Economic Dynamics: An Essay on Cyclical and Long-run Changes in Capitalist Economy.* 2. Impr. George Allen & Unwin.

Kaplan, G., B. Moll, and G. L. Violante. 2018. 'Monetary Policy According to HANK.' *American Economic Review* 108 (3): 697–743.

Keynes, J. M. 1930. *Treatise on Money: Pure Theory of Money.* Vol. I. London: Macmillan.

Kumar, V., S. Acharya, and L. T. Ho. 2020. 'Does Monetary Policy Influence the Profitability of Banks in New Zealand?' *International Journal of Financial Studies* 8 (2): 35.

Lavoie, M. 2014. *Post-Keynesian Economics: New Foundations.* Cheltenham: Edward Elgar Publishing.

Lima, G. T., and M. Setterfield. 2010. 'Pricing Behaviour and the Cost-Push Channel of Monetary Policy.' *Review of Political Economy* 22 (1): 19–40.

Liosi, K., and S. Spyrou. 2022. 'The Impact of Monetary Policy on Income Inequality: Evidence from Eurozone Markets.' *Journal of Economic Studies* 49 (3): 522–540.

Martins, N. M., et al. 2017. 'The Transmission Mechanism of Monetary Policy: Microeconomic Aspects of Macroeconomic Issues.' *Journal of Post Keynesian Economics* 40 (3): 300–326.

Mishkin, F. 1996. 'The Channels of Monetary Transmission: Lessons for Monetary Policy.' *NBER Working Paper Series.* http://www.nber.org/papers/w5464.pdf?new_window=1%5Cnpapers2://publication/uuid/E7FD0848-77D9-4893-A4F5-579BFFF16DE9.

Mishkin, F. S. 1995. 'Symposium on the Monetary Transmission Mechanism.' *Journal of Economic Perspectives* 9 (4): 3–10.

Modenesi, A. d. M., and E. C. de Araújo. 2013. 'Price Stability under Inflation Targeting in Brazil: Empirical Analysis of the Monetary Policy Transmission Mechanism Based on a VAR Model, 2000–2008.' *Investigación económica* 72 (283): 99–133.

OECD. 2015. 'The Labour Share in G20 Economies.' In *Report Prepared for the G20 Employment Working Group, Antalya, February.*

Padrón, A. d. R. S., et al. 2015. 'Por que a elasticidade-preço das exportações é baixa no Brasil?: novas evidências desagregadas.'

Palma, J. G. 2014. 'Has the Income Share of the Middle and Upper-Middle Been Stable Around the '50/50 Rule', or Has It Converged towards That Level? The 'Palma Ratio'revisited.' *Development and Change* 45 (6): 1416–1448.

Passos, N., and A. de Melo Modenesi. 2021. 'Do Public Banks Reduce Monetary Policy Power? Evidence from Brazil Based on State Dependent Local Projections (2000–2018).' *International Review of Applied Economics* 35 (3-4): 1–18.

Piketty, T. 2014. *Capital in the Twenty-First Century.* Harvard University Press.

Piketty, T., and E. Saez. 2006. 'The Evolution of top Incomes: A Historical and International Perspective.' *American Economic Review* 96 (2): 200–205.

Possas, M., and E. Dweck. 2004. 'A Multisectoral Micro-Macrodynamic Model.' *Revista Economia* 5 (3): 1–43.

Possas, M. L., E. Dweck, and A. C. Visconti. 2004. 'Um modelo macrodinâmico multissetorial.' *Texto para discussao* 3: 2004.

Rochon, L.-P. 2022. 'The General Ineffectiveness of Monetary Policy or the Weaponization of Inflation.' In *The Future of Central Banking.* Cheltenham: Edward Elgar Publishing.

Rochon, L.-P., and M. Setterfield. 2008. 'The Political Economy of Interest-Rate Setting, Inflation, and Income Distribution.' *International Journal of Political Economy* 37 (2): 5–25.

Rolim, L. N., C. T. Baltar, and G. T. Lima. 2023. 'Income Distribution, Productivity Growth, and Workers' Bargaining Power in an Agent-Based Macroeconomic Model.' *Journal of Evolutionary Economics* 33 (2): 473–516.

Samarina, A., and A. D. Nguyen. 2019. 'Does Monetary Policy Affect Income Inequality in the Euro Area?'

Samuelson, P. A. 1945. 'The Effect of Interest Rate Increases on the Banking System.' *The American Economic Review* 35 (1): 16–27.

Schasfoort, J., A. Godin, D. Bezemer, A. Caiani, and S. Kinsella. 2017. 'Monetary Policy Transmission in a Macroeconomic Agent-Based Model.' *Advances in Complex Systems* 20 (08): 1850003.

Sicsú, J. 2003. 'Políticas não-monetárias de controle da inflação: uma proposta pós-keynesiana.' *Análise Econômica* 21 (39).

Sicsú, J., A. Modenesi, and D. Pimentel. 2020. 'Severe Recession with Inflation: The Case of Brazil.' *Journal of Post Keynesian Economics* 44 (1): 89–111.

Silverberg, G. 1987. 'Technical Progress, Capital Accumulation and Effective Demand: A Self-Organization Model.' In *Economic Evolution and Structural Adjustment.* Springer-Verlag.

Smithin, J. 2004. 'Interest Rate Operating Procedures and Income Distribution.' In *Central Banking in the Modern World: Alternative Perspectives.* Aldershot: *Edward Elgar.*

Stockhammer, E. 2009. *Determinants of Functional Income Distribution in OECD Countries.* Tech. Rep. IMK Study.

Stockhammer, E., Ö. Onaran, and S. Ederer. 2009. 'Functional Income Distribution and Aggregate Demand in the Euro Area.' *Cambridge Journal of Economics* 33 (1): 139–159.

Summa, R., and F. Serrano. 2018. 'Distribution and Conflict Inflation in Brazil under Inflation Targeting, 1999–2014.' *Review of Radical Political Economics* 50 (2): 349–369.

Taylor, J. B. 1993. 'Discretion Versus Policy Rules in Practice.' In *Carnegie-Rochester Conference Series on Public Policy.* Vol. 39. Elsevier.

Taylor, L. 2009. *Reconstructing Macroeconomics: Structuralist Proposals and Critiques of the Mainstream.* Cambridge, MA: Harvard University Press.

Trotta Vianna, M. 2021. 'Monetary Policy and Stabilization in a Multisectoral Micro-Macro Dynamic Simulation Model.' PhD diss., Tese de Doutorado, Instituto de Economia–UFRJ, Rio de Janeiro.

Are Firm Markups Boosting Inflation? A Post-Keynesian Institutionalist Approach to Markup Inflation in Select Industrialized Countries

Guillermo Matamoros

ABSTRACT

Starting in 2021, the current inflation process has spurred plenty of discussion in academic and policy circles. This paper studies the relationship between firms' markups and inflation during the 2021–22 inflation surge in several industrialized countries. It begins by explaining markup inflation and its critics in the context of the current debate over the sources of inflation. Then it reviews the characteristics of markup inflation within the post-Keynesian theory of markup pricing and complementing it with the Institutionalist approach to inflation that distinguishes between basic inflationary pressures and propagation mechanisms. The second part assesses markup inflation for several industrialized countries using descriptive statistics and conventional econometrics. The main contribution falls in empirically estimating markups considering the contribution of material cost and controlling for changes in capacity utilization over time. It concludes that there is some evidence pointing at markup inflation and, importantly, the existence of markup inflation leads to rejecting any wage-price spiral.

Introduction

The recent years have witnessed a heated debate around the primary sources of the inflation process that started in 2021. Almost everyone agrees that part of the inflation comes from global supply-side issues pertaining to supply chain bottlenecks and industry-specific shortages caused by both the reopening of economies from the Covid pandemic and the Ukraine war. However, at least in industrialized countries, there is controversy over the source of the domestic inflationary pressures and how to fight them.

On one side, almost like a déjà vu of the 1970s, some economists revived Monetarism, whence they attributed inflation to the government deficits incurred during the Covid pandemic and unconventional monetary policies that significantly expanded monetary aggregates (Ambler and Kronick 2022; Dehejia 2022a, 2022b; Greenwood and Hanke 2021).[1] On the other, at least in 2022, New Keynesian economists like Olivier Blanchard

[1]Richard Vague (2017) provides an interesting empirical critique of this monetarist explanation where he looks at different measures of money supply growth and inflation for 47 countries, concluding that 'high inflation has

and Larry Summers (Blanchard, Domash, and Summers 2022; Summers 2022) pointed to an aggregate excess demand fueled by a supposedly overheated economy reflected in very tight labor markets and wages growing excessively — although Blanchard has recently changed his mind and contested this story (Bernanke and Blanchard 2023).

Nevertheless, there is a third explanation that has received less support among mainstream economists — or has been discredited with perhaps poor knowledge of it.[2] This view points out that firms' profits have risen to historically high levels even surpassing producer price increments in several cases, whence domestic inflation would be in part driven by rising profits as opposed to rising wages (Stiglitz and Regmi 2023; Storm 2022). In other words, despite the main drivers of inflation that are the supply bottlenecks and shortages that keep pushing costs upward, firms with higher market power acting as price-setters have not only pass on cost increments to prices — which is in and of itself inflationary — but they have also increased their markups pushing up inflation even further (Konczal and Lusiani 2022; Nikiforos and Grothe 2023; Weber and Wasner 2023).

This third explanation underlines that firms with high market power can raise their markups because of supply rigidities and bottlenecks specific to the pandemic and war context. Both bottlenecks and material cost shocks strengthen entry barriers (Storm 2022) and allow incumbent firms to coordinate unit price increments even above their unit cost increases (Weber and Wasner 2023). In this story, part of the current Covid inflation would be explained by increasing markups over normal unit costs (NUC) i.e., unit costs at normal capacity utilization rates following the standard post-Keynesian normal cost pricing. Yet how markup consecutive increments are translated into the current inflationary episode? I argue in this paper that the post-Keynesian conflict inflation model, jointly with the Latin American Structuralist theory of inflation — with clear Institutionalist roots (see Danby 2005; Câmara and Vernengo 2004) — both provide an appropriate framework.

The Structuralist/Institutionalist theory of inflation distinguishes between *basic inflationary pressures,* coming from supply-side rigidities and industry-specific bottlenecks (such as raw materials, agriculture, and certain imports) that are expressed in rising material cost, and *propagation mechanisms* that are all the policies and institutional channels that allow firms to shift cost pressures to other social groups e.g., market power, pricing mechanisms, monetary and fiscal policies, and so on (Noyola 1956). Furthermore, the post-Keynesian conflict inflation model provides the necessary formalization of markup inflation based on the notion that inflation emerges as a result of social groups trying augment or retain their national income share.[3] In the 2021–22 inflationary context, basic pressures would be located in the supply dislocations and bottlenecks

infrequently followed rapid money supply growth, and in contrast to this, high inflation has occurred often when it has not been preceded by rapid money supply growth.'

[2]Larry Summers, for example, defends that the high market consolidation in some industries cannot be blamed for the current inflation. Thus, he says: 'The emerging claim that anti-trust can combat inflation is "science denial"' (cited in Mintz 2022). I believe this assertion is misleading because it reacts to an over-simplified version of the argument that has been called 'price gouging' or 'greedflation'. However, as I will try to explain in this paper, this third explanation is much more sophisticated. It does not attribute the inflationary surge to market concentration, but it does argue that inflation would be lower if the market power by firms in some industries would be indeed lower.

[3]The seminal article of the Latin American Structuralist theory of inflation was written in 1956 by the Mexican economist Juan Noyola (1956). In it, the author recognizes the influence of Michał Kalecki regarding the concepts of the degree of monopoly and the supply rigidities that applied to developing countries (e.g., the inelasticity in the agricultural industry

caused by the pandemic and the war, and propagation mechanisms would be identified in the process of firms defending or increasing their income share by raising their markups and boosting the inflation surge.[4]

The objectives and contributions of this paper are twofold. First, I explore and provide evidence suggesting that part of the current inflation is explained by increasing markups in several industrialized countries.[5] Accordingly, I present descriptive and econometric analyses in a similar spirit as the IMF (2022) and Hansen, Toscani, and Zhou (2023) for a group of industrialized countries, Fiebiger (2023) for Australia, Cochrane (2022) and Stanford (2022) for Canada, Bivens (2022), Konczal and Lusiani (2022), Nersisyan and Wray (2022), and Storm (2022) for the United States; Schnabel (2022) for the Eurozone; and CMA (2022) for the United Kingdom. Nevertheless, as opposed to most studies, I estimate markups over unit material cost (UMC) and unit labor cost (ULC) that, at the same time, control for variations in capacity utilization rates. Second, I put forth a theoretical explanation of markup inflation using the post-Keynesian and Institutionalist approaches.

The paper is divided into four broad parts, including the introduction and conclusion. The second part presents the theory behind markup inflation that is primarily based on the conflict inflation model of post-Keynesian economics together with the Institutionalist theory of inflation. It starts by addressing whether markup inflation is theoretically possible. The second part of this paper analyzes the evidence on markup and inflation during different inflation periods for several industrialized countries, all which serve the purpose of shedding light on the relationship between markups and inflation in the context of a significant material cost shock. This part concludes by carrying out a pooled OLS regression of inflation on the markup while controlling for capacity utilization for a group of industrialized countries, where I found some evidence supporting markup inflation in 2022. The fourth and final part rounds up.

Theory

Can Larger Markups Generate Inflation?

Imperfect competition and markup pricing has been very common in Kaleckian economics, and more generally in post-Keynesian economics,[6] but in terms of the causes of price inflation, the possibility of markup inflation is not a subject free of controversy. As I explain further below, post-Keynesian models assume constant marginal cost, or

---

and the limited import capacity), and of Henri Aujac (1950) concerning his view of inflation as a particular expression of the more general issue of class struggle and conflicting claims over national output.

[4]To avoid confusions, it is important to distinguish the specific propagation mechanisms put forth by the Structuralist inflation theory, underlining the power relations, economic policies, and other institutional factors that are behind an inflation surge, and the conventional propagation or transmission mechanisms of monetary policy, related to the responsiveness of employment to changes in interest rates.

[5]In the same way as a wage-price spiral is conventionally defined 'as an episode of several quarters characterized by accelerating wages and prices (that is, in which both wage and price inflation rates rise simultaneously)' (IMF 2022, p. 53), a markup-price spiral or markup inflation is here defined as an episode of accelerating markups and prices.

[6]As explained in detail by Marc Lavoie (2022), Kaleckian economics might be considered one large strand of post-Keynesian economics associated with the contributions of the Polish economist Michał Kalecki, who, according to Joan Robinson (cited in Lavoie 2022), was better able 'to weave analysis of imperfect competition and of effective demand together and it was this that opened up the way for what goes under the name of post-Keynesian theory' (p. 49). Thus, hereafter I simply refer to post-Keynesian economics to encompass the Kaleckian and similar approaches to inflation.

unit direct costs (UDC), and decreasing unit costs (UC), which includes overhead costs, up to full capacity, but firms commonly operate with idle capacity. Hence, an increase in output does not affect prices because UDC remain constant, and unit costs decrease. The markup is defined in its simpler Kaleckian form as a margin over UDC or, more realistically, as a margin over NUC (see Lavoie 2022). An increase in the markup would thus raise prices proportionally, but the question is whether this can cause price inflation. From a purely accounting perspective, markup inflation (or profit inflation,[7] as Paul Davidson calls it, since it implies a growing profit share (Lavoie 2022, p. 594)) can come from a positive rate of change in the markup, at least temporarily since the wage share, $(1+z)^{-1}$, cannot decrease forever. However, a one-time markup hike would not, in principle, generate inflation.

For most post-Keynesians, inflation is always and everywhere a distributive phenomenon. This means that, in essence, price inflation results from incompatible income claims between social groups, say, workers and the owners of firms. This framework is focused on the determination of the inflation rate and the markup according to the bargaining power of workers and firms. However, the baseline model of conflict inflation is focused on wage-price inflation, i.e., how the inflation rate accelerates when firms have sufficient bargaining power to pass on every increase in the nominal wage rate so that the real wage and the markup rate do not change (see Blecker and Setterfield 2019; Lavoie 2022).

It is interesting to note that wage-price inflation has been always recognized in the broad economics literature, either in the form of rising wages and marginal costs through a positive output gap in New Keynesian economics, or in the form of greater social conflict triggered by workers pushing nominal wages too much. Nevertheless, this recognition is hardly the case with markup inflation, which signifies firms gaining larger bargaining power such that they can increase their target markup and income share. This might be in part because, as argued above, markups cannot rise forever since the profit share would approach unity and the wage share would tend to zero. Income shares are constrained to the zero-one space. More importantly, until 2021, there had not been a significant period suggesting the possibility of inflation pushed up by accelerating markups in industrialized countries. For instance, the long-run decline in the wage share that occurred from at least the 1980s to the Global Financial Crisis of 2008–09, was rather accompanied by low average price inflation (ILO-OECD 2015; Guschanski and Onaran 2021). Thus, if any, the evidence shows instead an era of wage-price semi-deflation that has been often referred to as the era of the flat Phillips curve (see Ratner and Sim 2022).

In fact, markup inflation would be what distinguishes the post-Keynesian analysis of Covid domestic inflation from the mainstream view that blames primarily the growth in wages. For example, the BIS (2022) Annual Report points out that the core of the inflation engine is the wage-price formation process. The report argues that inflation in history could be divided into low and high inflation regimes. High inflation regimes were seen during the First and Second World Wars, and in the 1970s and 1980s era

[7] The theory of monetary circuit, which has several common features with post-Keynesian economics, also considers profit inflation as a process in which firms constantly increase their desired rate of return on costs and this is reflected in a higher inflation rate (Parguez 1996).

following the oil price shocks. However, the transition from low to a high inflation regime depends on how first-round effects of price increments that are generally exogenous and assumed temporary, such as commodity price shocks, are transformed into second-round effects that are triggered by wage-price spirals.[8]

Summing up, wage-price inflation is hardly controversial, it is widely acknowledged by economists. The question is why this is not the case for markup inflation since, for example, it could be argued that first-round effects, or basic inflationary pressures (following Institutionalist terminology), can potentially morph into second round effects (though propagation mechanisms) that trigger an episode of markup inflation. And if so, how to distinguish between wage and markup inflation? To begin with, I first need to make sense of it in a model.

Markup Inflation in the Conflict Inflation Model

The conflict inflation model was developed by post-Keynesian authors that built on the idea that inflation is foremost a distributive phenomenon.[9] The model does account for changing markups that could contribute to price inflation (see Taylor 1989). Taylor and Barbosa-Filho (2021) underscore that the mainstream approach to explain inflation, focused on the equation of exchange PY = VM, is erroneous if one accepts that money is endogenous because V and M turn out to be determined inside the model. Thus, an appropriate approach must instead focus on the cost composition of production, i.e., gross value of output can be divided into gross profits, total wages, and intermediate inputs, which yields the following definition after considering that domestic inputs can be decomposed into profits and wages:

$$PX = \Pi + W\,L + e\,P_M\,M \tag{1}$$

where gross output is decomposed into profits (Π), wages ($W\ L$), and the value of imported inputs (where e is the nominal exchange rate, P_M is the price of imports in foreign currency, and M is the quantity of imported inputs). Mainstream economists underline the contribution of inflation that can come from wage growth, but from a pure accounting perspective, inflation can come from the growth in profits and/or in the value of imported inputs, as the authors argue:

> in addition to 'excessive nominal wage growth' from a tight labor market, inflation can also come from an 'excessive desired rate of profit' in structuralist models. The two effects have

[8]For instance, a passage in the mentioned report says:

> Sustained inflation ultimately involves a self-reinforcing feedback between price and wage increases — so-called wage-price spirals. Changes in individual prices can broaden into aggregate inflation. And they can also erode real wages and profit margins for very long spells. But, ultimately, they cannot be self-sustaining without feedback between prices and wages: profit margins and real wages cannot fall indefinitely. So, beyond the important impact of aggregate demand conditions on wage- and price-setting, a key question is how changes in relative prices that pass through to the aggregate price index ('first-round effects') can trigger feedback between price and wage increases ('second-round effects'). (BIS 2022, p. 46)

[9]The idea of inflation as a distributive phenomenon is not necessarily post-Keynesian. For instance, it has been sometimes attributed to Henri Aujac (1950) (see Noyola 1956). Yet there are some seeds of the idea in the analysis of German hyper-inflation of the 1920s by Joan Robinson (Câmara and Vernengo 2004), considered one of the indisputable founders of post-Keynesian economics. Part of the idea can also be found in former IMF Chief Economist, Olivier Blanchard, in the WS/PS model proposed in his article 'The Wage Price Spiral' (Blanchard 1986) in the *Quarterly Journal of Economics* (see Lavoie and Rochon 2022).

> the same importance, but changes in the firms' markup over cost have not been emphasized by most mainstream models. (Taylor and Barbosa-Filho 2021, p. 134)

Equation 1 might be expressed assuming that prices are fixed by adding a markup (m) over the sum of ULC and UMC in the following way:

$$P = (1 + z)[(W\,L/\,X) + (e\,P_M\,M/\,X)] = (1 + m)(\text{ULC } + \text{UMC}) \tag{2}$$

If ULC is computed at normal capacity utilization, m would be independent from the rate of capacity utilization up to full capacity and so higher markups would be explained by market power or other institutional factors.

In the context of the baseline conflict inflation model, a one-time jump in the market power by firms that leads to a higher markup, ceteris paribus, causes a higher rate of inflation in equilibrium. This is because a higher market power increases the target markup rate by firms, which means a lower target real wage by them. Since price inflation is defined as the gap between the actual and target real wage by firms, the lower the target wage the greater the wages gap and price inflation. In equilibrium, when the real wage and markup are constant, the inflation rate would be higher, and the equilibrium real wage lower, compared to before the initial rise in the target markup (see Dutt 1987; Blecker and Setterfield 2019; Lavoie 2022).

Besides, equation 2 clearly reveals that inflation may come up through growing UMC, as Lavoie (2023a) has put forth since labor cost comprises only a fraction of unit cost, whereby UMC (which includes domestic and imported intermediate goods and raw materials) accounts for another relevant share of unit cost. Thus, he argues, given a markup, if UMC grows faster than ULC, the price-ULC ratio would increase. Nevertheless, the conflict inflation model can easily incorporate UMC in the process of price formation. If so, in line with Lavoie (2023a), accelerating UMC would increase equilibrium price inflation and increase the markup (while decreasing the real wage). To see this, Setterfield (2022) included a stochastic parameter to the price inflation equation (equation 7), representing UMC shocks, such that rising UMC would increase price inflation and reduce the real wage in equilibrium for the duration of the supply shock. This is critical in the current context of Covid and war inflation because rising UMC is undoubtedly the main contributor of the 2021–22 inflation surge (Bernanke and Blanchard 2023), so to really make a case for markup inflation, it is necessary to disentangle the contribution of rising UMC from the contribution of rising markups.

It is very interesting to note that, due to the recent data pointing to a markup-price spiral that could be intensifying current inflationary pressures, some mainstream circles have ruled out a potential wage-price spiral (see IMF 2022, Ch. 2) or they are even open to the possibility of markup inflation (Boissay et al. 2022). This is because markups and profits have kept up with inflation and, in some industries, have outpaced price increments. For instance, a recent article published by the BIS claims:

> Firms' pricing power, as measured by the markup of prices over costs, has increased to historical highs [...] in a high inflation environment, higher markups could fuel inflation as businesses pay more attention to aggregate price growth and incorporate it into their pricing decisions [...] Indeed, this could be one reason why inflationary pressures have broadened recently in sectors that were not directly hit by bottlenecks. (Boissay et al. 2022, p. 4)

Finally, the Institutional/Structuralist approach to inflation also provides critical concepts to understand the rise in market power by firms due to the pandemic and war disruptions and how this is channeled towards accelerating inflation. Noyola (1956) and Taylor (1989), for instance, pointed out that supply-side rigidities or bottlenecks in price-inelastic industries, such as food and energy sectors, are translated into rapid price increments in concentrated industries. In this framework, basic inflationary pressures are represented by the UMC shocks and industry-specific bottlenecks and disruptions of 2021–22. Propagations mechanisms conveyed firms able to pass on fully or over-proportionally rising UMC to prices due to a market power reinforcement by surviving businesses after the pandemic turmoil. The combination of growing UMC and supply-side bottlenecks and industry-specific shortages, led to firms carrying over basic inflationary pressures to workers in the form of generalized price increments — instead of squeezing wages, like what might have happened in the early-2000s commodity boom (see Matamoros 2023).

In a similar vein, Storm (2022) underlines that not only several firms had to shut down due to the measures to contain the pandemic, thereby increasing market consolidation, but those surviving firms ended up in a privileged position to access input and foreign markets. The result was entry barriers becoming larger and enhancing oligopolistic power of incumbent firms. In fact, this process could be another important reason why average markups might have grown during the pandemic. As Lavoie (2023b) and Nikiforos and Grothe (2023) claim, average markups will necessarily grow up as firms with lower individual markups exit markets due to the pandemic severe crisis — because these firms have less market share and thus are less resilient. Therefore, a change in the composition of firms could be driving the rise in average markups despite no change in individual firm markups. Nevertheless, in my view, this would not invalidate the contribution of rising markups to inflation, which is the cornerstone of markup inflation.

Description of Markups

The existing evidence on markup inflation could be divided into two branches. First, the findings supporting a significant uplift in oligopolistic power during the pandemic years, in which case firms could have passed on cost increments to consumers over proportionally. Second, there is the evidence of markup inflation per se, that is, of accelerating average markups and prices during 2021–22. This paper focuses on the latter, such that it turns out critical to explain markups in theory and how they differ with the proxies that are commonly used in the literature.

For instance, Isabel Schnabel, member of the ECB's executive board, shows that a proxy for the markup, measured as the difference between prices and ULC, was the main contributor to inflation in 2021 for the Euro Area countries. She adds:

> To put it more provocatively, many euro area firms, though by no means all, have gained from the recent surge in inflation. The fortunes of businesses and households have diverged outside of the euro area, too, with corporate profits in many advanced economies surging over the past few quarters. (Schnabel 2022)

Strictly speaking, despite their recent popularity, price-ULC ratios (or equivalent measures) are different from traditional post-Keynesian markups. They have two important shortcomings, as underscored by Lavoie (2023a). First, at least in theory, they are dependent on changes in capacity utilization since ULC include overhead labor costs, and not just direct labor costs. As such, they would be rising with the reopening of economies during the Covid pandemic and the corresponding increase in capacity utilization. Second, price-ULC ratios do not include UMC, which would be very important to account for during the 2021–22 inflation surge, since rising price-ULC ratios could be the automatic result of UMC growing faster than ULC.

To better understand why, in theory, it is important to control for capacity utilization when computing markups, Figure 1 depicts a simple presentation of the post-Keynesian cost curves for the firm and how markups are calculated (see Eichner 1976 [1981] for a more complex exposition). Post-Keynesians assume that firms fix a markup over NUC, equal to the difference between unit price (p) and NUC, that is (p-NUC)/NUC in Figure 1. The problem with calculating markups over ULC and UMC — which both comprise UC — is that UC decreases as the rate of capacity utilization goes up (since they include overhead labor cost) up to full capacity (Q_{fc}). Beyond the Q_{fc} production level, UC and UDC start to increase. For instance, in an economic boom, production exceeds output at normal capacity, which means $Q > Q_n$ and NUC > UC, such that profit margins would be greater than markups computed at Q_n. In this sense, p-ULC ratios are procyclical whereas markups at normal capacity utilization would be relatively independent to variations in capacity utilization. In addition, traditional Kaleckian markups, as the ratio of unit price-UDC, would be also constant up to full capacity, as shown in Figure 1.

Lastly, it is worth to consider that the baseline conflict inflation model implies that every increase in market power by firms, ceteris paribus, brings about a higher

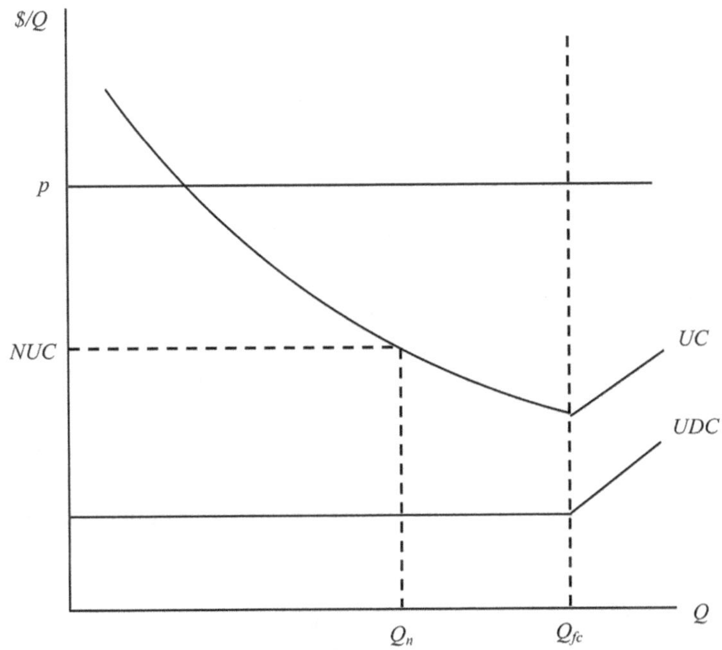

Figure 1. Post-Keynesian markup pricing. Source: Author's elaboration based on Lavoie (2022, Figures 3.8 and 3.9).

markup and inflation rates in equilibrium. Nevertheless, post-Keynesians have always kept in mind that the real world is much more complex than that. Increasing market power does not necessarily yield greater markups and inflation. It is not automatic, and post-Keynesian economics acknowledges that firms have multiple objectives other than profits (see Lavoie 2022, Ch. 3.3). Market share and sales growth, for instance, are critical objectives of the firm, sometimes even more important that short-run profits. Therefore, higher market power could lead to other type of business strategies like predatory pricing and vertical integration, which Khan (2017) has documented in the case of Amazon's company strategy. Does this invalidate markup inflation? I do not think so. Rather, the recognition of multiple objectives by firms advocates for carrying out research at different degrees of aggregation to complement and enrich the macroeconomic approach that I am using in this paper.

Evidence

Inflation and the Markup Equation

This section tries to look at the evidence to test the hypothesis that part of the Covid inflation is driven by increasing markups in several industrialized countries. To do so, I look at the evolution of markup measures and inflation rates across selected industrialized countries. But how do inflation and markups relate each other? In what scenario would markups contribute to inflation? For starters, simple markup equations emerge from the traditional post-Keynesian assumption that prices are fixed by setting a markup over UMC and ULC, as in equation 2. After taking equation 2 and defining the ratio k = UMC/ULC, the price equation in logarithms can be expressed as the following:

$$\log(P) = \log(1+m) + \log(1+k) + \log(\text{ULC}) \tag{3}$$

using the usual approximation of the limit of $\log(1+x) \approx \log(x)$ when x is small, and differentiating with respect to time, the price equation in terms of rates of growth is:

$$\rho = \mu + \kappa + \lambda \tag{4}$$

where ρ is price inflation, μ is the growth in the markup, κ is the growth in the ratio k, and λ is the growth in ULC. Equation 4 can also be interpreted as the simple markup equation depicting the difference between price inflation and the rate of change in total prime cost $(\kappa+\lambda)$ (Seccareccia 2015, p. 74). Logically, inflation is positive if, ceteris paribus, λ or μ are positive, or, as Lavoie (2023a) argued, if UMC grows faster than ULC (meaning positive κ and λ). Again, he put forward two reasons why inflation could be greater than ULC growth $(\rho > \lambda)$ with constant markups. First, if capacity utilization is rising, ULC will grow less than normal ULC, because in theory the former depends inversely on capacity utilization. Second, provided UMC is an important cost component, not controlling for the growth in κ leads to an omitted variable bias, which would overestimate the growth in the markup so long as UMC grows faster than ULC.

Despite that, if I control for changes in capacity utilization, whenever inflation is greater than the sum of κ and λ, it would be explained by a growing markup, which is nothing but markup inflation. This is precisely my objective in this empirical section, which faces some challenges. First, there is no data on direct or normal ULC to directly abstract from fluctuations in capacity. Perhaps because of that, some authors prefer to show just price-ULC ratios as a proxy for markups. Second, researchers must estimate UMC as well taking material cost indexes and adjusting its potential contribution to unit cost. Therefore, it becomes crucial here to estimate markups controlling for the variation in both UMC and capacity utilization. I divide the evidence in two subsections: one that addresses the issue of growing UMC using descriptive statistics; and a second subsection that accounts for both fluctuations in UMC and capacity utilization using conventional OLS regressions for a group of industrialized countries.

Markups, Inflation, and UMC Shocks

In this subsection, I calculate a markup over the weighted sum of ULC and UMC for six industrialized countries in three different historical periods where UMC grew significantly along with inflation. These periods correspond to the 1973 oil shock, the 1979 oil shock, and the 2021 energy price shock. I estimate markups over UC (i.e., ULC and UMC) based on equation 4 for six industrialized countries: Belgium, France, Germany, Italy, Netherlands, and US. For the estimation of UMC, I take two different indexes: the FIBER Industrial Materials Index, and the Commodity Research Bureau (CRB) Index, both pulled out from Haver Analytics. Furthermore, I utilize the country average of the share of imports in total supply at purchasers' prices as a weight in the UC sum when computing the rate of growth in the markup.[10] The implication of using this share as a country specific weight is that variations in UMC will have a stronger impact on the markup in countries that have a larger import share, such as Belgium and Netherlands, compared to countries with a lower import share, like the US.

The 2021–22 Inflation Surge

Figure 2 depicts the growth in markups and prices for the six industrialized countries mentioned, for the period 2019–22 in annual data. As a robustness check, I provide two estimations of markups with two different UMC indexes. As the name indicates, markup (FIBER) is calculated using the FIBER index whereas markup (CRB) uses the CRB index. Moreover, Figure 2 also displays the GDP deflator inflation and the CPI inflation, since the GDP deflator is used as the output price in the markup equation whereas CPI inflation gets more attention of central bankers and social groups.

For starters, what is commonly referred to as the pandemic inflation surge is the fact that CPI inflation started to pick up in 2021 and it accelerated in 2022. Also, GDP deflator inflation appears to be following CPI inflation except in 2021 in France and Italy. The year 2021 is clearly associated with the initial shock in UMC caused by the war and pandemic related disruptions and bottlenecks. In terms of markups, the UMC shock is very large such that markups could not catch up and instead they declined significantly in 2021. However, markups recovered and rose in 2022 — in all countries except in

[10] The share of imports in total supply at purchasers' prices is found as a percentage in Table 45 of the SNA at OECD Statistics. Despite the series only covers since 2010 for all countries except the US that starts in 1997, the available data shows that this share varies very little over time. For instance, the US share of imports in total supply in 1997 is 0.06 and in 2021 it is 0.07. I took the average of the available period for each country, which in the US is 0.07, as a weight in the calculation of the markup over the weighted sum of UMC and ULC. Of course, this share is much higher for smaller and more open economies, such as Belgium and Netherlands that both depict an average share of 0.26 for the period 2010–2019.

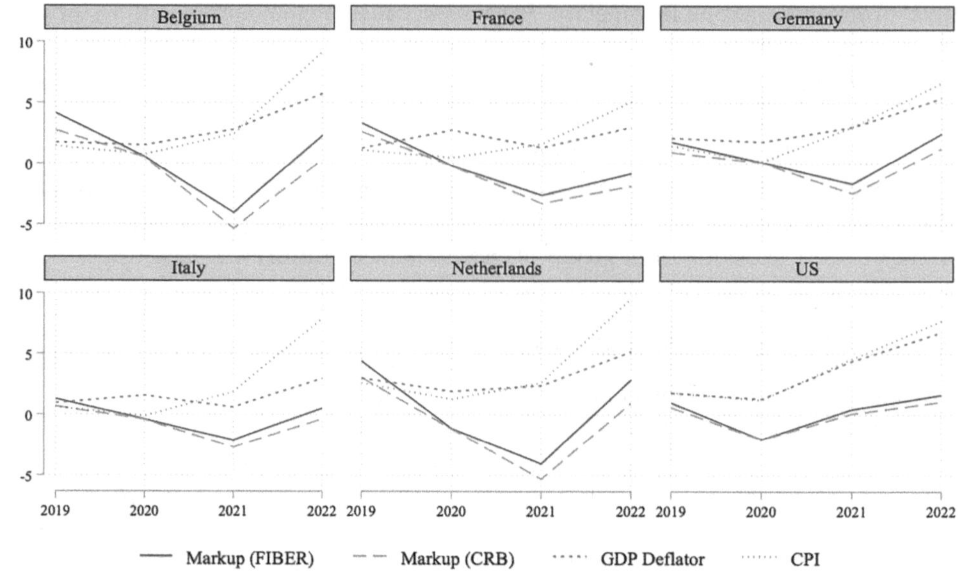

Figure 2. Growth in markups and price indexes, selected industrialized countries, 2019–22. Source: Own calculations based on data from AMECO, Haver Analytics, and OECD Statistics.

France — together with inflation and with rising UMC. Therefore, the evidence is mixed in the sense that 2021 shows rising inflation and decreasing markups whereas 2022 depicts even higher inflation and rising markups.

In other words, the year 2021 portrays declining markups that were driven by the initial shock in UMC. But inflation kept growing in 2022 and this price acceleration was accompanied by a solid recovery in markups. In principle, the evidence is consistent with the Structuralist/Institutional theory of inflation where the initial UMC shock in 2021 is the basic inflationary pressure that triggered further redistribution adjustments in the form of accelerating inflation in 2022. The propagation mechanism of inflation was firms able to catch up after the initial shock by raising markups in 2022 and this seems to be contributing to greater inflation rates.

Summing up, the price and markup evolution suggests that if there is a case for markup inflation, it was until the year 2022, when both inflation and markups rise together. In contrast, the 2021 inflation episode does not have to do with markups, but it could be primarily attributed to growing UMC. It is important to note, however, that although the two markup estimates seem to be evolving together, suggesting that material costs indexes follow each other closely, the rise markups in 2022 is dependent on the material cost index in Belgium and Italy. The growth in the markup is only positive in both countries when it is computed with the FIBER index, whereas it is negative or zero in case of the markup (CRB).

The 1979 Oil Price Shock

To support the story of the 2021–22 inflation dynamics in which markup inflation may have a role in accelerating inflation in 2022, I compare the inflation and markup evolution during an analogous period with a significant UMC shock. Figure 3 depicts the same descriptive statistics as Figure 2 but this time looking at the 1979 oil price shock. These two periods have been widely used for comparison since they share important characteristics, such as accelerating price inflation, low unemployment rates, and nominal wages failing to catch up (see, for recent comparisons, Hansen, Toscani, and Zhou 2023; Alvarez et al. 2022; IMF 2022, Ch. 2), although there might be some structural differences given the fact that, for instance, the bargaining power of workers has been declining since the 1980s and is very low during pandemic inflation (Ratner and Sim 2022) or that average households in the lower-income quintiles depict comparatively higher debt ratios (Costantini and Seccareccia 2020). Also, the fact that I am looking at these six industrialized countries is because of the lack of data on ULC and capacity utilization (which I will use in the next part of the paper) going back to the 1970s.

Figure 3 displays the rates of growth in markups and price indexes as in Figure 2 but for the period 1978–81 in annual data. Regarding inflation rates, they were rising from at least 1979 until 1980 and then they start to decline in 1981. As expected, the 1979 oil shock impacts positively inflation rates but they accelerate even more the year after in 1980. This behavior exactly mimics what occurred in the 2021–22 inflation surge. However, the markup response is less clear on this respect. Firstly, some of the countries with available data display a slightly declining markup in 1979 very likely due to the UMC shock, such as Germany, Netherlands, and the US, but the fall in the markup is more modest compared to the fall in 2020, whereas other countries depict positive rates of growth in the markup, like France and Italy. Secondly, the year after the initial shock, in 1980, sees positive but small rates of growth in the markup, except in France and Italy where they are positive and increasing.

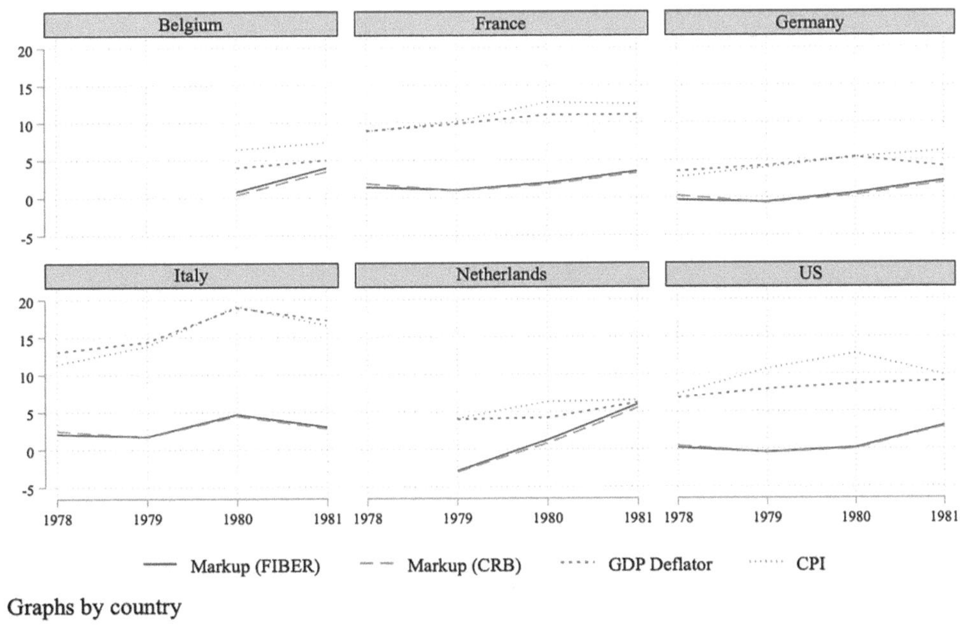

Figure 3. Growth in markups and price indexes, selected industrialized countries, 1978–81. Source: Own calculations based on data from AMECO, Haver Analytics, and OECD Statistics.

One important thing to note, however, is that inflation rates are comparatively higher in the late-1970s compared to 2021–22, such that the 1979 shock functioned as an additional inflation pressure that added up to an environment of close to two-digit inflation. In that sense, it is not clear by how much some of the positive rates of change in the markup in 1979–80 would be contributing to accelerating inflation. For this reason, I carry out econometric analysis of possible markup inflation for this period in the following part using some conventional OLS regressions.

That said, overall Figure 3 displays a roughly comparable pattern of markup and inflation behavior in 1979–80 with respect to 2021–22, both in terms of initial declining markups the year of the UMC shock and a corresponding subsequent increase in markups the year after, presumably due to firms trying to catch up after the rise in UMC and this process could have perhaps contributed to the inflation process.

The 1973 Oil Price Shock

Finally, I tried to go back in time even more to compare the first OPEC oil price shock as to its possible effect on inflation and markups with respect to the 2021–22 inflation. Unfortunately, I could only collect data for Germany, Italy, and the US for this period. Figure 4 depicts the evolution of markups and inflation rates for these three countries in the period 1973–75, where inflation is neatly growing in 1973–74 and then starts to go down in 1975. Thus, the inflation behavior is somewhat analogous to the two previous periods analyzed with respect to accelerating inflation triggered by a UMC shock that extends for about two years.

Nevertheless, the evolution of markups is not quite like the other inflation surges. For instance, Germany, and the US display negative rates of growth in the markup in 1973

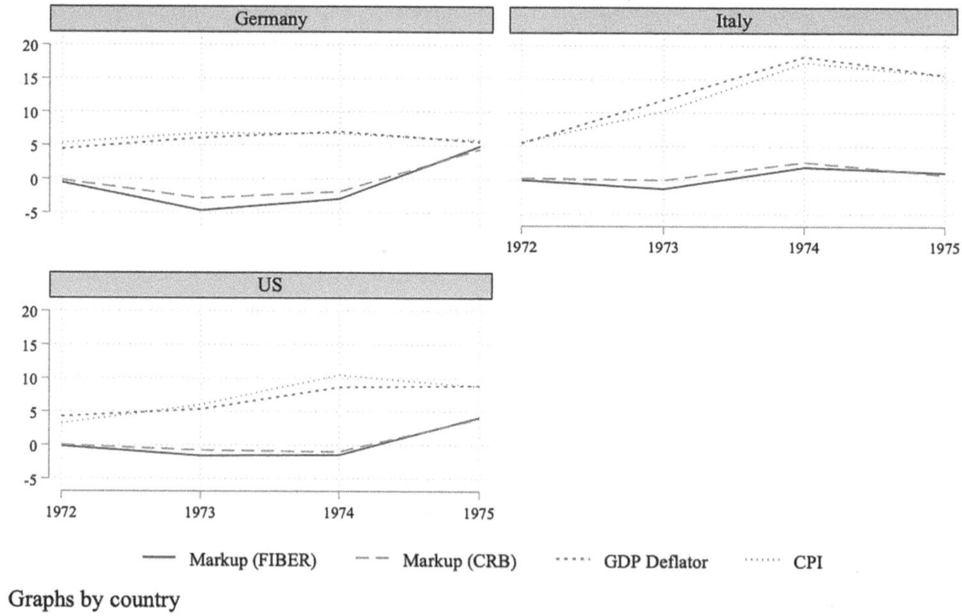

Figure 4. Growth in markups and price indexes, selected industrialized countries, 1972–75. Source: Own calculations based on data from AMECO, Haver Analytics, and OECD Statistics.

and 1974, although Italy does show a slightly declining markup in 1973 and then a rising markup the following year. In general, in this case markups do not seem to be contributing to inflation except perhaps in Italy, thereby contrasting with the inflation episodes in 1979–80 and 2021–22.

To sum up, it is safe to say that there is some descriptive evidence pointing towards possible markup inflation in 2022 driven by firms rising markups to catch up with the 2021 UMC shock in 2021. But further analysis is needed for at least two reasons. First, to measure the statistical association between growing markups and rising inflation in 2022 and try to assess the contribution of markups on inflation, and to compare it with the inflation episodes in 1980 and 1974. Second, and perhaps more important, to control for an omitted variable bias that in this case would be the fluctuations in capacity utilization, since post-Keynesian theory suggests that the growth in the markup over UC would be positively associated with the growth in capacity utilization, due to the inclusion of overhead labor cost. In the following part, I try to address both concerns with the use of standard econometric techniques.

Capacity Utilization, Markups, and Inflation

From a mainstream perspective, Larry Summers and others have argued (see Mintz 2022) that markup inflation is just an expression of a supply constraint that is exerting pressure on prices, so that rising markups are not really pushing inflation up, but it is markets that are too tight and firms that have reached full capacity. In short, markups are rising because inflation is higher. From a post-Keynesian Institutionalist approach, markups are independent of capacity utilization up to full employment while firms are always able to fix prices due to market power and other institutional features. But not only that, we know that in theory the markup over NUC would be independent of fluctuations in capacity utilization. The problem is that there is no data on NUC so that ideally researchers must control for variations in capacity utilization when estimating markups. This part primarily deals with this potential issue by estimating some POLS regressions for the six industrialized countries studied in the previous part, while at the same time tries to provide some estimates of the contribution of markups to inflation in 2022.

To start with, Figure 5 shows the evolution of capacity utilization rates for the period 1970–2022 in annual data. The first thing to notice is that utilization rates are not abnormally high in the years after the pandemic. Utilization rates seem to be still recovering from the 2020 drop caused by the pandemic measures, with the exception perhaps of the US where the utilization rate in 2022 is slightly higher than before the pandemic. However, it cannot be argued that the 2021–22 inflation surge is responding to capacity utilization rates because they are nor particularly high by historical standards. Secondly, utilization rates in the US are trending downwards over time, they were often above 80 per cent in the US before the 2000s, while they have been always below 80 per cent following the 2002 dot-com crisis. In the rest of countries, utilization rates do not have a clear historical trend. Moreover, it is easy to distinguish the booms and busts in the different economies by observing fluctuations in capacity utilization rates, notably the significant fall in utilization during the 1980s crisis and the 2008–09 GFC, and how these rates take some time to recover.

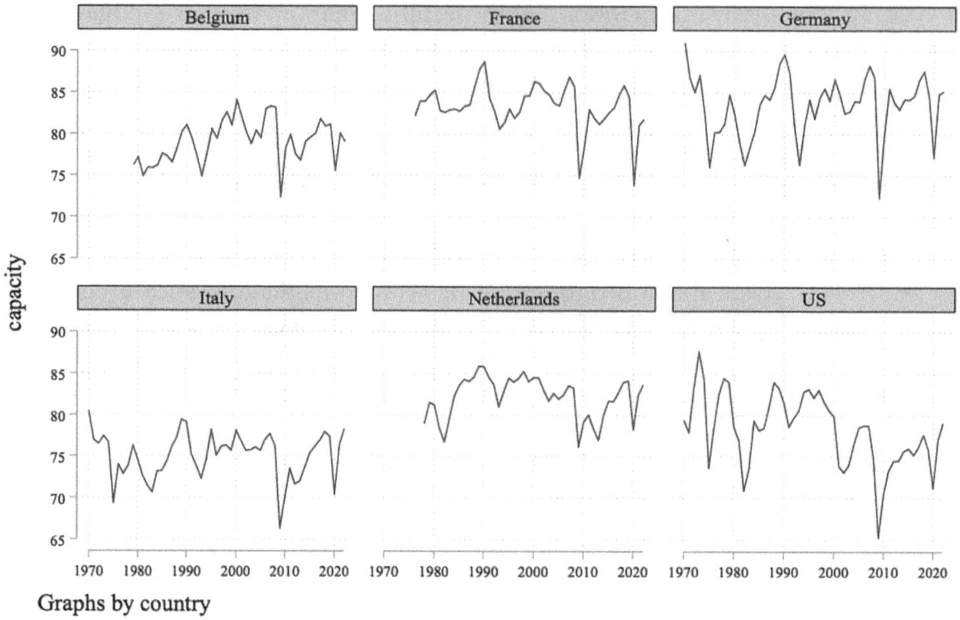

Figure 5. Capacity utilization rates, selected industrialized countries, 1970–2022. Source: Business Tendency Survey, OECD Statistics.

It can be argued, instead, that it is the growth in capacity utilization that is pushing markups up during the 2021–22 inflation surge. To see this, Figure 6 depicts the annual rates of growth in capacity utilization and ULC in the period 2019–22 for the six countries in the sample. As expected, there is a significant fall in capacity utilization in 2020 due to the pandemic, and then it bounces back in 2021 and afterwards it is positive but small in most countries in 2022 — except in Belgium where it is negative.

On the other hand, the growth in ULC moves somewhat in opposite direction to capacity utilization rates as predicted by the post-Keynesian theory of normal cost pricing, in the sense that when capacity utilization rates grow, this tends to attenuate the rate of growth in ULC because of overhead labor cost that is fixed over the economic cycle. Conversely, a decline in capacity utilization contributes to the increase in ULC provided that overhead labor cost is spread across a smaller number of units produced. For instance, when capacity utilization went up in 2021, the growth in ULC was very close to zero or negative in most countries. Then, in 2022, ULC grew significantly more than capacity utilization, which was positive but declining. This underscores the importance of trying to control for the growth in capacity utilization when computing markups.

Yet it is still to be seen whether the growth in capacity utilization affect markups over UC in the way predicted by the theory i.e., if the growth in capacity utilization increases markups per se due to overhead labor cost and whether this is translated into higher inflation rates. To do so, I carry out a POLS regression of inflation on markups over UC controlling for the growth in capacity utilization. The results of the regression are depicted in Table 1.

Columns 1 to 4 specify CPI inflation as the dependent variable and the rate of change in the markup as the independent variable. The first two columns depict the

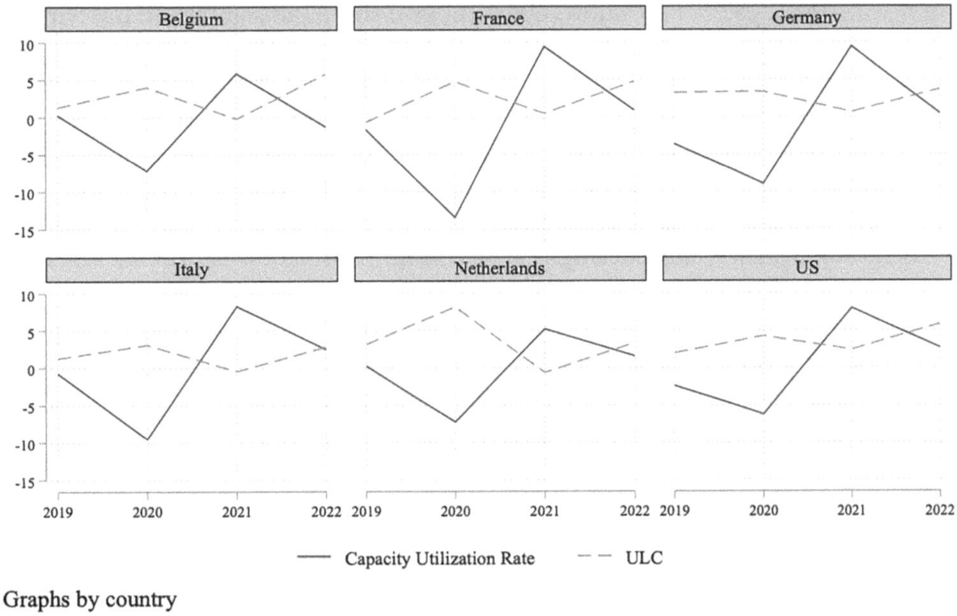

Figure 6. Growth in capacity utilization and ULC, selected industrialized countries, 2019–22.
Source: AMECO and OECD Statistics.

markup calculated with the FIBER index as UMC whereas columns 3 and 4 show the markup with the CRB index. Moreover, columns 1 and 3 control for the growth in capacity utilization to compare how the inclusion of this variable affects the estimation.

Table 1. POLS regression: CPI inflation (columns 1 to 4) and markup (columns 5 to 6), selected industrialized countries, 1971–22, annual data.

	(1)	(2)	(3)	(4)	(5)	(6)
Dependent variable:	CPI Inflation				Markup *(dx/dt)*	
	FIBER		CRB		FIBER	CRB
AR (1)	0.915***	0.904***	0.923***	0.911***		
	(0.0345)	(0.0338)	(0.0383)	(0.0376)		
Capacity *(dx/dt)*	0.0835***		0.0872***		−0.111***	−0.113***
	(0.0227)		(0.0233)		(0.0291)	(0.0320)
Markup *(dx/dt)*	−0.132***	−0.163***	−0.149***	−0.179***		
	(0.0471)	(0.0489)	(0.0455)	(0.0457)		
Markup $_{2022}$ *(dx/dt)*	2.209***	2.255***	1.233	1.286		
	(0.348)	(0.342)	(1.626)	(1.647)		
Markup $_{1980}$ *(dx/dt)*	1.649***	1.664***	1.559***	1.569***		
	(0.129)	(0.134)	(0.111)	(0.113)		
Markup $_{1974}$ *(dx/dt)*	1.427	1.547	0.577	0.729		
	(1.248)	(1.169)	(1.180)	(1.128)		
Constant	0.323***	0.384***	0.370***	0.433***	0.758***	0.731***
	(0.0965)	(0.100)	(0.108)	(0.111)	(0.114)	(0.120)
Observations	283	283	283	283	289	289
R-squared	0.858	0.850	0.827	0.818	0.048	0.046

Note: Robust standard errors in parentheses.
***$p < 0.01$.

To start with, the capacity utilization coefficient is positive and significant, implying that a one percentage point increase in the rate of growth in capacity utilization is associated with a 0.1 percentage point increase in the rate of inflation on average, regardless of using the FIBER or CRB indexes. This is a very small correlation though. The markup coefficient for the whole period is negative and significant in all specifications. A one percentage point increase in the growth in the markup is associated with a decrease of between 0.1 and 0.2 percentage point in the inflation rate on average. Again, this correlation is very small, for instance, considering that the mean of inflation is around 3 per cent, and the standard deviation is 3 per cent as well.

To measure the extent to which markups would be contributing to inflation during the acceleration of inflation in 2022, I introduce an interaction term referred to the markup in 2022, that is, what would be the correlation between inflation and the growth in the markup conditioned on the year 2022. The results show that in 2022, the increase of one percentage point in the growth rate of the markup is associated with an increase in 2 per cent in the rate of inflation, when the markup is calculated with the FIBER index (columns 1 and 2). This association is independent of variations in capacity utilization since the coefficient does not change between columns 1 and 2. Furthermore, results are consistent with the markup inflation narrative positing an important contribution of markups to accelerating inflation in 2022. However, if the markup in 2022 is computed with the CRB index (columns 3 and 4), the markup coefficient is positive, but it is not significant anymore, such that the statistical significance of markup inflation in 2022 depends on the proxy of UMC. On top of that, this result is robust regardless of controlling for capacity utilization, thereby suggesting that in this case controlling for the growth in capacity utilization is not statistically relevant.

In addition, I include two more interaction terms referred to the markup conditioned on the years 1974 and 1980, which were years of accelerating inflation following a significant UMC shock. On the one hand, the markup coefficient in 1980 is also positive and significant, which means that a one percentage point increase in the growth rate in the markup is associated with roughly 1.5 per cent increase in the inflation rate on average in 1980. The markup interaction coefficient in 1980 is like the 2022 coefficient, suggesting that markup inflation might have played a role in 1980. Also, this result is both robust to controlling for capacity utilization and for changing the UMC index. Although it must be said that average inflation rates in those years were significantly higher on average in the late 1970s compared to 2021–22. On the other hand, the markup coefficient conditioned in 1974 is not statistically significant in all specifications. Unlike the years of 2022 and 1980, markup inflation does not seem to play any role during the 1973–74 inflation surge.

Lastly, columns 5 and 6 depict results of a POLS regression where the growth rate in the markup is the dependent variable and the growth rate in capacity utilization is the independent variable. This is just to try to shed light on the relationship between capacity utilization and markups given that the capacity utilization coefficient is positively associated with inflation, despite the size of the coefficient is very small (columns 1 and 3). It would be expected that growing capacity utilization would likely increase markups in theory, but the capacity utilization coefficient in the last couple of columns of Table 1 suggests that the relationship is negative and statistically significant, hereby this relationship is more complex and there might be also a countervailing effect playing out, for instance, à la Kalecki through growing markups that lower real wages and this in turn decreases both effective demand and capacity utilization.

Overall, there is evidence suggesting significant markup inflation in 2022 after controlling for capacity utilization. However, this evidence is dependent on the measure of UMC utilized to compute the markup. On the other hand, it seems that the growth in capacity utilization does not play a very important role in the evolution of markups, after controlling for it, but UMC does matter in assessing markup inflation. Perhaps more research is needed at the industry level in determining empirically the industry pass through of UMC shocks towards markups to conclude whether markup inflation in 2022 was a generalized phenomenon. For instance, Fiebiger (2023), in the context of inflation in Australia, distinguishes between the resources and non-resources industries, in which it would be worthwhile to assess the differential impact of UMC shocks on their prices and markups. Despite all that, the comparison with other historical inflation periods shown in this paper pinpoints that markup inflation after an initial positive shock in UMC is relevant in the 2022 and 1980 inflation years.

Conclusion

The previous analysis puts forward that markup inflation is relevant in the context of the current 2021–22 inflation surge. The views that simply discredit markup inflation on theoretical grounds are not consistent with the conflict inflation model of post-Keynesian economics and the Institutionalist theory of inflation were basic inflationary pressures — in this case a positive UMC shock — interact with firms raising markups as a response to catch up (propagation mechanism), thereby contributing further to the initial inflation shock. Also, the opinions that disregard markup inflation by pointing to a supposed lack of evidence are, to some extent, contradicted by the evidence put forth in this paper for six industrialized countries. Nevertheless, the evidence on markup inflation in 2022 is not entirely conclusive given that its significance depends on the measure of UMC to compute markups.

Moreover, this paper provides a comparison of different inflation episodes along with the 2021–22 inflation surge, with respect to markup behavior and controlling for variations in capacity utilization, in which the basic inflationary pressure was a UMC shock, such as the 1979–80 and the 1973–74 inflation episodes. In this regard, markup inflation is also observed in 1980 whereas it does not show up in 1974, whence pointing out that, despite the common UMC initial inflation pressure, markup behavior responds differently in magnitude and direction in each case. In other words, it is not automatic that following a UMC shock, markups would raise subsequently to catch up, it depends presumably on the institutional factors at hand. On top of that, controlling for the growth in capacity utilization when calculating markups does not make a significant difference on assessing markup inflation.

In line with recent evidence on the 2021–22 inflation process (see Bernanke and Blanchard 2023), this paper argues that propagation mechanisms are not identified in wage-price spirals rooted in a more militant and powerful working-class. Instead, for some industrialized countries, increasing market power of firms is contributing to inflation through increasing average markups. However, accelerating markups could be explained either by firms on average raising markups or, as Lavoie (2023b) points out, by increasing market concentration among the firms with higher markups i.e., a change in the composition of incumbent firms with no change in markups at the firm level. I would argue that although the latter does not imply that firms raised their individual markups, this is still markup inflation since it is explained by increasing market power of firms and how this ultimately contributes to price inflation.

As it has been well documented (see Ratner and Sim 2022; Taylor and Barbosa-Filho 2021), the long-run erosion of labor bargaining power has prevented workers to put enough pressure on wages and prices. Thus, specific class conflict in the traditional view reflecting workers successfully fighting for the distribution of resources has not been the primary factor behind Covid and war inflation. In short, there is no evidence of a wage-price inflation spiral.

Yet, it is also true that markup inflation would account for only one part of the current inflation surge. Therefore, the fight against it must address primarily the basic inflationary pressures located in the supply-side disruptions and scarcities in specific industries. However, solving these issues might help as well to reduce the excessive market power by firms and so inflation could be further reduced by weakening entry barriers and special market access for incumbent firms.

Finally, this paper falls short on some aspects. First and foremost, I was only able to assess markup inflation at a country-level aggregation while conclusive evidence on markup inflation would need to be complemented with industry- and firm-level data on markups. Apart from that, the markup measures utilized in this paper are estimates of the theoretical markup measure, which is the markup on NUC that both includes normal ULC and UMC. As a result, the lack of available data of any of these costs measures implies that they must be substituted by proxy variables. Clearly, it can always be debated whether the proxy variables are appropriate. My feeling is that this very fact must lead to both investigate and provide further evidence with additional markup measures. For example, more research could look at more disaggregated markup measures to reveal other aspects of the markup inflation process. Lastly, the sample of countries is limited to some industrialized countries with available data. Ultimately, inflation (or the lack thereof) is always and everywhere a distributive phenomenon, and we all know that the class conflict over income distribution has its own historical features in each country and region.

Acknowledgements

I would like to thank the many helpful comments and suggestions from Mario Seccareccia, Marc Lavoie, Simon Power, and two anonymous reviewers. Any errors and omissions are entirely my own. A much more substantive version of this paper is part of my PhD thesis at the University of Ottawa.

Disclosure Statement

No potential conflict of interest was reported by the author(s).

ORCID

Guillermo Matamoros http://orcid.org/0000-0001-7137-4710

References

Alvarez, J., J. Bluedorn, N. Hansen, Y. Huang, E. Pugacheva, and A. Sollaci. 2022. 'Wage-Price Spirals: What Is the Historical Evidence?' Washington, DC: International Monetary Fund, IMF Working Paper 22/221.

Ambler, S., and J. Kronick. 2022. 'Money Talks: The Old, New Tool for Predicting Inflation.' Toronto: C.D. Howe Institute, Commentary No. 623. July.

Aujac, H. 1950. 'Une hypothèse de travail: l'inflation, conséquence monétaire du comportement des groupes sociaux.' *Économie Appliquée* 3 (2): 279–300.

Bernanke, B., and O. Blanchard. 2023. 'What Caused the U.S. Pandemic-Era Inflation?' Hutchins Center on Fiscal and Monetary Policy at the Brookings Institution. Conference Draft, May 23. https://www.brookings.edu/wp-content/uploads/2023/04/Bernanke-Blanchard-conference-draft_5.23.23.pdf.

BIS. 2022. 'BIS Annual Economic Report 2022.' Bank of International Settlements, June.

Bivens, J. 2022. 'Corporate Profits have Contributed Disproportionately to Inflation. How Should Policymakers Respond?' Economic Policy Institute, April 21. Accessed June 2, 2022. https://www.epi.org/blog/corporate-profits-have-contributed-disproportionately-to-inflation-how-should-policymakers-respond/.

Blanchard, O. 1986. 'The Wage Price Spiral.' *The Quarterly Journal of Economics* 101 (3): 543–565.

Blanchard, O., A. Domash, and L. H. Summers. 2022. 'Bad News for the Fed from the Beveridge Space.' Peterson Institute for International Economics, Policy Brief 22-7, July, 2–16. https://www.piie.com/sites/default/files/documents/pb22-7.pdf.

Blecker, R. A., and M. Setterfield. 2019. *Heterodox Macroeconomics: Models of Demand, Distribution and Growth*. Cheltenham: Edward Elgar Publishing.

Boissay, F., F. De Fiore, D. Igan, A. Pierres-Tejada, and D. Rees. 2022. 'Are Major Advanced Economies on the Verge of a Wage-Price Spiral?' Bank for International Settlements, May 4. BIS Bulletin No. 53.

Câmara, A., and M. Vernengo. 2004. 'Allied, German and Latin Perspectives on Inflation.' In *Contemporary Post Keynesian Analysis*, edited by L. Randall Wray and M. Forstater. Cheltenham: Edward Elgar.

CMA. 2022. 'The State of UK Competition.' Competition and Markets Authority, 158, April. Accessed August 4, 2022. https://www.gov.uk/government/publications/state-of-uk-competition-report-2022.

Cochrane, D. T. 2022. 'The Rise of Corporate Profits in the Time of Covid.' *Canadians for Tax Fairness*, April.

Costantini, O., and M. Seccareccia. 2020. 'Income Distribution, Household Debt and Growth in Modern Financialized Economies.' *Journal of Economic Issues* 54 (2): 444–453.

Danby, C. 2005. 'Noyola's Institutional Approach to Inflation.' *Journal of the History of Economic Thought* 27 (2): 161–178.

Dehejia, V. 2022a. 'Opinion: The Bank of Canada Needs to Get Serious About Inflation.' *Financial Post*, March 24. Accessed June 6, 2022. https://financialpost.com/opinion/the-bank-of-canada-needs-to-get-serious-about-inflation.

Dehejia, V. 2022b. 'Witness Testimony, Opening Remarks, House of Commons Standing Committee on Finance.' *Vivek's Newsletter*, May 24. Accessed June 6, 2022. https://vivekdehejia.substack.com/p/witness-testimony-opening-remarks?s=r.

Dutt, A. K. 1987. 'Alternative Closures Again: A Comment on "Growth, Distribution and Inflation".' *Cambridge Journal of Economics* 11 (1): 75–82.

Eichner, A. S. 1976 [1981]. *The Megacorp and Oligopoly: Micro Foundations of Macro Dynamics: Micro Foundations of Macro Dynamics*. 1st ed. New York: Routledge.

Fiebiger, B. 2023. 'Profit Margins, Inflation and Productivity in Australia.' *Monetary Policy Institute Blog*, no. 80. Accessed July 20, 2023. https://medium.com/@monetarypolicyinstitute/profit-margins-inflation-and-productivity-in-australia-685cf15122f9.

Greenwood, J., and S. H. Hanke. 2021. 'On Monetary Growth and Inflation in Leading Economies, 2021–2022: Relative Prices and the Overall Price Level.' *Journal of Applied Corporate Finance* 33 (4): 39–51.

Guschanski, A., and Ö. Onaran. 2021. 'The Decline in the Wage Share: Falling Bargaining Power of Labour or Technological Progress? Industry-Level Evidence from the OECD.' *Socio-Economic Review* 20 (3): 1–34.

Hansen, N., F. Toscani, and J. Zhou. 2023. 'The Role of Import Prices, Profits and Wages in the Current Inflation Episode in the Euro Area.' Washington, DC: International Monetary Fund, IMF Working Paper 23/131.

ILO-OECD. 2015. 'The Labour Share in G20 Economies.' Report Prepared for the G20 Employment Working Group. International Labour Organization-Organisation for Economic Co-operation and Development.

IMF. 2022. *World Economic Outlook: Countering the Cost-of-Living Crisis.* Washington, DC: International Monetary Fund.

Khan, L. M. 2017. 'Amazon's Antitrust Paradox.' *The Yale Law Journal* 126 (3): 710–805.

Konczal, M., and N. Lusiani. 2022. 'Prices, Profits, and Power: An Analysis of 2021 Firm-Level Markups.' Roosevelt Institute, Working Paper. June 21.

Lavoie, M. 2022. *Post-Keynesian Economics: New Foundations.* 2nd ed. Cheltenham: Edward Elgar Publishing.

Lavoie, M. 2023a. 'Some Controversies in the Causes of Post-Pandemic Inflation.' *Monetary Policy Institute Blog*, no. 77, May 14. Accessed June 9, 2023. https://medium.com/@monetarypolicyinstitute/some-controversies-in-the-causes-of-the-post-pandemic-inflation-1480a7a08eb7.

Lavoie, M. 2023b. 'Profit Inflation and Markups Once Again.' *INET*, June 15. Accessed July 5, 2023. https://www.ineteconomics.org/perspectives/blog/profit-inflation-and-markups-once-again.

Lavoie, M., and L. P. Rochon. 2022. 'Olivier Blanchard and Inflation.' *Monetary Policy Institute Blog.* Accessed January 18, 2023. https://medium.com/@monetarypolicyinstitute/olivier-blanchard-and-inflation-219f195125fe.

Matamoros, G. 2023. 'Once Again on Profit Inflation: A Follow-Up on Marc Lavoie's Blog.' *Monetary Policy Institute Blog*, no. 82, June 5. Accessed July 3, 2023. https://medium.com/@monetarypolicyinstitute/once-again-on-profit-inflation-a-follow-up-on-marc-lavoies-blog-78f2986e3a39.

Mintz, J. M. 2022. 'Jack Mintz: Blaming Inflation on Big Corporations is "Science Denial".' *Financial Post*, June 10. Accessed June 10, 2022. https://financialpost.com/opinion/jack-m-mintz-blaming-inflation-on-big-corporations-is-science-denial/wcm/7fd6e6be-30fb-4e8a-a70c-debf780b7d7a/amp/?utm_source=pocket_mylist.

Nersisyan, Y., and L. R. Wray. 2022. 'What's Causing Accelerating Inflation: Pandemic or Policy Response?' The Levy Economics Institute Working Paper Collection, 1003, March 4.

Nikiforos, M., and S. Grothe. 2023. 'Markups, Profit Shares, and Cost-Push-Profit-Led Inflation.' *INET*, June 6. Accessed July 5, 2023. https://www.ineteconomics.org/perspectives/blog/markups-profit-shares-and-cost-push-profit-led-inflation.

Noyola, J. 1956. 'El Desarrollo Económico y La Inflación En México y Otros Países Latinoamericanos.' *Investigación Económica* 16 (4): 603–648.

Parguez, A. 1996. 'Financial Markets, Unemployment and Inflation Within a Circuitist Framework.' *Economies et Societés* 10 (2–3): 163–192.

Ratner, D., and J. Sim. 2022. 'Who Killed the Phillips Curve? A Murder Mystery.' Washington, DC: Board of Governors of the Federal Reserve System, Finance and Economics Discussion Series 2022-028.

Schnabel, I. 2022. 'The Globalisation of Inflation.' In Conference Organized by Österreichische Vereinigung für Finanzanalyse und Asset Management, Vienna, May 11. https://www.ecb.europa.eu/press/key/date/2022/html/ecb.sp220511_1~e9ba02e127.en.html.

Seccareccia, M. 2015. 'Pricing and Financing of Investment: Is There a Macroeconomic Basis for Eichnerian Microeconomic Analysis?' In *Money and Macrodynamics: Alfred Eichner and Post-*

Keynesian Economics, edited by M. Lavoie, L-P. Rochon, and M. Seccareccia. New York: Routledge.

Setterfield, M. 2022. 'Inflation and Distribution During the Post-Covid Recovery: A Kaleckian Approach.' Hans-Böckler-Stiftung, FMM Working Paper 82, October.

Stanford, J. 2022. 'A Cure Worse than the Disease? Toward a More Balanced Understanding of Inflation and What to Do About It.' Centre for Future Work and Canadian Labour Congress, October.

Stiglitz, J. E., and I. Regmi. 2023. 'The Causes of and Responses to Today's Inflation.' *Industrial and Corporate Change* 32 (2): 336–385.

Storm, S. 2022. 'Inflation in the Time of Corona and War.' Institute for New Economic Thinking Working Paper Series, 185, May 30.

Summers, L. 2022. 'Three Key Issues for Post-pandemic Monetary Policy.' Cato Institute Policy Forum, USA. Accessed June 8, 2023. https://policycommons.net/artifacts/3365178/three-key-issues-for-post-pandemic-monetary-policy/4163843/.

Taylor, L. 1989. *Stabilization and Growth in Developing Countries: A Structuralist Approach.* 1st ed. London: Taylor & Francis.

Taylor, L., and N. H. Barbosa-Filho. 2021. 'Inflation? It's Import Prices and the Labor Share!' *International Journal of Political Economy* 50 (2): 116–142.

Vague, R. 2017. 'Rapid Money Supply Growth Does Not Cause Inflation.' *Evonomics.* Accessed October 31, 2022. https://evonomics.com/moneysupply/.

Weber, I. M., and E. Wasner. 2023. 'Sellers' Inflation, Profits and Conflict: Why Can Large Firms Hike Prices in an Emergency?' *Review of Keynesian Economics* 11 (2): 183–213.

Index

Note: **Bold** page numbers refer to tables; *italic* page numbers refer to figures and page numbers followed by "n" denote footnotes.

FSC
www.fsc.org
MIX
Papier | Fördert gute Waldnutzung
FSC® C083411

Kolibri 360 GmbH
Ferdinand-Jühlke-Straße 7
99095 Erfurt, Deutschland
produktsicherheit@kolibri360.de